ON CREATIVITY

JOHN TUSA
ON CREATIVITY

Interviews exploring the process

Methuen

First published in 2003 by Methuen

10 9 8 7 6 5 4 3 2 1

Published in Great Britain in 2003 by
Methuen Publishing Ltd
215 Vauxhall Bridge Road,
London SW1V 1EJ

Methuen Publishing Limited Reg. No. 3543167

A CIP catalogue record for this book is available
from the British Library

ISBN 0 413 77299 3

Designed by Bryony Newhouse

Typeset by SX Composing DTP, Rayleigh, Essex

Printed and bound in Great Britain by
Creative Print and Design (Wales), Ebbw Vale

CONTENTS

FOREWORD

It was some three years ago that Tony Cheevers, then heading radio production at Mentorn Barraclough Carey, asked if I was interested in doing a series of in-depth interviews with major figures in the arts world for BBC Radio Three. From his point of view the aim was to revive what was in danger of becoming a moribund form: the extended face-to-face conversation. This remains a classic form for radio but it had slipped into comparative disuse.

There was another impulse behind the proposal. Many major arts figures were, indeed, the subject of interviews. Usually, they were asked to speak only when they were promoting a new film, play, book or exhibition. These were, therefore, exalted commercial plugs. Additionally, a handful of these figures were known as being good at topical interviews on matters of public controversy. In this role they were in danger of overexposure and overfamiliarity.

What was missing was the interview with someone with a proven record of achievement, unconnected with a moment of promotion, detached from current controversy, but with a career and a life to examine and explore.

This would be a series positively defined by what it was not, as well as by what it was.

But the positive impulse behind the series was crucial: who

were the major figures in the arts whose look back at their life and career was worth hearing in its own terms? And, at this point, another important negative came to mind. We would not engage with the 'stage army' of the familiar, the overexposed, the establishment orthodox. In fact, Tony Cheevers and I sat down and drew up a list of people – great names in their own right – whom we would exclude from our invitations. They have had their say, many times over. Wild horses will not draw from me who was on that list, but a look at those who appear in this book can point broadly to those who are not. They will survive anyway without my attentions.

But we regret nothing of the choices we made and the artists in all disciplines we pursued. Hardly any whom we approached declined to be interviewed. Some were surprised to discover that they were facing questioning about their entire career rather than about the latest manifestation of it. Once they realised, all joined in the spirit of the exchange as it evolved. I am very grateful to them for their time and their engagement.

The series would not have existed at all without Tony Cheevers's promotion of it. It would not have had the range and quality that it did without Tony's sheer professionalism, judgement, and skills as producer, editor and colleague. I am very grateful to him for the effort and imagination he put into getting, shaping and editing the interviews.

Roger Wright, Controller, BBC Radio Three, has supported the series with good placings and regular repeats in the summer.

I am grateful to my editor, Max Eilenberg at Methuen, for his enthusiastic adoption of the idea for the book and his vigorous supply of ideas to make it as good as it could be. My long-standing friend, Ilsa Yardley, copy-edited it with understanding, patience and devotion.

A word about the text. The spoken word comes out in its own form – informal, colloquial, loosely grammatical, implicitly punctuated, driven by feeling rather than by sense, conveyed through intonation, inflection and speed as much as by actual sentence structure. Transcribed on to the page in literal form, it would be unreadable and frequently unintelligible. Working from the transcripts and the original recordings, I rendered the text into a form that looks comfortable on the printed page. In doing so, I put clarity above informality. I am absolutely confident that in imposing a degree of order on the informal and the spontaneous, I have not in any way violated or distorted the sense of my interviewees' words.

In the course of this process I have been hugely assisted by my wife Ann, whose eagle eye for clarity and precision has made the text even more accessible. In particular, her ability to use punctuation as an instrument to achieve understanding, and her instinct to prepare text with the sound of the individual's voice in her mind's ear, have provided an authenticity to the texts that I had not dared to hope was there. As a result of being so close to the material, Ann has also been very fertile in suggesting linkages, connections and themes in common for the introductory essay. I am most grateful to her for her interest and engagement.

I must add a word of thanks to the Corporation of London – my employers at the Barbican Centre, and generous ones at that – who, as part of my contract, have given me the time to do these interviews. In particular Michael Cassidy, Chairman of the Barbican Centre Committee for the last three years, has been never failing in his support and encouragement for the Barbican's work and my personal activities.

It has been a wonderful process of privileged discovery to learn how such a wide variety of creative artists work. Each is different and distinct. All are wholly exceptional. All are exceptional in being entirely individual.

I hope these interviews throw some light on particular roads to artistic creation. Those roads remain, in the end, the particular mysteries of their owners. No one else can travel down them. Yet their value to the rest of us is immeasurable.

ON CREATIVITY

On the face of it, fourteen individuals working in six different art forms can have little in common with one another. How can the approach to work of a sculptor – such as Anthony Caro – resonate in any way with the concerns of, say, a novelist, such as Muriel Spark, or a composer, such as Harrison Birtwistle? Surely, the difference in the materials being handled – metal, words, musical notes – would lead to quite important differences in the processes of handling them? As we planned these interviews, they were not conceived as a coherent series, likely to be united by common themes. We had no belief that a group of such widely varied artists could be forced into a conforming set of patterns and we had no interest in trying to create patterns where none existed. It would have been a foolish exercise. Every interviewee was approached because of the intrinsic interest of his or her work, and because we believed that they all had something to reveal about themselves and how they worked. They would not have been the artists they were if they had not been utterly individual and distinct.

And yet as time went by, what emerged was that for all their differences, there were points of common outlook, of shared experience. Each, for want of a better word, was an artist, a slippery word that does conveniently straddle a range of disciplines and activities. 'Creative', 'creation', 'creativity' are some of the most overused and ultimately debased words in the language. Stripped of any special significance by a generation of bureaucrats, civil servants, managers and politicians, lazily used as political margarine to spread approvingly and inclusively over any activity with a non-material element to it, the word 'creative' has become almost unusable. Politics and the ideology of ordinariness, the wish not to put anyone down, the determination not to exalt the exceptional, the culture of oversensitivity, of avoiding hurt feelings, have seen to that.

If the origins of this ideology can be traced anywhere, they surely lie in a generation of primary schools where anyone's Playdo model, anyone's finger painting, anyone's clay bowl was deemed as praiseworthy as anyone else's. The trouble was that a laudable recognition of worthiness – 'this is the best you can do, you deserve respect for your effort' – sidled evasively into the proposition that everyone's faltering acts of creation were as 'good' as anyone else's. This was manifest nonsense; but as the desire to protect feelings was judged more important than the desire to stimulate real creativity or instil respect for special achievement, so the very notion of the exceptional, the excellent, was dealt a body blow through the critique of elitism and exclusivity. In consequence, 'creativity' re-emerged as a blanket phrase to acknowledge almost any activity possessed of originality and a spirit of individualism. In the process of valuing every individual's worth and effort, the definition of creativity was extended so widely that it almost undermined any belief in its true meaning: the exceptional act of imaginative discovery and expression in an art form.

And yet! Although the people interviewed in this book themselves shy away from the grand words when it comes to self-description – 'overheated words', Anthony Caro calls them – the only word that adequately sums up the exceptional nature of what they do in a variety of disciplines is 'creative'. To explore how they achieve the exceptional in their particular field can only involve an exploration of creativity. That is what I believe these interviews do. What the individual artists have in common turns out to be – at a deep level – remarkable and often eerily consistent. There is something shared and similar about the multifarious, complex processes of discovering the exceptional, the different, the original. These processes cannot be codified for imitation or application by others. They cannot be replicated; they have to be painfully rediscovered. But they exist in a strikingly shared framework of experience learned and won the hard way, seemingly regardless of the precise activity involved. The practice of working creatively is more important than the particular art form in which the work finds expression.

Yet why does creativity matter? Why is it worth exploring at all?

The answer, in part, is because any society needs to renew and add to its stock of imagining. Just as scientific research is needed to prevent intellectual stagnation, so creative innovation is vital to the process of understanding ourselves, of seeing the world differently as it presents itself anew, of presenting novel propositions about the way we see, hear, look and conceptualise. While the process of scientific research generally occurs within the boundaries of formal institutions – led, of course, by outstanding individuals – artistic originality and creativity are almost always the product of the individual. Achieving the breakthrough to the unique and innovative insight cannot be planned into a programme of systematic research. It has historically come about through the intensely personal vision of a single individual, often reacting against his or her basic background and education, though sometimes egged on by an enlightened teacher. Artists may not always be revolutionary in the full sense of the word; but they will often jolt, frequently question and occasionally transform.

This is what makes them original, exceptional, cherishable and essential. It also marks out artists from the rest of us, and in the fields where they work, as better than us! Not better as human beings, but so distinctly exceptional that not to recognise their different worth is self-defeating. None of us is – or should be – diminished by acknowledging that artists do many things better. We need them to be better than us. If we cannot admit to ourselves the true worth of such people, then the poverty of spirit behind our failure is miserable indeed.

7

In the course of talking to this diverse range of creative artists, certain common themes emerged, not conclusively but in various suggestive ways. For a start, artists often seem to spring from perfectly ordinary, not to say routine, backgrounds. Some were positively discouraged from pursuing what appeared to be an inevitably penurious and useless future. Others were pushed towards the arts as children because it was a way of keeping them off the streets, out of mischief, and could possibly lead them to a better standard of living than their family's. Some found their unexpected talent greeted with total disbelief and puzzlement – even a degree of regret – by their bewildered parents. On the evidence of the sample in this book, there is no sign that a privileged background or a basic education leads to the production of a creative person. In class terms, the home backgrounds represented here are often lower middle class, with an aspirant tinge.

Do these childhood experiences suggest that outstanding ability descends in a pleasingly unpredictable, almost egalitarian, way? If so, then there is an important lesson for governments. The possibility of individual creativity must be recognised as open to children of all classes and backgrounds. Everyone has the right to be exceptional. This right has to be proclaimed as a goal available to every individual, not a right to be granted only when many can achieve it.

Then, too, there is a common thread in the importance of teachers. Most of those interviewed can point to someone who fostered an enthusiasm, provided an example, or nudged in a particular direction. Some had a teacher who demonstrated a way of approaching work rather than a particular method of expression. Some had to break away from teachers who were so sure of their achievements – or maybe so uncertain – that they looked for acolytes and admirers rather than potential rivals. The lucky ones had a teacher or friend who indicated firmly at a critical stage that the only road to follow was the one instinctively understood by the young artist, however peculiar that appeared to be. The truly original seem never to be mere followers; they are usually uninterested in becoming leaders; for the most part they remain solo travellers whom others can take as an example if they want. They are available rather than overpowering. The courage involved in their decisions, in the choice of direction at the crossroads that defines the innovator from the journeyman, is impossible to overestimate. Yet the taking of such decisions was often a necessary, defining moment for the truly creative.

For the process of making, painting, writing is, by and large appallingly lonely. While some artists – sculptors in particular – need studio technicians to do the physical and technical labour, most work alone. No one else can endorse or confirm what they are doing, though occasionally friends or critics can play a marginal part in the process. But the artist is driven by a strong sense of the direction in which he or she should go. They possess a deep instinct for when something is 'right' – a word much used – when a piece of work has become 'right' or when it is 'true'. Many of those interviewed speak of the moment of recognition when their work reaches a point of rest, a moment of completion. When the word 'true' is used in this context, it signals a reconciliation with their internal sense of truth, with their understanding of personal integrity.

The fundamental loneliness of the artists' work is compounded by the fact that they can never know in advance if what they think is right and true will find an answering recognition from the public and the critics. To be driven internally in one creative direction and to fear that the outside world will not recognise it, or might actually reject it, must be the ultimate personal nightmare. Most of us could not take such risks with ourselves, our time, our lives.

Just as bad, or conceivably even worse, is the period of sterility, of creative barrenness, of imaginative block. Many artists spend time simply looking at their work, scribbling in their notebooks, turning things over in their minds. These may be the times of fallow; or they may be devices to buy time, to delay a crucial decision, subtle evasions. Yet there are, too, times of constructive stillness, allowing the intensely self-critical gaze to be directed at the work in progress, testing it against the inner sense of purpose and direction. Those times when the moments of stillness do not reveal anything bursting to emerge, when the inner voices are silent and the deeper instincts remain mute, these are the crises of the spiritual despair which the rest of us might recognise but can never fully understand. We have a job to go back to, a task to perform, the everyday supports of the routine to help us. The creative artist faces only emptiness.

What also emerges from these conversations is the variety of ways of working. Nowhere does the sheer difference of the individuals show through more. No one should imagine that artists of all kinds do not work regularly, daily – some work every day of their lives, long hours, too – systematically and intensively. Composing music is sheer hard work, a detailed grind, where it takes days of concentrated effort to create something that is played in a few seconds in the concert hall. Very few artists go straight from the idea to the execution, though one instance of doing so exists in this collection. Most reach their end by repeated addressing of the problem, whether on the canvas, the poet's notebook, or the composer's score. Some attack the work almost physically, finding the resolution of the problems through the elimination of earlier attempts. Some continue to revise work even after it appears to be completed. All are looking for that understanding of rightness, that revelation of personal truth, which represents their own essential guide to when a work is complete.

In almost every case the acts of creation represent a huge accrual of effort, of second and third thoughts, doubts, hesitations, uncertainties and inner debate. Being creative is not a dilettante pastime, an occasional involvement, a diverting hobby. It is often painful, an urgent necessity, a driven work. And tantalisingly, for some artists, there exists the deep understanding that the very moment when it seems that a particular problem has been resolved may be the exact moment when that solution has to be rejected, perhaps because it represents too easy a solution. The easy answers, it seems, can seldom be the right ones. It takes courage to admit and to act on the admission.

The sheer intensity of the artist's work emerges time and time again. Making things is a physical business, expressed in effort and sweat. It will range from the sheer burden of lifting sculpture, to the drive to write through the night while the inspiration lasts, to actual shouts and physical movements around the canvas while painting. David Sylvester, the authoritative writer on the visual arts, describes the physiological intensity of his reactions to looking at art with a critical eye; it hits the spine, the solar plexus, the hands, even creating the feeling that layers of skin are being peeled off, so intense is the sensation of response. At all events, for many artists there is nothing polite and pretty about creating. It is not a period of quiet reflection but a real intellectual and physical engagement with the material.

Working on and completing a particular work is not just an end in itself, a moment of particular conclusion. The activity of making one work opens up possibilities for what is to be done next. Artists discover in their current work sometimes what they want to express next, sometimes solutions to ideas that have lain around unsolved in the past. In the current act of making, an awareness of continuity into the next work – which may well be very different in nature – lies hidden until it is discovered.

This idea of a seamless, instinctive continuum to the creative process is very strong. Each work throws up fresh ideas, new problems and the possibility of new solutions. It is the reverse of repetition, of a formulaic approach to work. Continuity involves continuous and instinctive innovation, but an innovation that is evolutionary as well. It points, too, to the very uncalculating way that artists move from one type of work to another.

Artists of whatever discipline differ from one another more than they resemble one another. Yet they have more in common with other artists than with the rest of us who are not involved in the awkward, obstreperous, messy, difficult business of creation. They share a unique sense of themselves and of what they need to do to be true to themselves; most do not create for themselves alone, even if they avoid being driven by the overt demands of the public. Even when they are apparently driven by the most powerful creative instincts, the need for a deep order, for some binding logic, some ultimate coherence possesses their work. There is nothing impulsive or slipshod about the true work of creating. That is what sets it and those who engage in it aside. That is why it is worth thinking about them.

To maintain that most of us are not creative in the ways described above is not to diminish ourselves or to exalt the artist to an absurd level of exclusivity and exceptionalism. It does recognise the precious nature of their creativity and to acknowledge its value. If it can never be explained, it is worth trying to understand it better. But to pretend that everyone has it, to imply that everyone might have it, or even to hint that creativity should be spread more thinly in order to be more equal is to delude ourselves and to diminish society's capacity for innovative imagining.

EVE ARNOLD

'Something happens to flesh after fifty'

Some fifty years ago, a young woman called Eve Arnold was given a camera by her boyfriend. She had worked as a photography supervisor at a mass film-processing plant in New York. She thought that she wanted to become a professional photographer and, attracted by the already legendary names of Henri Cartier-Bresson and Robert Capa, she applied to the Magnum collective to see if they would have her. They accepted and that was the start of a prodigious and prolific career as a photographer, ending with a name recognised around the world. Eve Arnold's pictures are some of the abiding images of our time; images of Joan Crawford, Marilyn Monroe, Malcolm X, Marlene Dietrich. She worked for years on the *Sunday Times Colour Magazine*. She covered the making of dozens of feature films and travelled the world to show people, famous and ordinary, as they are.

As you go along the street, do you find yourself compulsively taking pictures for yourself, even if you don't have a camera in hand?

It is very strange, but I am going through some kind of change at the moment, where I don't miss not photographing. I had a very serious back operation about a year ago and I found that I had reached some form of plateau. What I missed was words, I had been writing a lot.

Are you worried by this, that suddenly the habits of a lifetime, of needing to see the world through the camera, that these have changed?

I am not upset about it, because every time I tried to think of something that I might do, I found I'd already done it, and I have done a great deal in a long lifetime. And it seemed to me that it was time to try and see if I can exercise another skill, so I have been writing and it is lucid. I don't know how good it is and I don't care, because it is expressive and it says what I wanted to say, and at the moment I am working on three books. One is a book on hands doing various things around the world. These are about four hundred photographs that I photographed in Afghanistan and Zululand, and the book is called *The Hand Book with Foot Notes*; it is a light-hearted little book. I had put the pictures in a drawer for forty years and they are now coming out for publication. Another book is on the forty films that I worked on, did stills on, films around the world, and the third book is a reissue of a book on Marilyn Monroe.

But just at the moment you are not driven by the need to photograph?

No. Time was when I could hardly wait to get out of bed to go for the camera.

And would you always carry a camera with you?

No, I never did. My colleagues were always after me, saying you must be missing something. I felt that little black box and seeing the world through it would sometimes be too much for me.

I suppose it is a fairly neurotic reaction, isn't it, the thought that any moment there might be the world's greatest photograph about to happen and if you are a professional photographer and don't snap it, somehow you've failed?

No, I never just went along on the streets and photographed like so many of my colleagues did. I would think of a project that I wanted – and I was fortunate to work on my own idea so that I would guess that about ninety per cent of what I did are things that I wanted to do.

I would like to take you back to the very beginning because what strikes me about how your life was worked out is how practical you always have been. The first five years that you spent as a routine supervisor of this mass photo-processing works in Brooklyn, Standby Pictures – how important was that for you later on?

No, it was never routine for me, because it read like a Ford plant, with conveyor belts, and these pictures, hundreds of thousands, millions of them going down the conveyor belt. And I had to train people, it was during the war, there were very few trained people about, including me. I was an amateur and bluffed my way through this. During the war you hired whomever you could get your hands on and although I was very young and inexperienced I was imaginative, I like to think, and I wanted to make things work for the people who came and worked for us. Because it was amateur photographs coming in for processing, we had all sorts of things going down the line and they were mainly of school children. And because they were amateur photographs, usually their first picture would be in the snow, and they would put the camera aside and then they would pick it up for a beach scene. And then since we had snow and beach, to be used either in the summer or Christmas, we would be able to teach these people who are doing the processing what to look for.

But that's what I mean: your response was a very practical one. I wonder how much you learnt from that about the business of running your life thereafter – because you took on this big responsibility when you were a comparatively young woman.

It was fun, it was a challenge, it was a way to look at the world. Most of the pictures were dull. Occasionally, we would get a picture of a nude and usually we were not permitted by law to send it through the mail, which is why we returned these pictures, with a little note, a printed note, saying, 'Well, we couldn't print it.' And we would put it aside and I had a key to a file cabinet, just put everything in the file cabinet, and once a month one of the big bosses would come over to Hoboken as it was, not Brooklyn, and ask for the key and you'd hear a great guffaw of laughter coming from this man. And they were deadly dull!

They just happened to be nudes, but they were dull?

They were unattractive, you know. And what would come back is a letter from the man you had sent notes to saying 'sorry, we can't deliver these to you, because of the law', and always, invariably, they would write back and say, 'It was my wife.' There was nothing we could do about it; we couldn't mail it, we couldn't hand it over. Whatever statutes there were about it simply didn't tell us what to do with it. So it piled up year after year of all the five years that I was there!

Was this when you were interested in the idea of looking at people at work, photographing people at work, because that has been a constant theme in your photography?

I looked for a sense of reality with everything I did. I didn't work in a studio, I didn't light anything. I found a way of working which pleased me because I didn't have to frighten people with heavy equipment. It was just that little black box and me, and £5 worth of film in my pocket, or maybe it was only £2 in those days.

But the theme of work – and it strikes me in a number of your images – what you like photographing is what I would call mind and spirit. I know there is a wonderful photograph of a nun making her bed; it's a transcendent, wonderful picture. Or one of a musician tuning a string. Does that sense of engagement of the spirit with work particularly appeal to you?

I find that enormously appealing. I did a book recently, called *All in a Day's Work*, that illustrated the point that you are making. You get closer to people when they are in their work. If you got a lacemaker, let's say, I would get her at her loom. If you got a writer, you might do something as mundane as a typewriter. But if it was William Carlos Williams, it was poetry, because of the way he moved and the way he looked at the words on the typewriter, and you got a sense of the person, the defining moment that I was looking for.

Do you think that you quite did justice to the grinding nature of physical hard labour? Looking at your books, it's as if you yourself can't bear to show the physical degradation that goes with the hard labour that so many in the world still have to undertake.

The grinding labour is part of their work; and because I respected them and didn't want to savage anybody, I hope you found that it was a concern for the people and not a misunderstanding of what they were.

At some stage you defined yourself as being a photographer informed by a woman's sensibility. Is what you've just said a reflection of that woman's sensibility? You have also said that you are not a 'woman photographer'.

No, I am photographer. And you don't say 'a man photographer'. So it seems likely that I am a photographer.

So what is the woman's sensibility that you say you always brought to your photographs?

It's hard for me to assess what I brought because each time you pick up a camera and point it at a person, you're trying to define that person, so to talk generally is difficult because I have to think of a given image in order to conjure up what we're talking about. I don't think of it again as groups of people running through my lens.

No, of course not, and indeed, every single one of the images in your book about work is characterised by the sense that it is a particular person to whom you're responding.

Well, very often there was no language, so it was done with a sort of pantomime because I didn't like to have an interpreter around, because it changed the atmosphere slightly – like litmus paper turning blue – when there's a third person. It's bad enough when there are two. So I would be there alone with the person and with their work, and very often travelling through a souk in Afghanistan would show you something. There would be a man with a pan with bits of wood that he was burning. Those bits of wood would cleanse the house at the end of the winter, and I had no idea what this was all about. He didn't tell me; after I had worked, I got an interpreter to tell me what was going on. But very often it might have been purely visual, because you think obviously visually, and that's a way to capture the image. I come to blows very often with my colleagues who don't like the captions, they feel it disturbs their deathless photographs. I feel that you owe the viewer information.

About how it was taken?

Well, more about what's going on. Where you are, what's going on, who this man is, what he's done.

I can see that your colleagues might say a photograph is self-sufficient; if it is absolutely right, it tells the entire story. If you've had to embellish it with words, then somehow you haven't caught it on the image.

I disagree with that wholeheartedly. If I couldn't gauge what was going on exactly, then I wondered whether my viewers would be any brighter and understand better. At any rate, now the vogue is to put the caption in the back of the book and you keep flipping back and forth, caption, picture, picture, caption, and I think that's arrogant.

Yes, it's imposing a burden on the reader or the viewer, isn't it? Let's talk directly about your career with the great Magnum photo collective. What did you know of Magnum before you joined it?

They had just started a branch in New York. They started first in Paris, I think in 1948, and I think in 1950 they started a branch office in New York. I had just begun photographing. I hadn't a clue that they would even think of me as a member. These were exalted characters, like Cartier-Bresson, or Robert Capa, George Rodger, or David Seymour, the four founders. But I had a desperate need to find out if I was on the right track. So one day I gathered up my courage, called and made an appointment, and I was seen by Maria Eisner, who started with them in Paris and had come over to the United States to get this office moving. And I had done one story, a picture story on migrant labourers in Long Island where I lived, and on the strength of that I became a stringer, which surprised me. Oh, there was a published story as well, of fashions that I had done in Harlem, and that had been published in England in *Picture Post*, which was a really wonderful picture magazine.

And then you moved up from being a stringer to being a fully fledged member of the Magnum co-operative. At the outset, were you more drawn by Cartier-Bresson, whom I suppose we call the poet, or by Robert Capa, the journalist? Or were you still prepared to find out for yourself where you'd lie between these two?

Well, I learned a great deal from them. I learned what not to do in many cases, what to do in some cases. I looked at them and tried not to make their work influence me too much, but I veered between both of them. At one point it would be what Capa was doing, but I never went to war so I don't think I should talk about that. He was very important to me because he would look at my pictures and analyse them. At the time that I started, I was working with a larger format than normally, two and quarter inch square, with a Rolleicord – a $40 Rolleicord was all I had, and I had no money. So I had to make these images on an inferior camera and speak for whatever I had to say. And over the years I have come to the conclusion that it doesn't matter what instrument you use; it's the eye behind it and the brain, I hope.

I think you have written that Capa taught you to take risks. He said, 'If your pictures aren't good enough, you aren't close enough.' Did that strike a chord with you? – because a lot of the pictures that you publish in your books, they are not brutally up front in the face and the body. They have this sense of detachment in allowing the figures to speak for themselves. So, was that advice of Capa's something that you didn't take because it wasn't relevant to your work?

It is hard to analyse what I did take from these people. There were so many instances when one of them would look at my work and we would talk about our work. So it was not just them looking at mine, they would talk to me about their work as well and you absorb it like osmosis. I don't know how much of it came from them, how much of it came from looking at books, how much of it came from my own need to say something. There are so many factors that it's hard – for lack of a better term 'the creative process', but I think that's too grand for me – it is hard to analyse and shouldn't be.

Of course, the whole time you had to be yourself. Did you ever look at what you'd done and say, 'What I was doing there was taking a fake Cartier-Bresson'? and you had to pull yourself back and say, 'That is not me'?

No, I never felt that I had, because there is only one Cartier-Bresson, and his work has a magnificence about it because, somehow or other, he bonds with nature or in their world, but generally that only exists in art. And I don't think he can be copied, he is unique.

I wondered whether subconsciously you found yourself, because his influence was so strong, mimicking Cartier-Bresson, and that was something you would then have to work out of your system?

No, because he worked on the streets. I went into people's homes. It was an entirely different way of looking at the world.

One of the formative moments that you write about was when you observed to the journalist Janet Flanner that some of Robert Capa's photographs weren't well designed. And you said that Flanner said to you, 'My dear, history does not design well.'

That knocked me back. I was startled at that. Because I had been quite nasty in my mind about Capa's pictures. And there he was in the middle of war and I wanted him to design his pictures! I mean, what stupidity that was, I thought afterwards. And she spoke it very well to me, and it meant a great deal to me after that.

Certainly when I was looking at your photograph taken during the Republican National Convention when Eisenhower defeated Taft, and Ike's in the foreground, Taft is hardly visible, and what the photograph

does capture is the extraordinary turmoil of that moment. It is
wonderfully not well designed, if you know what I mean?

I know, because after that, I started to look at my photographs
with an eagle eye. If the moment was there, you shot it and you
didn't wait to design it, it was important to say it. What happened
at that moment can't happen now. When the convention started
I was late, I didn't get there until three days after. So I didn't have
any pictures to go on at all, and these were for *Picture Post*, your
magazine here, and I was very upset about it. And I tried to think
of what was going to go next and Eisenhower had booted Taft
(the leader of the party, really, you know) out of the system. I
thought they had to heal the wounds of the party, so they'll have
to get together. Will it be public and if it is public can I go there
and do what I can? I found that they were going to be at the
Blackthorne Hotel (I think that's what it was called). And I went
there, and NBC was setting up to take pictures when the two men
arrived. The NBC crew arms were making a circle and with great
generosity they let me into the circle, and that's what the picture
is. Now nobody would do that nowadays, there isn't that kind of
generosity around.

I want to ask you a few questions about the approach to taking
photographs and the words used to describe it. You have observed that
the vocabulary of taking a photograph is almost entirely made up of
masculine aggressive words. You 'grab' an image; you're 'shooting' the
whole time. You 'capture'. Can you suggest some non-aggressive words
that are used for taking the image?

Well, in some cultures it is considered taking the soul. The
Hopi Indians grabbed the back of my camera and wrecked it
because I was photographing them doing their dancing. I don't
think it is solely masculine, I think it is just an aggressive way of
working; there is no other way, it seems to me. If you are going to
work on the streets or even when somebody takes you into their
home, you very often find yourself wanting to transgress that
hospitality. Because what you want to do, you want to go as
deeply into them as people as you can. But usually what happens,
if you're careful with people and if you respect their privacy, they

will offer you part of themselves that you can use, and that is the big secret. It has more to do with the relationship of the photographer to the subject than it has to do with anything else that might be happening.

Yes, 'offer' is a very good word. In your mind, you would not even think that the words I just mentioned – 'grab', 'shoot', 'capture' – are words which inform how you approach your work?

No. They're too harsh for what I have tried to do. What I have tried to do is involve the people I was photographing. To have them realise, without saying so, that it was up to them to give me whatever they wanted to give me. So I would get somebody like Joan Crawford stripping down nude – granted she had been drinking! But Malcolm X: there's a tough man who let me into his life – granted it was at a time when he wanted press in *Life* magazine. Granted he was under threat from Elijah Mohammed, the head of the Black Muslims, and wanted to be seen by the white press so he wouldn't be murdered, which he was in the end. But for two years, he made it possible for me to photograph the Black Muslims and the way they worked.

Now did you think that because he was being so co-operative, that because he had a reason for wanting a favourable image put over, that was why he gave you access? Did you ever say to yourself, 'I'm becoming part of his publicity machine'?

I don't think there is any such thing as detachment when you're photographing. You have a point of view; and if you haven't, your pictures don't show anything about the people you are working with.

But were you using your point of view there or were you reflecting his point of view? Who was using whom?

I think we were both using each other. I don't think there was any such thing as my saying, 'Well, I'll do this and I'll do this.' It moves so fast when you're working. There isn't time to analyse and if you do analyse, you get exactly what you thought you were going to get when you talk to these people at the beginning. So the idea is to keep as far away from a commitment of trying to work on their terms or your terms. You don't care. It isn't important.

What is important is what's going on at the moment, and it moves rapidly with involvement from both sides.

Joan Crawford was the other one that you mentioned. She insisted on your photographing her in the nude, didn't she?

Yes. She stripped down in a dressing room where she was trying clothes on.

Absolutely naked?

Absolutely. And she was to be photographed with her daughter. And I said, 'Can we wait for Christine' and she said, 'No, I want to be photographed now.'

Why didn't you say no?

Something happens to flesh after fifty, and she was well past fifty. And I felt that she would hate it when she'd sobered up. I wouldn't want that to happen to me or anybody I knew, and I felt that it was only fair to let her know what she was doing. And she insisted. And I never used the photographs. I gave them back to her. She had started her career doing blue films, making blue films, and as I went around the world afterwards, I found that every once in a while somebody would tell me that they had a print, because from a print you make a negative. It's an endless flow of pictures, if you want them. And because I had been generous enough and didn't use them and didn't exploit them, years later she gave me the most explicit kind of pictures to show what it took to stay at the top of the heap, the heap being Hollywood, for thirty years.

I'll ask the question, I think I know the answer. Were you ever tempted, even for a moment, to make those photographs of Joan Crawford in the nude public?

No. And selfishly, because I didn't think they would do me credit.

A very honest answer indeed!

Well, yes. You know, I was not unselfish about this. I had in mind a long career and it just was counter-productive. In those days we did work for four or five months, or a year, or whatever it took to get a story, because *Life* magazine felt film was cheap, labour was cheap. What was important was the most explicit or individual photograph. And so they would let you go off for months at a time. Now they talk about a photo opportunity which is seven and a half minutes, because that's what you get.

Did you find that that time was always well spent? After you'd been with, say, Joan Crawford or Marilyn Monroe for weeks or months, didn't you find yourself saying, 'I think I know this person, I really can't be bothered to spend another month or two months working with them'?

No, that never occurred to me. What did occur to me was that if they were willing to give, then I was willing to photograph. In Marilyn's case, at the end of her life, after she had spent months and months working on *Misfits*, and I had worked on that film for two or three months, she was getting a divorce from Arthur Miller, and I was going up every day for a week with packs of contact sheets. She had a set, I had a set, we checked the pictures and she would say she wanted to use that picture; if she didn't, she had the right of refusal.

So she was manipulating her image. She was in control of her image, I suppose?

She was in control of it when we photographed. She always was. She knew more about the camera instinctively. She was not a cerebral character, as you would know. She had an instinct about things.

And didn't that produce in you a countervailing reaction, that you thought, 'This woman is such a brilliant manipulator of herself, I want to find the moment when she is not presenting an image of her own choice to me'?

You couldn't. There was no way to get around her. She was brilliant at what she did. She knew what she could do; she couldn't have explained it to you. But in the beginning when we met, we were two young women starting out. She was a starlet, no place yet in the Hollywood hierarchy. Neither one of us knew anything about our craft and that was a bond between us. So I don't know where she ended and I began or I ended and she began. We fed each other for ten years on this.

Did you ever envy her and think, 'She's famous!'

Oh God, no. Oh God, no.

From a very early stage you could see there was, in a sense, no future for her life?

She was always trying to outsmart, and she was street smart, she was very clever. But it never occurred to me that she was manipulating me or I was manipulating her. I think we both were. We produced something between us. She couldn't have done it without me and I couldn't have done it without her.

You mentioned The Misfits *and there is that absolutely devastating portrait of Clark Gable, which must be one of the sexiest 'come-ons' ever recorded. Was he manipulating a direct sexual come-on at you?*

You know when he went to hospital – because he took me home the week before he had his heart attack – but when he went in the hospital, *Life* magazine called me up and I was doing a story on Gable for them, and they said, 'Can we have the picture that you took of Gable looking the way he looked on Broadway?' And I said, 'You mean *Machinal*' and the editor said to me, 'How did you know that?' I said, 'That's what he was talking about when the picture was taken.' But he was wonderful with me. He'd never let a photographer go home with him. He invited me home for lunch. When I was ready to leave, he said, 'When are you going back to New York?' and I said, 'This afternoon.' And he said, 'Let me give you something.' And he found a book – a murder mystery, I think, nothing very special – and he wrote in it, 'Hurry back, we'll miss you, love, Clark.' And I had established a friendship with him. And the reason I had established it was because I had gone to watch the rushes of the film when they'd come in every day, because Marilyn didn't want to go and she wanted me to go and I didn't want to go.

Why didn't you want to go?

Because it put a responsibility on me I shouldn't have had, because the director would have my throat!

You mean you would have had to tell him whether you thought it was good, or Marilyn whether she thought it was good?

She talked to John Huston and he told me to come. And one day when we had seen the rushes and Gable had done a wonderful scene, which is normally done by a double, because he gets drunk, tips on to the bonnet of the car, he falls off and no actor would generally do that, but Gable did that. And when we watched the rushes, the lights came up. I heard somebody behind me say, 'What did you think, Mrs Arnold' and I thought it was one of the grips because they were teasing me. And I said, 'Knocked me on my ass – oh yes, Mr Gable, it did!' And a guffaw of laughter from him, and he said, 'You know you've wanted to do a story on me for *Life*; I didn't want to do it, but I'm going to do it for you because', he said, 'you're a good sport about it.'

You've been talking about the relationship that you strike up with people. You photographed Margaret Thatcher. I don't think you followed her around for a very long time. She certainly bossed you around. Was there any sense in which you were taking revenge on her when you photographed her surrounded by those huge stone busts of Winston Churchill?

Oh, no, no. No way revenge. I was working for the *Sunday Times*. I had been following her for months and I was getting nothing. She was telling me where to stand, the light was not flattering to her – and I couldn't use those pictures because it made me a bad photographer. And then one day when I'd been on it for months, Michael Rand, who was the Art Director at the *Sunday Times*, called and said that it was time for him to see those pictures, and I said, 'Michael, Mrs Thatcher looks dreadful, the pictures are terrible.' And he said, 'Oh, you couldn't take terrible pictures.' I said, 'You want a bet?' He said, 'Well, I'll come and have a drink tonight and you'll show me the pictures.' We showed them to him and he said, 'They're terrible.' And just as we were talking, her publicist, Gordon Reece, who was responsible for new dentition and clothes and all of that, he called and said, 'Eve, can you do the Conservative Party a favour?' And (going back to the question) I said, 'What do I do?' And he said, 'Can you show Maggie in the footsteps of Churchill?' I said, 'How do I do that? He's long since cold.' And he said, 'We have these statues by a man called Oscar Nemon who was a friend of Churchill's, and if you can show Maggie with the statues, and Nemon is sculpting Maggie as well, we'll have a story.' So I said OK. And she showed up and this time it was my turn to say, 'Stand here, stand here, stand here', and when they were turned in to the *Sunday Times* they were delighted with them.

She looks very cross.

She looks . . . Well, she looks the way she wanted to look. I just followed her lead. She was standing where she was. She tried to be Churchillian in her stature.

She looks uncomfortable as well.

She is. She hated photography. Didn't like women very much. At any rate, we all thought, and I was worried about it, that we were going to damage her. I found out afterwards that it helped a little to get her elected.

Can I ask you about a very different area of your work, where you were doing photo coverage of an entire country such as China, Russia and, indeed, South Africa? Now, after shooting in South Africa, at the time of apartheid, you say that you fell ill and a doctor could only explain your symptoms by describing it as a broken heart because of your reaction to what you'd seen. Is that right?

Yes, yes. I came back from four months in South Africa absolutely shattered. And my GP sent me to a heart man, and I went, and he prescribed something. Still it went on for months. And he said, 'The only way I can describe it is that you are suffering from a broken heart.' It was such an emotional reaction. I got into the black areas of the homelands, because I found that the police, where I had to check in where I was working and bring my papers, they came at nine o'clock in the morning; they started work and left at five in the evening. So if I came in the homelands at five o'clock in the evening after they'd gone, I could work if I left before nine the next day when they came back to work. But it was a hellish time for everybody in South Africa.

Do you remember the sort of things that caused you so much pain and distress?

The poverty, you can't express it. What happened that broke my heart was that the men would go around, leave for the mines, they would come back once a year, and because they had no way of knowing about birth control, the wife would be impregnated again. They sent very little money home and you saw these woman struggling. And one series of pictures that I did was of children suffering from kwashiorkor or from malnutrition, dying children in mothers' arms. And it was heartbreaking to see these kids dying of kwashiorkor or no food.

Were you also angry?

Yes.

And did that affect how and what you shot?

I suppose I deliberately went out of my way to show how terrible it was, because it was terrible. What else would you do with it?

Now when you were in a very different sort of country, clearly also a very cruel country, such as the Soviet Union, you didn't have that sort of reaction. Your pictures of people in psychiatric hospitals in the former Soviet Union have a terrible cold bleakness as well. What was your reaction to witnessing the systematic authoritarian cruelty in the Soviet Union?

To use your word 'cold', I guess in terms of heat, South Africa would be hot, Russia would be cold. It was very grey, and very depressing and slow, and it seemed to me that that was the tempo of it and it came from them, not from me. What I tried every time when I picked up the camera was not to impose what I thought was there, but hopefully to let it come up from beneath. So if that's your reaction, I guess that's what I saw.

But you never thought that your reaction was to come in and do a photo essay where you say, 'This is a cruel exploitative totalitarian regime'?

Well, if you look at the photographs from the insane asylum, these are political prisoners, they're not insane people, and the Russians are giving them hydrotherapy, they're in bathtubs. I think it depends on the way you read things. First of all, these people were suffering enough without my imposing and asking this upon them. They were long-suffering and you can see it now, a lot of them want to go back to what they had before. You know, you didn't have to pay for your gas or electricity, the state provided it, and it was that kind of bleakness that I saw and I felt. Now if you didn't feel it, then I failed.

I want to come back to some more practical things. How much of the work of making the image is done in the lab, and with editing and cropping?

No cropping in general. Yes, a good print will make a great difference, but a bad print can't spoil a good picture.

From time to time, you've been understandably very cross when people have cropped your pictures in an unauthorised way. There is this lovely image of three Anglican vicars, sitting on a farm gate in the countryside, and over their left shoulder is a cow, and on one occasion one newspaper cropped out the cow.

I know. Well, there's one photographer, who shall be nameless, who asked me if he could have a picture of mine of Marilyn Monroe, and the thing that makes the picture is that she is studying her lines for a scene in *The Misfits* out in the desert. And somewhere near her is a sound boom. My friend wanted that picture without the sound boom, which makes the picture. And you get people who have their own ideas of what your pictures should be like. These are my pictures and they are going to be on my terms.

When you talk to photographers today, the world in which they work, the world of digital images, instantly transmittable back through modems to the news desks of their newspapers – this is such a difference from the world that you or Robert Capa lived in. Are you attracted by the sheer facility that the digital camera now provides?

I have never been a very good technician. I never cared particularly. It doesn't matter if you use a box camera or you use a Leica, the important thing is what motivates you when you are photographing. And this I would like to think is what I have been doing.

What do the younger generation of photographers say to you about their life?

It depends. I ask them why they want to go into photography. Some of them want to do it for the glory, because they would make money and they might, if they are lucky, achieve some notoriety or fame or status. It's tougher, it's much tougher now than it was when I started. It was a new field, there were not many women in it. I am not sure I could do it now.

You say it's the eye and the head and the fingers that count?

And your ability to entrap – that's an emotive word I used deliberately.

To entrap the subject?

To involve them, to have them care enough, to have them feel that you are not going to savage them.

So that's universal, that hasn't changed?

What has changed is that when I photographed, most people that I photographed don't have the right of refusal on their work; it would take Marilyn Monroe at her height to be able to dictate that. Nowadays, if you do a set of pictures which is saleable, you have to sign a release if it is a famous person, that they will get part of the monies in perpetuity that you make. They will have the right to go through and destroy negatives. All that is very different today.

Did life change for you, when instead of being 'here is a young photographer called Eve Arnold coming to take some photographs', it became 'Eve Arnold, the Photographer, is coming'? Did it make life easier or more difficult for you?

I found it pleasant. I liked the idea that people knew my work. I don't care about myself, but I do care about my work. I take my work seriously, I don't take myself seriously. But it did help, you know, when I was under contract for the *Sunday Times*, and they were the only colour magazine in Britain at the time, it was an adventure playground for people like me. I was under contract six months of the year for ten years. Michael Rand and I would talk on the phone. The only instruction he ever gave me was 'make sure you get back in time for the Christmas party'. That doesn't happen now.

What you've just said about work and personality brings us back rather neatly to the very beginning. That you define yourself by your work, which is what I think you do in so many of your images. There is a certain consistency in how you think of yourself and how you photograph other people?

I suppose that's true.

FRANK AUERBACH

'The truth is something that hasn't been captured by painting yet'

I'm very lucky. I have a Frank Auerbach on the walls of my office. Not that I own it, you understand, but I have it on loan and I've got more and more involved in the thick paint, the gashes of colour, the bold gestures of the painting. It's very recognisable, as indeed Auerbach's pictures are. They're only in oil or charcoal, occasionally acrylic now, only portraits of a very limited number of sitters, or of landscapes around Camden Town in north

London. For fifty years since leaving art college, Auerbach has ploughed the deepest of furrows – some say too narrow, perhaps – with an obsessive intensity. He seeks to capture reality, to create something new, create something living, as he puts it, to add something to the world. Frank Auerbach belongs to no school though he has been linked to his friend Leon Kossoff, to Lucien Freud, to Francis Bacon. He has followed no -isms, belonged to no active coterie. He works intensively, slowly and doggedly to achieve the rawness that he seeks. It's a very long way from the eight-year-old German-Jewish boy who arrived in England in 1939, sent from Berlin by his parents to escape Nazism. He never saw his parents again.

What do you remember of family life in Berlin from 1931?

Very, very little indeed. I remember vaguely the flat that we lived in, although I don't think that if I was shown it now, I would recognise it. I remember very little about the streets through which I went to school and I have the haziest possible recollection of my parents. Partly because I was under eight years old when I came to England; and partly because it was a total and utter change. I didn't see for many years anybody I'd seen before. So it was like being picked up and transported into a different world. And if there are no attachments, if there are no associations, then one doesn't remember.

Do you remember them as loving parents?

I remember my father as an indulgent father. I had one of the few sort of tags of memories of him taking pleasure in buying a particular sort of bun for me, and sitting opposite and seeming to take pleasure in the fact that I was greedily eating it. I think my mother may have been a little cooler. Very understandably – because we were Jewish and the Nazis were in power – such memories as I have of my mother have to do with anxiety. I remember once that somebody gave me a sweet in the street and I was put to bed for two days because they thought it might have been poisoned.

Do you understand why they didn't leave Germany when they sent you away?

Well, firstly they were rather elderly parents; I'm not certain of their exact age, but I think I was a late arrival. And then I think that they possibly thought it might all blow over, and that this was rhetoric and nothing would come of it, things would settle down, that they would go on as they had before. And I think they were persuaded that it would be a good idea to send me to England and they made, at least, that decision.

Did you feel abandoned by them?

Absolutely not at all. Partly because I went to this rather remarkable school, which was much more than a school but a sort of community, a small republic.

Called Bunce Court in Kent?

That's right, and – perhaps this is some sort of fantasy or gloss – there is a sort of slight feeling of alienation, which might lead to a life in one of the arts. And I never really quite felt at home with what I remember as a rather bourgeois life where one was put into smart clothes and taken for walks in the park by a nanny, and I somehow felt that this wasn't what life should be like. It seemed to me to be overprotective.

So you were much more at home at the school that you ended up in, this progressive, rather arty school.

Well, not really arty. The emphasis was on community spirit. There were no frills and the woman who ran it had been a German-American Quaker who'd come back to Europe after the First World War, looked after a lot of starving children in Europe and then decided that she would rather look after a hundred children properly than five hundred thousand in the abstract and founded the school. No, the emphasis was on community spirit and culture, and culture was regarded as something that wasn't in any sense dangerous. She had a Michelangelo print on her wall, and we had Brueghels over the dining tables, but it wasn't really arty. You know, there are arty schools where children are encouraged to express themselves. We weren't encouraged to express ourselves; we were encouraged to be part of a community and to have community spirit.

Was it at that time that you saw in a children's encyclopaedia a black-and-white reproduction of Turner's The Fighting Temeraire?

Yes, it was in my first year – I think that I was ill – and I saw *The Fighting Temeraire*. We had these huge volumes and I was looking through them, and I do remember being stirred by the picture and perhaps also by the poem opposite, and I've never quite forgotten it.

It's too facile to say that, because of that, some idea that you might become a painter stirred. But do you know when the idea that you might turn to painting began?

I remember being given a paintbox in Germany. I remember vividly what seems to me to be putting a brush for the first time on to a cake of watercolour. And I think one of my tricks – like you get a dog to roll over – was that I did little drawings and in my case they were of Red Indians on scooters, which I was asked to draw. I can't have been more than three or four. And so it was always a possibility. I'm not certain that I specifically wanted to paint but I do think that I wanted to do something that was what's called creative. I was to some extent attracted to acting and I wrote, as many, many children do, poems and made a translation of the beginning of *Faust*. So it wasn't focused in that way but I think I knew very definitely that I wouldn't want to go into an office, to have that sort of life. And I think perhaps I'd hoped that I might be able to do something inventive rather than routine.

Going back to the question of the stability of the environment: is one of the reasons why you've spent nearly fifty years in Camden Town a reaction to leaving Germany? You have needed to put down roots in one place in a compensatory way?

No, I think the habit was formed by extreme economic instability. I hadn't quite realised when I came to London and went to art school that most of my fellow students had a little money in the building society or somebody would help them buy a flat. I had found a studio that I rented, which had an outside loo and was damp, and a very, very indulgent landlord. And I was in continual fear of being thrown out of this or something going wrong. I may say that before it was rebuilt the Council, if they'd seen it, would have disapproved of it. And I needed this space, so I clung to it like a drowning man to a raft.

Sheer economic need?

Sheer economic need. I needed the studio. If I had been thrown out, I wouldn't have been able to afford or find anything else. And for thirty years that was the situation. I've become far better off but my habits have been formed.

Back to the early years as an art student and the absolutely formative influence of David Bomberg at Borough Polytechnic. What did he teach you?

I'm not certain that Bomberg on his own would have been sufficient. But Bomberg was firstly innately rebellious. There was an official biography some years ago and it hadn't said what I learned later from another book, that although he was a brilliant student at the Slade, he was so stroppy that they threw him out at the end. And he was also a deeply intelligent man with an instinctive plastic sense and education that I think went deeper than that of most other painters in the country. And yet he couldn't have been ingested by the system. He was difficult. What he taught wouldn't have equipped any of us to pass any exam, and there used to be art exams.

So what did he teach you, then?

I also had another art education – all sorts of intelligent people taught what was generally taught. What Bomberg taught was that whereas the drawings that one did in other classes were a sort of addition of various parts – a piece here, a bit there, try and fit them together so that it becomes coherent and is true – he had this idiom that allowed one to go for the essence at the very beginning; to adumbrate a figure in ten minutes and then to redo it, and then to find different terms in which to restate it, until one got something that seemed to contain the mind's grasp of its understanding of its subject. Firstly, the gestures could be very large; secondly, it could be totally incomprehensible as anything but an abstract. And it never was an abstract – its essence lay in the fact that the balance and rhythm were exact; it was an experimental journey. And this was not what was taught in art schools. We were taught by very intelligent people to produce something that could be justified, and that would display one's control and one's intelligence and one's understanding. This wasn't a question of display. This was a question of a private quest, which had certain results. And of course the very great masters are in pursuit of a private quest, which has results that become more and more visible.

'Seeking the spirit in the mass' is, I think, a Bomberg phrase?

It certainly is, yes!

And also painting without inhibition, painting very, very freely. Did he ever try to convert you to Vorticism or anything like that?

No, but he had all these things in him. He had after all copied Holbeins when he was a student. He had been a prize draughts-man at the Slade. He had been a Vorticist and, for me, by far the most talented of the people who worked in that neo-Cubist idiom. He had been an extremely adept landscape painter of very, very topographical landscapes – marvellously done in Palestine in the twenties. So, this wasn't a man who had some sort of single mission. He had a mission and he had an idiom, and I think it probably would have developed. But he knew a great deal about painting; had a deep knowledge of painting from all sorts of angles. And, of course, you can't stand in a class where people are drawing and keep mouthing principles! He came up behind you and said, 'Look at the model, it's doing this, it's doing that. I suggest this' and so on. So it was a practical course of instruction, which actually took up most of the time – but what people remember are the slogans.

Leon Kossoff was a friend of yours and I think you got him to go along to Bomberg's classes, and you're always associated with Lucien Freud, Bacon, Michael Andrews and so on. Did that mean anything at the time apart from being together and sharing some sort of values and interests?

The relationship with Leon was close. When we were both

students at the Royal College of Art and nobody would sit for us – and I think in both of us there was a certain hunger for continuous work from a model, which wasn't provided by the art school – we sat for each other for a year, one day a week. So that Leon would sit for an hour and I would paint; and then I would sit for an hour and he would paint. And what's more, you know, nobody's looking over our shoulder and we can't but have affected each other by the way that we worked. And I saw a great deal of him for a long time after that, and saw his work as it was being done and was very often inspired by it, as he saw my work as it was being done. So that was very much a relationship which is not rare among young painters. They often have one other person whom they work with.

You must just tell me – why would nobody sit for you?

Well, because who's going to sit for an art student who does incomprehensible paintings and who can't pay you and who scrapes the thing off so often and goes on for ever? It doesn't seem a very worthwhile project!

So you were already scraping things off at the time?

Yes, willy-nilly because it wasn't to do with the desire to scrape up. It sounds a sort of drama. But if you're trying to make a whole image that works, that is as it were one thing, and it doesn't work, then there is very little alternative but to paint over it and to scrape it off. And as the paint becomes ludicrously thick, there's no alternative at all – you have to scrape it off. The time I'm talking about it is after about six years of being a student. First, there was something called the Hampstead Garden Suburb, then I was at the Borough Polytechnic for two years, then I spent four years at St Martin's School of Art and then three years at the Royal College of Art, so I spent eight years altogether being a student. And at St Martin's, at one point, they said that if we continued to attend Bomberg's class they would throw us out. But we went to Bomberg and told him this and he said, 'Well, don't kick against the pricks, just keep coming to the class and don't tell them that you're coming,' which I thought was very good advice.

On your style of painting it's been said: 'As drips are to Jackson Pollock and spots to Seurat, so gashes of thick paint are to Auerbach.' Just as a straightforward description, does that mean anything to you?

I'm not so much aware of it. I don't think Seurat would have been aware of the dots – he would have been aware of what he was trying to do, the dots were an instrument. I don't think Pollock would have been aware of the drips, because sometimes there weren't drips after all – some impressive paintings were done with the brush. Seurat's first painting of *The Bathers*, that we've got in the National Gallery, is as grand as a Masaccio in its discovery of three-dimensional sculptural form. And I don't think I'm going to do a thick painting; on the other hand, it's a by-product and I can't, I don't, disavow it and I'm not ashamed of it. And nor am I interested in other people's thick paintings – it's not the essence of the matter.

It's a technique to achieve the essence of what you're doing. The technique, the expression of gashes, vectors and so on, is incidental to the search for meaning?

Absolutely, and in some sense I'm hardly aware of it until it's pointed out. For years now, twenty-five or thirty years, because my paintings are so much thinner than they were, I think of them as being thin rather than thick paintings.

They're three-dimensional – they're almost sculptural, like Giacometti – particularly the earlier ones, aren't they?

The early ones are, yes. It wasn't that when I saw this happening, I stopped it. I was quite prepared to accept something that looked outré and strange, but that wasn't the first thing I wanted to do. The first thing I wanted to do was to state the truth, and the point about the truth is, the truth is not a painting. The truth is something that hasn't been captured by painting yet. As soon as you do something that looks like a painting, there are all sorts of ways of making it work (precisely because it's already been done) that are presented to you. But you've got to venture into unknown territory where you're trying to state the thing, without having these handholds and grips and assistance of previous practice. And so when the paintings became these strange lumps of thick paint, I was very interested and I pursued that line.

That implies that there was an important element of discovery between yourself and the painting. You didn't set out to say, 'I'm now going to paint something a few inches thick.' It happened that way.

Absolutely, absolutely – that's precisely what happened.

Is this element of surprise still there? I think you've said that sometimes you set out to put a mark on the canvas in a particular place and when you get to the canvas, the mark goes somewhere else!

Yes, I think that is true. You know, none of these things are unique to me. I think that to paint a picture with a foreseen conclusion . . . I don't think very many painters do this. I think there's always an element and sometimes a totality of discovery involved in the process – otherwise it would be so boring, wouldn't it? It would be handicraft.

The word that you've often described about your work is 'raw – a quality of rawness'. What does that mean to you?

Well, it's not my work particularly, but when I look at Hogarth's *Shrimp Girl*, there she is, with a great grin on her face. When you look at it closely, it's actually a rather remarkable object because it's an underpainting by Hogarth, which he then started making a more final version – painted the head and, by a miracle, it all hung together and he left it. But I'm aware of the girl. In the recent Vermeer exhibition, there was a little painting of a girl with a red hat. Well, it's a marvellous painting and in a sense, in retrospect it's not unlike a Matisse. But I was aware of the girl looking out at me. And unless the painting reconstitutes itself – not necessarily as a physical object in the world, but something that is adumbrated by the painting and that then settles in one's mind – it becomes a smooth surface behind which something is happening but which doesn't affect one.

You have this store in your mind's eye of some of the world's great images – the Rembrandt in Kenwood, or a Matisse cut-out. What are the other really key images that you have in your mind?

It's an endless list but it changes all the time. I'm one of these people that has art books open on the floor, not always, but very often when I work. And I love, for instance, Mexican sculpture and Frans Hals. It's an endless list of great, great images. Painting isn't dependent on being able to understand the language or assemble an orchestra. All artists who've been curious about their metier, and I think that is almost every artist, have got a vast store of images in their minds. That is a help in the sense that it sets a standard. It's also sometimes an embarrassment in the sense that sometimes you get something that looks too much like something that's already been done – and there's no point in doing it!

You say 'setting a standard'. You've said that you feel like a worm when somebody else – this refers to contemporaries – pulls off something really daring. And you admire it, but also think, 'Why haven't I done that?' or 'I must do as well as that!'.

Well, I do. I challenge anybody to feel, faced with Picasso, any sort of vanity or megalomania at all. What that man's done, it's absolutely incredible. Even if five thousand of the paintings are only very accomplished and very charming, there's thousands of great images and inventions and the marvellous, marvellous sculpture – great sculptures, engravings and drawings and so on. I don't see that there's anybody who's lived through the past century, who hasn't felt in a sense like a little dog following a brass band.

And Rembrandt of course?

Oh, absolutely, yes. I think people at Michelangelo's time must have felt the same. It wasn't the fact that he was so prolific – although he covered a fair amount of space – but the mastery is so great. Yes, or a Rembrandt. Absolutely, I've been haunted by Rembrandt all my life. Even apart from the marvellous painting, it's actually very touching that somebody who was such an assiduous painter, goes on so long, and so painstaking, is such a witty and lively and prolific and brilliant draughtsman. I mean, the dichotomy there is just stimulating and marvellous.

You admire his doggedness; I think you said it's an interesting quality?

I admire the doggedness, yes, I do. Well, this was an exemplar when I had no other choice. I wasn't brilliant, I had to be dogged.

But his drawings are not dogged. The drawings are just abso-bloody-lutely brilliant. I mean, they're just brilliant. It's tender and exact. A drawing of nothing, of a woman bending over and adjusting a child's dress, is both grand and the forms as varied as they are in life. The air circulates around them, and it's like nothing else – brilliant.

You have this extraordinary historical sense, a sense of continuity. I think you've said that from Giotto onwards, it's one school of art and you're part of that. In what way do you feel connected to what Giotto was doing?

Well, firstly, I haven't seen all that much art in the original. But I was in the Giotto chapel in Padua, and I was struck by the radicalism. Firstly, it's very interesting because the light has faded the frescos at one's own level, at ground level, and because light hasn't attacked the frescos as they go into the darker ceiling, they're pretty fresh up there. And there was a guide going round and saying, 'Here somebody's weeping about something, some biblical scene' and you looked, and that's what they were doing. He represented the emotion and the drama directly. I think they're done in response to feelings, so that the gesture would not be done with any view of correctness firstly in view. But if someone touches somebody gently, or the cherubs are blubbing because of death, it's done out of feeling. It seems to me that these are fresh and radical paintings done in response to feeling.

And wonderfully innocent?

Yes. But then, in a sense, there's a sort of element of innocence in great art. There's an element of innocence in what was perhaps the most sophisticated painter who ever lived – that's Velazquez. And yet if you see a portrait of Philip IV – I think, 'There he is.' You don't think this is Velazquez being clever. It's just he's ingested it and made this marvellous image.

We've been talking about your historical influences, also your very strong rootedness in your contemporaries. But do you have any sense of connection with the sort of things that are being done by the young Auerbachs of today: installation art, video art?

Yes. I must say I feel considerable loyalty to everybody working in art and I rather despise some of my colleagues who do not. And I have a very great sympathy with somebody who's trying to do something new, because that's what I am trying to do in a different idiom. And it really has very little to do with uniform, you know. I mean, there are all sorts of people called Cubists – Picasso and Braque were never called Cubists and they rather despised them. There are all sorts of people called Abstract Expressionists. Finally, it's a question of the individual spirit within the idiom. And it's not that one idiom is better than another; as long as it is capacious enough to do something of a large scale in. And when the dust has all blown over, it finally comes down to spirit and quality and perhaps human quality, and nothing to do with the idiom in which people work. And I can see that people got impatient with the picture on the wall for all sorts of reasons – perhaps there are too many of them, too many of them were in museums, it didn't any longer seem a vivid way of presenting experience. I've got total sympathy with people trying to do different things. I think myself that if there's any sort of conflict or battle, it's largely in the head of journalists. Because after all, there's nothing much you can say about painting – which is pretty dumb in the sense of silent activity – and it's there to be looked at. And what are you going to say? So if you can find a conflict or a fight, or talk about prices – well, that's something to talk about!

So you would approach video art, installation art – all the new forms of art – by the same sort of standards that you apply to yourself. Your aim, you say, is to create something which is like a new species of living thing?

Absolutely!

The instruments of expression don't matter?

No they don't, as long as they're capacious enough. Some things are so limited that if somebody types texts and puts them on a wall, good luck to them. But I can't see that this is actually going to stir the sense that responds to plastic art, although perhaps it might. And of course, the reason why I persist in what I'm doing – this is a slightly naughty caveat – if you're working in video or something, in a sense you're in a provincial situation, this is still a very small world, like being the greatest Cubist in Bulgaria! Not very much has been done and I can see that this is very exciting and this has its own stimulus. But to work in a field where an enormous amount of stuff has been done is also exciting, so there it is – there are different ways. And my admirations go to quality rather than to idiom.

Let's talk about your working habits which are now the stuff of legend: seven o'clock in the morning to nine at night, three hundred and sixty-four days in the year. Where does this come from? Was this just an economic drive, or who taught you to work like that?

I don't know, really. I'm not unique, you know. Perhaps I've made more fuss about it, that it should be attributed me, but I know other painters who work like that. It's partly, of course, that there was very little paraphernalia in my life and I was able to do this. But it's simply there's nothing else I really want to devote myself to. And since, for a long time, the business of finding the time to paint (I used to teach) and the space to paint and the colour to paint with, was such a difficult thing to achieve, I now feel perhaps that it would be ungrateful to start mucking about in my last years doing something else. And to be quite honest, sometimes I think, 'Why don't I do something else?' And then there's nothing else. Even if I'm tired and jaded and so on, the idea of picking up a brush and trying to paint just seems more fun to me.

Don't you ever long for the easy canvas, the one that really presents itself to you comparatively early?

Absolutely. I think I start every painting I've ever started with the hope that I'd be able to take the brushes and the colour, put all the colours in the right place, get something that is coherent and alive and fresh and new and true, and I'll be able to leave it. And it just hasn't happened yet – it hasn't happened. What I usually find is that I see something that reminds me far too much of paintings I've already done or that is just simply wrong in some way.

We must talk about your portraits and this very special quality to them. You never do portraits for commission – or is that right?

No, no. I've done two or three portraits on commission. In fact, David Landauer who's sitting for me now – the first portrait was a commission. And I painted a lady called Renee Fedden; somebody asked me to paint that. But it has been very rare and I've made very heavy weather before they started, saying that it would go on for ages, that the place would be a mess and they would have to be reliable. But there are no more than three or four, in my life.

So the vast body of the corpus is this small group of people who sit for you, absolutely regularly, once a week at the same time. And they are sometimes friends, sometimes relatives – occasionally, I think in the case of David Landauer, an Oxford academic, a stranger?

He was a stranger; of course he's become a friend now. A most remarkable man, he is. But he actually came to see whether I would do a drawing of the professor who was Master of Worcester College – I think it was Asa Briggs. And I wrote him a letter and said, 'If he's prepared to go to a messy studio and he's prepared to have somebody work in a rather intemperate way, and if he is prepared to go on sitting for perhaps two years or longer, I'd be prepared to do a portrait of him. And if you want to assure yourself that I am not exaggerating the squalor of the surroundings, you can come and call on me!' So he called, in a beautiful suit, what I think were hand-made shoes, looking immensely neat and Italian, which is his background. And we discussed this and he said, 'No, I don't think the professor would stand this.' And then, as he left, he turned round and said, 'Would you consider doing a drawing of me?' And I looked at him, and I thought, 'I don't think you'll be able to stand this, you look far too sheltered!' And I said, 'Yes, if you're going to be reliable, I will.' Well, he's been sitting for me for . . . I don't know, seventeen or eighteen years. He's a marvellously reliable sitter.

Doesn't the man ever go on holiday?

He goes on holiday, and then he has a substitute sitting for the one he misses. And he has to travel on business and all sorts of things, but he always makes up for it – you know, we do a morning sitting or something for the sitting that he's missed, and it's marvellous, you know.

Why do you like having this group of people – many of whom have sat for you for ten, fifteen, twenty years? Why do you need this to produce your portraits?

Well, some of it is patent in what I've already said: I don't think many people would put up with it. But there's also, I think, a factor on both sides of self-forgetfulness. If they've sat long enough, they're not self-conscious as a sitter. And they become used to my behaviour, and as they become used to me, I can behave freely without any constraints of wondering whether I'm shocking them or anything of that sort! And then it never seems to end to me. Say I've done a head of them; well, that's all right. And I think of the person, I think, 'Well, there's more to them! If they turn slightly, it would be different; if I did a half-length, it would be different.' At any rate, the head only represents an aspect, although it perhaps hangs together and although it seems to me to look like them, there are other things that wait to be portrayed, and so one goes on. And I'm extremely grateful. It's also immensely useful to have somebody to come at the end of the day and sit. It gives one a charge of energy; you know you've got to work, there they are, and I think somehow one gets a charge from the presence of another person.

Do they become different as they become tired, because they'll sit for two to three hours?

Yes, they do. I think people do become tired and it's not a doddle, sitting. You get backache and sometimes you feel rebellious. I mean, I have sat and sometimes it's perfectly all right, sometimes you daydream, sometimes you become desperately impatient. But they keep on doing it throughout these changes of mood.

Do you see them challenging you sometimes?

There is a certain amount of telepathy involved. I sometimes get a sense of something like that, of impatience from them and so on, and that arouses an impatience in me. I do get some of those feelings but, on the whole, it's a present, it's a gift and I'm very grateful for it.

I think you should try to describe (because your models have done so) what you're like when you are painting a portrait. How do you behave?

Well, I'm not putting it on but I don't really know how I behave. They are in a much better position to describe what I do than I am. If things are going really well and I feel that it's almost as though something arose on the canvas of its own accord – you know, the various attempts one's been making come together and an image seems to call to you from out of the paint – when I'm actually in pursuit of this, I really haven't the faintest idea what I'm doing and I may behave somewhat excessively and mutter.

Because you talk to the canvas?

Yes, yes, I may do but I'm really not aware of it. It's to do with the fact that I no longer quite know what I'm doing because all my conscious energies are engaged in this pursuit of the possibility that's arisen on the canvas.

Then despite all that, at the end of each sitting, you will look at it and then you scrape the paint off?

No, not immediately. No, at the end of the sitting I'll put it on the floor and look at it and turn it to the wall. And these habits change. I used to leave it like that until the next sitting and then I would scrape it off and go on. But partly because the paintings have got thinner – and it sounds ridiculous but I can't actually cope with the paint as thick as it used to be – usually after three or four days I blot it off with newspaper so that I have the image. The fact that it looks like a painting has gone but I still have a sort of flattened version of the image, which gives me a basis to go on the next time but without the paint on it. And then I hack away sometimes, when they are on board or something, I hack away at the painting of the dried conglomerations of paint on the picture.

You've used the word about our being destructive. Is this one aspect of the creative process: that you have to destroy?

I think it absolutely is. I think it absolutely is. Yeats said, 'Destroy your darlings.' If one begins to cherish and like what one's done, one's actually on a very slippery slope indeed, selling oneself one's own paintings, and there's nothing to do. One's got to heed one's conscience. And if one feels a slight unease, even if the thing seems plausible and presentable and nobody else might notice that it's no good, one's got to destroy it.

So that's why, even sometimes when it's been framed and comes back from the gallery, you look at it, and you say 'No, that won't work' and you redo it?

I've occasionally done that, yes.

Would the word 'aggressive' have any resonance? Is part of this an aggression?

Well, I think, I feel I'm aggressive, it's partly, of course, age. I've always felt myself to be aggressive and perhaps I am. But on the evidence of other people, I think they thought of me as rather quiet.

Why do you think that you're aggressive?

Most people are aggressive, you know. Life's a battle. We're taught by our genes to be aggressive because it's still in us. We're hunter-gatherers and competitive.

But do you feel that this resolves itself when you paint?

Absolutely. That's precisely what it does!

It sounds as if, given the length of time that it takes to do a portrait or a landscape, you can't be a prolific painter?

No, I'm not a prolific painter. You asked me why I have this routine. It's partly because I am so slow. And firstly for practical and then for reasons of vanity, I'd like to have something to show for it. So I go on a long time with pictures and unless I did that every day and every evening there would be very little indeed to show. This year I think I've done five paintings, finished five paintings. They're relatively small, so I'm not very prolific. But I have been going on a long time and now there's an exhibition at the moment and it's not all my work – it's about a quarter of it.

Now, that's your work inside your studio. Then, there's your beloved Camden Town. I suppose it is beloved rather than habitual, is it?

Well, it's beloved in the sense – I've said this before but it still seems to me to be true – people become fond of their pets. They get a kitten at a pet shop and you don't know what sort of kitten it's going to be. It might be a placid cat, or it might be an irritating cat, or a scratchy cat but you become fond of it – it's your cat. And I live in Camden Town and I pass those streets every day and it's my part of London, so I've become extremely fond of it.

How much work from the life and in the exterior do you do? You don't, like Monet, take your canvases out and then paint in the open air on Primrose Hill?

No, I don't. I do drawings and I tend to do them every day before I start, so that they're drawings, they're scribbles really but they're drawings of a different sort. At the beginning, I simply record and find how many windows there are in the building, and where exactly the chimneys are situated and all sorts of things because I don't know them, and it seems to me to be more interesting. People used to talk about the aleatory element and luck and chance in painting. Well, it's all chance if you go out and draw; you don't know what anything's going to be. Then buses come across and people move and then you do more drawings and all sorts of sensations about pace and speed and the plastic coherence of the material that you're dealing with. And people walking across begin to appear in space, and you just make these drawings and take them back to the studio. And it gives you an impetus to do something with the painting you're working on.

Was there never the drive to say, 'I've really got to have a new visual stimulus. I've got to look at somewhere different, I've got to paint the Grand Canyon'? Or like your friend Michael Andrews, who went out to Australia and painted Ayers Rock; that search for the exotic?

Well, the exotic is only in the title. There is a chimney in Mornington Crescent which I've passed for the past fifty years. I've looked at this thing and it is very exotic. It's very remarkable – like Cleopatra's needle or something, stuck in the middle of the Crescent. And I've thought it's really, really important that I should paint this thing because I'm the only person who knows about it properly. And then a few years ago I started painting it. Well, that wasn't like anything else, and the configurations to the building seem like canyons sometimes to me. And there's a set of three tower blocks with different coloured headbands on them and I put those into a painting. Somehow it seemed to be a challenge that I should attempt to record this. It looked so daft that it seemed to make some sort of formal point. Finally one's response to things in painting is wordless. And these three primary colours on top of these buildings seemed to be a sort of challenge, so I painted those!

You say it's a formal response. It's not a social response. It's not a narrative response either, to life in Camden Town?

No, not really, not really. Buses and people and so on appear and I suppose, in some sense, the fact that it is inhabited and perhaps that it dwarfs the people does sometimes surface. But it's not a conscious drive to comment in that way at all. Although sometimes, when the painting is finished and done, there seems to be some sort of comment in it and that's fine.

Now, you're painting your studio, and you're finding this very, very difficult. Why do you think this is? Because you have got so much of yourself in it?

No, none of these sort of emotional, introspective things work very much on me. It's partly because I've never done anything quite like it before and I've put myself into the picture painting and the whole composition is unfamiliar. But perhaps most of all is the fact that, by my standards, it's a large canvas, and my pictures are not terribly large. And it may be that I find it hard to access the energy to get the whole thing freshly organised – it is a complex picture; there's a lot of stuff in it – to get the whole thing organised in a fresh and daring way so that it hangs together. I don't give up, I shall keep on trying but I may never finish it.

What would you say to a young artist starting off from art school today?

It seems to me to be a bit of an impertinence for me to say anything to a young artist, but I'll try. I think subject is terribly, terribly important. It's implicit, it isn't only the labelled item, as it were: the head or the tree or the factory or the abstract. One has certain deep feelings which express themselves in a plastic way. But there must be some experience that is your own, and try and record it in an idiom that is your own, and not give a damn about what anybody else says to you. I think that is important and I think that the key word there's 'subject'. Find out what matters most to you and pursue it.

And is there one of your own paintings or charcoals that you feel most closely matches up to these criteria?

Well, there's two, at the moment. They're both early and it may have to do with the fact that they were the first. One is a large head of *EOW* that's actually in the show at the Academy, which I went on for ages and which now seems a very strange object and still looks like the person. And it seems to me to stand up by itself, perhaps, and not have a great deal of reference to other art. And the other's a painting that's called *Earls Court Road Building Site* which is just a few very thick lumps of black and white and red ochre. All the experience of making the painting, which was actually very elaborate at many stages, is buried there, and it seems to me to be a remarkable object. And though nobody else may be aware of it, I am aware of the amount of painting experience that's buried under those heavy lumps of black and white and ochre.

HARRISON BIRTWISTLE

'It takes ten seconds to play but
two days to write'

                        In the second half of the last century,
British musical life was dominated by the names of Benjamin Britten and
later Michael Tippett. A generation behind, there was a trio of composers
who had met in the early 1950s at the Royal Manchester College of
Music: Alexander Goehr, Peter Maxwell Davies and Harrison Birtwistle.

Born in Accrington in 1934, Birtwistle entered the college as a
clarinettist and initially kept quiet about his serious interest in

composing. It was another decade, after further periods of study and making a living teaching and playing, before Birtwistle decided to concentrate on composition alone. Scores from the mid-1960s such as *Tragoedia* and *Punch and Judy* marked him out as an independent voice. They were the first major scores to draw on what have been the continuing interests of Greek theatre, myth and ritual in his work.

In 1975, at Peter Hall's invitation, Birtwistle became Music Director at the National Theatre – appropriately at a time when he was midway through his then largest stage work, *The Mask of Orpheus*. Three more operas have followed – *Gawain*, *The Second Mrs Kong* and *The Last Supper* – and another is in its early stages. These have been complemented by a series of major orchestral scores confirming Birtwistle as the leading British composer, with conductors like Rattle, Dohnányi, Boulez and Barenboim championing his works internationally and with honours and teaching positions at some of our leading musical institutions. But he refuses to compromise, and audiences have yet to take his music to their hearts as they did with Britten and Tippett. They respect; they have yet to love.

Talking about your work you've said, 'My music always causes problems.' Do you enjoy that?

Enjoy is not the word. Surprised, because I don't know why there are problems. I don't understand what the problem is.

But there is a sense in which you have this interesting dual image at this stage in your life: the elder statesman, whom everybody wants to commission; and also the bad boy of music, the person whose music often causes controversy or problems.

Well, I can only ask questions. I ask the question why is it music that always causes this? You don't really get it in the art world quite so much, and even if you do get the problem like the Tracey

Emin bed, at least people are inquisitive about it. And the problem with music is, first of all you can't buy it and you can't own it. So it's very often a fait accompli that you go to the thing, so therefore you're trapped and you have to listen to it. And I think that is one of the problems about it: that you can't own it and you're trapped sitting there having to listen to it. But there are more interesting things about music and the comprehensibility of music, because I think the comprehensibility of music is really about tonality. Our ears are accustomed or conditioned by tonality. So therefore, if there is a piece of tonal music that we've not heard before, there is already something in which the journey of tonality helps you through it. Now if that doesn't exist, this different sort of journey, this different sort of continuity – I think it's more about that than the dissonant noises – I think that people get lost in it. I think that's where the problem is. But I don't think that's unique to me.

It's not as if you write atonal music?

Far from it, far from it. I seem to be an emblem for that; that's when I say I can't understand it. Why me? Because it would seem that I am part of the establishment and yet the establishment doesn't know the music I write.

But which establishment? You're commissioned by Glyndebourne, you're commissioned by Covent Garden, you're that part of the establishment. But the social and political establishment couldn't be more confused and bewildered by what you write.

Yes, but I've heard people say that 'it sounds like a load of Birtwistle to me' – you know, that sort of thing. And the thing about my piece *Panic* at the Proms, for instance, I don't think it was *Panic* that was the problem there, it wasn't me. I think that any piece of modern music in that context would have caused that sort of problem.

So the problem was not Harry Birtwistle the composer, but John Drummond the Director of the Proms for deciding that he was going to provoke the Last Night audience by commissioning a piece from you. Let's blame it all on John!

That's not true either. I wasn't commissioned to write a piece for the Last Night of the Proms. And secondly, John didn't ask me to write a piece for saxophone. I had to go and see him in his office to solve this problem that I wanted to write this piece for John Harle, the saxophonist. And it wasn't until I had written quite a lot of it that I was told it was going to be on at the Last Night of the Proms. So there was no sort of set-up or trying to do anything.

This was not Birtwistle cocking a snook at the music-loving audience by writing something as provocative as he could?

I wouldn't know how to do that. And I wouldn't be interested in doing it. It's not what I am in the business of writing music about.

But I seem to remember you actually got hate mail, didn't you?

Yes. I got a lot of letters. I got a lot of good letters as well. And the tabloid press got into it and I heard people denouncing it who hadn't heard it.

But did it upset you when you got the hate mail?

Not in the least. No. You can't be worried about that. I know what the issue is and I don't write music in order to irritate anyone.

Let's go back to the very beginnings for a moment and the thing which pitchforked you into music: your mother insisting that you take up the clarinet. Did she have to insist or was it just a normal thing for a parent to do?

I think there were two things. It was the ambition of my parents to give me music, otherwise I wouldn't have even known what it was. And secondly, she said that she wanted me to do it to keep me off the streets. Because I lived in a working-class area of Lancashire and I think she wanted me to be occupied in directions that she thought – otherwise I would have been doing something else.

Did you resist and say, 'That's not the sort of thing that my friends are doing'?

No. I understood it was a flute that I was going to be taught, and it turned out to be a clarinet. And as soon as I could read music, I wrote it. It seemed to be quite the natural thing to do. I was eight.

So you were writing pieces for the clarinet, you were writing songs?

I was writing music to play and of course the clarinet is a single line. And I think that aspect of music is something that has carried me forward, that I identified in retrospect as being something of the way that I think about music. It doesn't begin through harmony, it begins through a sort of linear idea about music.

Lyrical? Tunes?

Melody. Melodic. I think we could have a discussion about the difference between tune and melody.

How are they different?

Well, a tune is 'Lilliburlero' – with a beginning and an end. And a melody is something which is contour, so a tune can also be a melody.

Does 'lyrical' then have overtones of meaning, or is just a more general description?

That's a description of melody, that it can be lyrical, yes.

And linearity, which is sometimes used, is that just a rather more technical word for looking at things in melodic ways?

Well, it's more than that with me because it really comes back to what I was saying before about a very self-conscious attempt at a different sort of continuity. Because I'm very often asked, 'Are you ever surprised at the music that you write?' And I think that what the question means is that if you took a tranche of it, a slice of it, and listened to a moment, 'Are you surprised at the noise it makes?' And I am never surprised by that. But what I am surprised about is how things unfold in time, how things speak and how time works in music. And because we are no longer restricted by this tonal procedure, this logic of tonality, then it's open into different sorts of continuity. And this is something that I have self-consciously attempted to take on. There are certain things in my music – progressions if you like, certain sorts of continuity – which would be very difficult to have if you had tonality. This is what I feel I am free from. But I think you lose an awful lot through not having tonality as well.

What did you know about this whole process when you were a young student at the Manchester College?

I didn't know anything about it. Absolutely nothing.

What did you know about composition, then?

Nothing. I was a clarinettist when I was a student, I wasn't a composer. My colleagues, Maxwell Davies and Alexander Goehr, were composers. I was a clarinettist, but I always knew that I was going to write music. I just sort of played around with it, as far as they were concerned. But I had written a huge amount of music before I became a student, this is the important thing. So consequently when I was confronted with official tuition, I found it very difficult to compare what I did with what I was being taught. So I left off and waited until time elapsed and I could not be a student any more and could get back to where I left off.

And what was being taught? Was it still essentially the pre-war English Pastoralist tradition?

No, that wasn't taught either. In England at that time, you were not taught composition; there was no composition being taught. Now I feel that there is maybe too much composition being taught. But to be a composer was . . . well, it was what Beethoven did, it sort of happened somehow!

So there you were, these young men, early 1950s, post-war atmosphere, a very different world, a world opening out again?

Absolutely fantastic. Because first of all, modern music was not played. So it was all absolutely new and it was something that you became involved in. For me it was just extraordinary.

What were you hearing? What modern music was available?

None, nothing. I learned my music from the Third Programme. And also a lot of other things. If you ask me where I was educated, I would say the Third Programme. I remember hearing Beckett on the Third Programme. You see, I came into a world of modern music. There was this sort of English pastoral thing; there was something that happened before the war and that we didn't have access to and it was called Hindemith and Schoenberg. But nobody really knew the difference between Hindemith and Schoenberg. I certainly didn't!

So what did you know of serialism, as a student or just after you left the college?

I learned serialism from Sandy Goehr.

And what did you think of it?

I thought that it was another way of writing music; it was the future, and everybody thought that this was the future. I think there are two important things that have happened in the last century in the arts. One is Cubism. And one is serialism. And you ignore them at your peril. I think that Cubism changed the way that we looked at the world and serialism changed the way that we listened or thought about music. And even if you react to it and you write in C major, it has had a huge influence on C major really. But it was something that I couldn't make work for myself.

Your exposure to serialism didn't make you think that was the way for you to write music?

Well, maybe for a short time I thought that it was the way to write music, because that was the way that people wrote music then. But the problem was applying it to the music that I had in my head. I couldn't make a comparison between the music in my head and serial music. I couldn't make serial music be what I was looking for.

That must have been very brave, mustn't it, to say this is not for me because it won't allow me to reveal what I can hear?

Well, I don't know whether it's brave. I don't think there was any alternative. It seemed to me that it was simpler for me to improvise, to improvise a chord that I liked, that was directly from my subconscious state, if you like. I would play a chord and I would think, 'Well, this is quite interesting, this has something in it which is of interest to me.' And then to put that under a microscope, to look at it and see what it was made of and what were the things in it. It always seemed to be made of inconsistencies. Whereas in serialism, it was the opposite. I could never make these chords with serialism without cheating.

And what is the point of cheating?

Well, what is the point of cheating? So, if I make a chord, if I say that this seems to me the chord that I like, then I can commit that to analysis and I can make more of them. I find a way of then proliferating the situation, a method of composition if you like. I would hate to think that I have a method of composition because it is something that happens, is quite ephemeral, what I do. I'm doing one thing one day and a year later I notice that it's not quite what I was doing before. So there is a sort of process of change of the way. And it's never a sort of light in the sky, like a bolt from the blue and 'oh, that's an interesting idea'. It sort of creeps in, the way that I do things. And then over a process of time, if you come back to my chord, I realised that it was a sort of modality, which was to do with situations which have increments, which have more of one thing than another. And I think that that is why modal music sounds like it does, like a pentatonic scale that has a certain flavour. So I suppose that what I am is a sort of a modal composer, but a mode in the sense that it's to do with hierarchies, you know, more of one thing than another.

And that could be anything from volume to instrumentation, to orchestral colour, anything like that?

And that's where it becomes a formal thing, that's where it starts to become a sort of system.

But it's your system driven by the particular circumstances in which you're composing?

Yes. And it never came out of an academic situation. Nor have I ever done anything apart from using these methods of composition to express ideas. The idea comes first and then I look for the material to express it. I haven't got a book in which I look back and think, 'Well how do I do this?' But the biggest thing that I found, the most important thing, apart from pulse, is that I realised that the pitch instance – pitch instance is A or B, which is the essence of serialism – this was the problem, in that what was more interesting for me was the interval. The interval has a definite character, it comes down to the mode, comes down to the pentatonic scale. The pentatonic scale is a scale of limited intervals. And intervals are the things that are flavours. A minor third is a very specific interval; an augmented fourth is a very specific interval. And so in thinking in intervals, more than pitches, this is where a whole vista opened for me.

Can I clear one thing up? You've never had any impulse to follow anything connected with the classical disciplines? Sonata form doesn't mean anything to you; symphonic form doesn't?

No. No, because it doesn't have any direct reference to the music I write. And I have a problem with music that apes sonata form and then is not tonal. You see, I think it goes through the motions of music. It's a set of rules that we're familiar with. But the interesting thing for me is to make forms which are in a sense unique, where the music speaks in a different way, so it's a different sort of continuity.

You have said the moment you began to appreciate that you could write the music that you wanted, you were profoundly affected by Messiaen and the Turangalîla *Symphony. When I first read that, I thought I can think of few works that I would associate with Harry Birtwistle less than the* Turangalîla *Symphony! So what did Messiaen do for you?*

Well, you see, it is not Messiaen directly. You see up there is a picture of John Wayne in the corner, John Wayne in *Stagecoach*. Now, people have been in here and said, 'Why are you interested in John Wayne?' I'm not interested in John Wayne as such. His entry in that movie is, for me, a very interesting moment; how things are introduced, how things gather. And that moment is extraordinary. And Messiaen to me is rather like that. The first Messiaen that I heard, I thought there is another way of writing music! And he sort of explained it. I think that I performed in the first performance of the *Quartet for the End of Time*. But at the beginning of the *Quartet for the End of Time* is that little chart about rhythm. And that was pretty moving because I thought, 'It gives you courage. What have I been on about! Somebody else is doing it, maybe there is something there.'

This was Messiaen's own way through, without anybody else's rules, his own way of writing music?

Yes. To talk to him about it, to listen to him talking, you'd think that he was in the tradition of music from the beginning of time. But he really did invent a sort of music in one go and he was still doing the same thing at the end of his life. He managed to shuffle the cards in different ways but there were melodies at the beginning, which were the same melodies at the end.

Let's talk about theatre and the huge role that theatre and writing for theatre has had. Punch and Judy *– 1967 I think it was, at Aldeburgh – your first major work, music theatre, not opera. What was the real driving impulse behind that?*

Well, there are certain things, which were inside the music, which I thought could manifest themselves in a theatrical context; it was a natural extension. That's purely a musical thing. But because of the sort of music I was writing, it also suggested a sort of theatre. If you have a narrative, linear narrative requires a particular sort of music. Now, I was not writing linear music.

And you weren't writing narrative music either, were you?

I wasn't writing narrative music either. So that suggested a sort of theatre, that's one aspect of it. But there is another aspect to it. Right from the beginning of my childhood, theatre was pretty important to me because I used to play for the amateur dramatics. I would be obviously older than that, but probably twelve or thirteen, and the amateur dramatics, they had musicals: *Bless the Bride, No, No, Nanette* – and there's one about a Mountie.

Rose Marie! And that ignited your feeling that when something happened on the stage there was a sort of magic?

There's that side of it. And it always happened before Christmas. And there was a time when the pantomime came and the pantomime was a sort of fourth-rate pantomime and the amateur dramatics always had a professional orchestra, I don't know why. Professional in the sense that we were paid. And that was really extraordinary because it was a sort of theatre that was from the music hall tradition really. You were given a book and it wasn't clarinet and saxophone parts, it was just a book with music. And they put it together and you played what bit you liked and you learned to play it from memory. And there were all sorts of devices. I remember they used to shout 'Happy for tabs'. Now, 'Happy for tabs' is 'I want to be happy'. And he'd just shout it. The band would play it, you see, and that would get everybody off stage. And as the season went on, fewer people came and the band got smaller and I was left in the end, seriously, with just the bass player, a drummer, a saxophone player and me. And I was just a kid. And it would run. We would do about a month, I think, a week before Christmas and then about three weeks after until it sort of packed up.

I think the wonderful thing about that is that it shows that what a young person takes in almost doesn't matter. It doesn't have to be serious. It doesn't have to be listening to Beethoven. It's just an incredibly rich lode of experience.

It really was. I think I only understood the experience in retrospect, but nevertheless, I do think it was a major influence on me. And also a roughness, you know, there's a sort of roughness that I quite liked. Something slightly raw and like theatre probably was a long time ago.

Of course, theatre wasn't raw when you went to the National Theatre?

Well, some of what I did was. When I did the *Oresteia* that was pretty raw.

You were making things up with the musicians and the actors at the time. Do you think that was a conscious evocation of your experiences as a twelve-year-old in the pit for the music?

Maybe. It's just a different way of working because the theatre works in a completely different way. I was talking to you before about writing opera and you said, 'When are you going to write your next piece?' And I said, 'Well, the opera companies talk in ridiculous terms, like 2012 or something' – which doesn't mean anything. The interesting thing about the theatre is that they only know what they're doing tomorrow. And you go in and in eight weeks you have a piece. And so, consequently, I can't have the situation where I sit here and write it out and then turn up and say, 'So this is the music!' You can't have that relationship with theatre. You have to go in with your two boots, with your wellies, and do it and there are ways of doing it.

So while you were doing this incredibly informal, spontaneous, rapid, journalistic work at the National Theatre, you were also struggling – because you were struggling – with your first really big opera, The Mask of Orpheus. How did those two processes, the instantaneous and the very considered, work together or not work together?

Well, they are two separate things. There are certain things which are cross-referred. There are things which relate; one does influence the other. I mean, the directness of it is something which is important, particularly in opera. And I think that is what I brought to the National Theatre. I like to think that what I brought was a sort of formality which music can describe. It can underline and underpin a formality in the theatre which is something that is part of my armoury, which I think that I can bring to it.

But at the same time, it took you five or six years to write The Mask of Orpheus.

It was ten years in writing it from beginning to end, but it took me five years to write it.

Did that reflect huge difficulties in doing so, rather than just the complexity of the score and its length?

No, just time. I gave up in the middle because it wasn't going to be performed. And I said, 'I'm not going to finish it unless it's going to be performed' and then it was performed. I picked up the threads, and I remember it was like doing research into some sort of obscure sort of Egyptian papyrus when I came back to it. I unfolded these things and of course I'd changed in the meantime. You don't just pick it up and think I'm the same person as I was five years ago. I find in the continuity of my work here, I find it very hard to lay off. I can only believe in what I'm doing for the moment. If I get to a point in my work where I think I know where I'm going and I go away and leave it, when I come back, I very rarely continue in the way that I thought I was going to continue!

So the moment you have some sense of certainty or predictability, you think, 'Forget it, I've got to keep on surprising myself'?

Yes. Very often I can't understand why. But very often, if I ever need a solution to something, and I find it, I walk away!

Looking around, we are in your work room. Do you use the word 'work'? Do you think of it as work, rather than 'it's the most wonderful thing I want to do in the morning'?

It's the most terrifying thing to do. It causes me a great deal of pain and I am not being romantic or, you know, 'the artist must suffer'. I'm not into that syndrome. I worry a great deal. Keeps me awake at night. I dream in the abstract – can you imagine that? Can you imagine sort of cogs, wooden cogs that are meant to fit, but don't. And then you try to put them in another way and they don't, and it's difficult to describe but it's a sort of abstraction, it's not a sort of psychodrama!

Do you solve anything in those dreams?

No.

Looking around here, your scores, written in darkish pencil, look terribly neat. But what have you had to do before you put pencil to paper? Are there all sorts of rubbings out which I can't see?

There is a pile of paper there, which are the notes for this. And what you're looking at is a finished thing. So there's one, two, three, four journeys until you get to what you see there. And even in doing that, I will change things.

Four journeys in the sense of four attempts at a solution?

One is a sort of shorthand; then you gradually bring it into focus and there are certain logistical problems to do with an orchestra. It is a much smaller place than you think. There are never enough instruments. I don't mean to make more noise. So it's always a situation of compromise.

And the piece that you've got here is a commission from the Cleveland Orchestra. Does it matter that it's a commission? Of course, it's money and you know it's going to be played and so on. But does it actually have any effect on your creative process?

No. No, it doesn't. I try to make my commissions be what I want to write next. And I've been lucky in my life in managing to do that. And if a commission comes along and it doesn't fit into a sort of context, I then put it on the back boiler and hope that by doing something else, then it will come, then it will have a context. But this piece is a dark nocturne. It's the ultimate nocturne.

Very dark and very slow?

Yes. It's getting faster. The other day, it started doing something which I never thought it would: it started ticking!

This is Harrison's Clocks *coming back to haunt you?*

Well, maybe it is. Now it does sound as if I'm saying that I have no control over the thing. But what I can never do in writing a piece is have a sort of pre-compositional scheme. I can't be an architect and then, you know, then you build the building!

I thought you did a lot of working out with numbers, and having a lot of very formal sketches?

Yes, but that's to do with the moment, it's not to do with the superstructure of the piece. It's not to do with the journey of the piece, it's only to do with the detail of the piece.

You talk a lot about the resemblances or not between composing music and painting. You envy people like Cy Twombly, Bacon, Jackson Pollock, who can put their intuition directly on to the canvas, whereas you've said that's not something composers can do. 'What I'm mainly doing', you've said in the past, 'is technical, technical, technical.' Looking at your score, one can only sympathise!

Yes. Because there is no equivalent in music of being able to take a big brush and make a gesture and see what the effect is.

A big noise needs particularly detailed working out?

You build it up by pebble, by pebble, by pebble.

Do you have no idea how many pebbles you're going to load on at any particular time?

No. But at the same time, the thing about spontaneity, the sort of spontaneity that I'm talking about . . . Heaven forbid that I would want to take a big brush and do that, but there are people who have done that. The actual amount of time it takes is the opposite to spontaneity. Because the initial thing is that you might want this gesture, but then you have to start with your Lego and then you build it up and build it up and build it up. And so consequently, the next bit of spontaneity is a long way from the last one. I mean, just look at that piece of page there. It takes about ten seconds to play and two days to write!

By the time you've ground it out in this meticulous detail, is the detail so great that there is no life in it?

Well, maybe. I don't know until I hear it. My big neurosis with this piece, my *Night Vigils*, if you like, is the fact that it's a slow piece and being brave, if you like, of keeping it like that. Of not wanting to make it a bit more interesting, by saying 'move it on a bit here'. You've got to sort of keep your eye on the ball, I think. That's the risk I'm taking.

It's interesting what you said, because somebody to whom you taught composition said, 'Harry is very practical, he'll say things like, "Have you tried making it louder?".'

Yes. One of the things I have found out about students is to make them realise and identify what the idea is. Very often they are dealing with things that they've never identified. And so, I also might say, 'Don't make it louder. Why don't you just keep it like that?' But this question of the analogy between painting and music, I don't really think there is one. You see, if you look at my pictures that I have in that room, they're minimal pictures. What would be the equivalent?

The equivalent to your music?

Yes, or any music. There was a student who wrote a piece called *Barnett* and it was influenced by Barnett Newman and he came in with this big score, this beautiful white paper, and turned it over and there was a list of instruments down the left-hand side. Not a note on the page, just barlines. OK? Turn the page, nothing! Nothing. Nothing on the page. So at about page ten, the whole orchestra played 'bbaaagghhh!' And then it stopped.

Now, the equivalent in music is a negative equivalent. What he hadn't understood is that all the white pages should have been filled. He should have written white noise. He should have done something and started, and done something that represented whatever that was, and then when he got to the loud noise it would have been sound because that's how music works.

But the art that you've got around you is minimalist. But minimalist music has nothing to say to you, does it? Or you for it?

What we call minimalist music doesn't mean anything. I find it very simple-minded. The only true minimalist is Webern; that's what I would call minimalist music. And the equivalent to the minimal painting that I have – I would like to think it has more in common with Webern than with minimal music, with Steve Reich.

Why do you think minimalism is so popular?

Because you don't have to listen to it! My problem with it is, because it goes through a process, my brain gets there before the music does. You know, for me it's like waiting for a bus. I can understand it in this sort of dazzly way, and that it's a complete reaction to Webern. I mean, Webern was the great influence of the twentieth century, maybe more so than Stravinsky. And it's the opposite to that. I think it's a total reaction to that aspect of thinking about music.

You have this evolving sense of the music that you write. When it comes to a major collaboration, such as working with librettists, with their own artistic integrity, how much of a problem is this? How does that tension work?

Well, it depends how the text works. If the text is conventional in the sense that it's linear, a linear text, then it's difficult. But if you do something like I did in *The Mask of Orpheus* – which is something I intend to pick up again and it is something that I feel that I have not really exploited enough – there is the question that if you're dealing with a myth and you're dealing with a known subject matter, then you can deal in the elements of it in a musical way. For instance, if somebody is in the underworld and looks back, you know exactly what that means. And if you know that it's Orpheus, even if you started an opera on Orpheus with somebody looking back, you know exactly what it was. So therefore, you're free of the subject matter. There is a known quantity before you go to the piece. I can see no point in composers who just simply set a play to music. For me, that is just something else to applaud. It's just making a modern equivalent of what already exists. Because opera is not in our vernacular any more. The cinema is the thing that is. So for me in working in the theatre or working in opera, it has to be something about opera. The subject matter is incidental. It has to take on the form, because it's a unique thing. It's something unique within the nature of theatrical expression. I could tell you of a project that I have started working on, and I've already spent a week on it, and I was given the facilities at the National Theatre to work on it. The way that I'm trying to do it is not with a text and somebody writing it and then me setting it. What I am doing is I am going to make a scenario; I am working through a storyboard without any text and using actors to do it, and then I'm going to write the music to that. So that all the timings, and the length of things and that, that's going to be my scenario and text is only going to come into it where it is necessary.

*Then looking ahead still further, another opera on another absolutely
key classical myth, The Minotaur.*

Well, there again it's the same thing. Because I want to assume
that we know what the story is before we get there. But I have an
interesting idea about this: to use the idea of a labyrinth as a
metaphor, as a musical metaphor, so that within the piece we
might begin and go to the end three times, so the opera will begin
three times and end three times. But in the course of the journey
through it, we will touch on different aspects of the narrative.

*So you're carrying that around, that idea is at some level of your
mind, while you're working on other pieces?*

Yes. It's not simply a question of thinking of an interesting story
to tell. It's really an interesting story to retell and something where
I can deal with my preoccupations as a composer of pure music in
the theatre. So the same journeys that I make through a piece of
music, I can make in the theatre. Now, this idea of going through
this labyrinth three times has come out of my musical thinking. I
didn't think of it as a theatrical idea, I first thought of it as a musical
idea. And it's kind of interesting, isn't it, that you might be able to
begin and end a piece three times?

ANTHONY CARO

'I don't know where I am, and I love it'

Anthony Caro is widely regarded as Britain's greatest living sculptor. After a brief period working with Henry Moore from 1951 to 1953, he turned to making sculptures out of steel after a visit to the United States in 1959. In 1960 Caro made his first steel sculpture: a parallelogram, square and circle welded together and called, simply, *Twenty-Four Hours*. Since then, Caro has explored the world of steel, steel detritus, industrial offcuts, in a prolific career, his work being in public and private collections all over the world. In recent years he's had exhibitions at the National Gallery, the Tate and represented Britain with a group of other artists at the Venice Biennale. His latest involvement has been in the Millennium Footbridge over the Thames at Bankside and he became a member of the select Order of Merit earlier this year. He is the grand old man of British sculpture with all the vigour of a very much younger one.

When did you know that you wanted to be a sculptor?

I wasn't sure what I wanted to be early on because I think a sculptor was something that you were not allowed to be in my family. You were not allowed to be a dilettante and any sort of artist was a dilettante in my parents' book. So I wasn't sure what I wanted to be, and in fact I tried architecture, engineering, and they didn't grab me and it took a long time. And I went into the Navy – it was the end of the war – and finally I said to my father, 'Look, I am going to make a living at this, I am going to do it properly, I can teach.' 'Well, you're going to be very uncomfortable, you know; you're not going to be able to have a family and you're going to live in squalor, but if that's what you want to do . . .' So I went ahead and did it. And yet my father was very supportive, actually, in the end, very supportive.

Did you have the faintest idea then what kind of sculptor you were going to end up being?

No, I didn't, John. I thought, really, that being a sculptor meant doing a portrait of a general on a horse or a figure portrait like an Epstein portrait or something. I didn't know what it meant at all. I just knew that I liked the reality of clay, the stuff that I used to make it with. I worked during my holidays with Charles Wheeler, in Charles Wheeler's studio, and he was very kind to me and I think I just got the idea that this was the right material for me. I mean: I loved drawing, I didn't like painting because I wasn't into colour at all, and so sculpture was what I wanted to do.

What made you go to Henry Moore in 1951, after you'd finished at the Royal Academy?

Well, I hadn't really finished at the Royal Academy. I was still a student there because it was a five-year course, a very long course. But I felt I'd come pretty well to the end of it, and I was being taught then by old academicians who did these sorts of generals and I felt there must be more to it than this, there must be more. So I found out where Henry Moore lived and went and asked him, 'Can I come and do some assisting?'

Just like that, without any forewarning?

I'm afraid so. He was very kind, he took me in. I went to him six months later, and worked for him for two years and went and lived out in Much Hadham; and we had a little cottage there and we rented it, and I used to bicycle up the hill to Henry's every day and work away there. We were working a lot on waxes and on a certain amount of bronze casting because he'd made a foundry, a little foundry down the end of the garden, which he'd made quite wrong. We'd made it too wide for the size of the crucible, so we could never get the bronze to actually melt. We got more and more hot, the coke went bright red and then we had to put more coke in, it burned down and so we would be pumping this actual physical bellows, big pair of bellows. We pumped them until two o'clock in the morning! That was when we finally poured. It was great fun, it was like a sort of party, but it was not a very good way to do bronze casting.

What did you learn from Moore, apart from avoiding certain practical mistakes like that?

Oh, I learned a lot from him because he was very generous with his books, with talking about art to me. He knew I liked to talk about art; I liked to think about it. He let me borrow a book. Probably I borrowed two or three books and then changed them, so I'd take home a book at night on Negro art or on Surrealism. We hadn't seen any Negro art. I was at the Royal Academy Schools; you didn't know about Negro art. It wasn't something that was on our syllabus.

Entirely classical and classical plaster casts?

Absolutely. They looked horrible. They all looked brown because they were covered with shellac, so they didn't look a bit like the real Greek things or the real Renaissance things at all. They're still there, by the way, they're still there.

Was there anything that you did not learn from Henry Moore? Did you begin to think, 'The man is a great sculptor, he's a great artist and a great man but there are things that he's doing that I know are not for me'?

I think I discovered that at the end. I remember coming into the Tate Gallery and seeing a Francis Bacon and seeing some Picassos, and I felt that here was a looser way of working. And I thought that I could learn from that. But that wasn't really until the end, because when I think of the two years I was there, the change was pretty big from sheer academic work to thinking like Henry.

And then there was the period of about six years that everybody knows about in your history. In 1959 you went to America and suddenly you were told, I think by Clement Greenberg, the critic, that if you really wanted to do things differently you had to think differently. You just had to approach the whole business of art and sculpture differently. How shocking was that – or were you actually ready for change?

Oh, that was exactly what happened. I remember meeting on the boat, because we went across by boat, and meeting another chap who'd got the same scholarship as I had but in film. And he said to me, 'Of course I'm going to the States but I'd rather have gone to Italy!' And I was amazed. I couldn't believe that anybody would rather have gone to Italy – because I wanted to go to the future; I didn't want to go to the past. And I think that at that time, Abstract Expressionism was beginning to get accepted and I was beginning to notice it. It had been going some time but it was percolating to me by then and I felt this was where I was going to learn. And I knew that my art had come to a moment where something had to happen. And that was when I told this to Clem and he said, 'Well, if you want to change your art, change your habits,' which was a good open sort of remark and I took it to mean 'try different material'!

By that stage, of course, you already knew David Smith, the great American sculptor who worked in metal. Or did Greenberg introduce you to him?

No, I met him in 1959. He was one of the people that I met. Lawrence Alloway, who was there and knew a lot of Americans, gave me a list of people that I should call and David Smith was among them. I didn't go up to David Smith's place. There was a big party, I remember, that the Motherwells very kindly gave for me – Bob Motherwell, Helen Frankenthaler – and there I was, sitting at a table next to Hedy Lamarr and on the other side of it was David Smith.

What do you remember of Hedy Lamarr? Was she very sexy?

I think she was more taken with David Smith than she was with me, much to my annoyance!

So, the decision to work in steel was made there but your first sculpture, in steel, wasn't made until 1960 when you were back in Britain?

Oh yes. I didn't make a decision to work in steel at all. I said, 'I've got to work in something that's new to me'; and I thought to myself, 'Well, what can I use? Shall I use aluminium, shall I use steel, shall I use wood? What shall I do?' And I chose to use steel. I went down to the docks and found these bits of stuff and I didn't know how to stick them together. I remember saying to Frank Martin, who was a teacher at St Martin's, the head of the department with me, 'How do I stick two pieces of steel together?' I mean, I knew as little as that. I thought it was something you either bolted or you welded and I didn't know how to weld. I didn't know even how you make a hole in steel. I learned bit by bit, those things.

Did you make your first piece – the one that we mentioned called Twenty-Four Hours, *a parallelogram, square, circle (painted brown and black, which we shall come to) – did you make that by yourself or did you already need a lab assistant?*

No, I think I had a friend to help me lift it, you know, to actually put it into place and give me a hand!

Was that the breakthrough for you as a sculptor in steel?

It was the breakthrough with the public, yes. It was not the breakthrough because, in a way, I had been making it for three years but, yeah, that was the moment that I got noticed and it was thought to be outrageous at that time.

Now it was also painted, wasn't it? And for a long time you painted your sculptures. Why was this?

Because I didn't want them to get any credit by looking like sculpture ought to look – that is, by looking like bronze. I didn't want them to look like sculpture; I wanted them to look like something fresh and you said, 'That moves me.' Not 'put it in that box. It's got to move me because it is in the box.' I wanted it to say, 'Here's a new box. Try that.'

And to insist on looking at shapes.

And to insist on looking at shapes, and so on. And then I started actually by painting them brown. You've got to protect steel anyway and so I painted them brown, a couple of them – like the first one you mentioned – and then I thought 'why not try some other colours' so we tried, I tried, various other colours.

Bright yellow, bright red, blue . . .

Sometimes I got it wrong and my wife, who is a painter, gave me a lot of guidance on that and would say, 'You know, I think that red's the right colour for that'; and it got into the feel of it, the sculpture.

But we, as viewers, are almost trained to look at texture: this is the surface, this is where it's been worked on, this is where it has aged. So it is extraordinary that you were denying yourself this. Were you wanting us to look at what you were presenting which was plain shapes, relationships, not surface?

I still do. I still do, in a way. I don't want you only to look at plain shapes and relationships but I want you to look, as opposed to feel. I don't care for sculpture that you run your hands over, sculpture for the blind and so on. It seems to me that, by and large, that's not the area I'm into, and by and large, I don't actually think it's the right way to look at sculpture. Sculpture is something to be looked at. To be seen in a visual way, not a tactile way.

Clement Greenberg wrote many years ago, 'There are no volumes in

Caro, only planes, linear forms and shapes.' He was describing what you did then, but were you perfectly happy with that as a description of what you intended to do and what you have continued to do?

It's not true now. Because there are shapes and there are even recognisable things in them, sometimes. But yes, I was happy. I mean, Clem was very good at expressing those things. But where his real strength was, I think, was in the studio – because he would come into your studio and American critics do this: they come into the studio, not all of them but some of them, and you can talk to them while you're in the process of making art, which is wonderful. 'What do you think of this?' 'Well, I think you're in trouble on the right-hand side' – you know, that sort of thing. Very visual. Things you can do with other artists, too; this is lovely. Now our English critics don't do that. English critics look at the finished job and write a criticism about it. They scarcely meet the artist in that sort of way.

Do you think that is their background and that they feel a sort of need to keep a professional distance, an ethical distance, rather than writing reviews about artists with whom they have almost collaborated in the studio?

I don't know. I think probably yes. And I think quite a few of them come from a more literary start. I mean Greenberg, as an example, was originally a painter; he was a failed painter and he decided to be a writer.

But it helped even to be a failed painter in this context?

Well, he knew what it was like in the studio. There are some critics that still do that in America and there are some here that I can talk to quite intimately about art and some who teach in art schools and so on – so it is breaking through.

Let's talk about work in the studio because, after all, you're dealing with a heavy material. First of all, is it hard work physically?

I don't only deal in steel now; I deal in all sorts of things. But is it hard work physically? It is if you're trying to lift something which is right on the edge of what you can do, when you really ought to be using a machine; and you say, 'No, but I can lift it, I know I can' and that's when you put your back out! But by and

large, you use a machine if you can, or we have a simple gantry in
the studio, which we made ourselves. It works perfectly well; we
can lift heavy things up to two tons. Not terribly heavy things, but
heavy enough things, yeah.

*But the actual cutting and the welding, is that always being done by
a studio assistant?*

Wherever possible. Whenever possible. I can do it. I don't
enjoy it. It's like sticking stamps on really, except it can be done
well or badly and I'm very lucky because I have Pat Cunningham,
who has worked for me for thirty years and he's wonderful. And I
have some younger people who help me, who have come out of
art school and so on, and they're terrific, actually, and I really
enjoy working with them. But I'd rather spend my time usefully,
which is to say, 'Let's make that differently, let's change that.' In
other words I'm using my eye aesthetically rather than using it
from a practical point of view. I've never been very practical,
actually, I know sculptors are meant to be very good at putting up
shelves but I'm very bad at it. Mine can be guaranteed to fall
down.

*But therefore, you don't need to be involved in a tactile way with the
material?*

Well, I think you do, insofar as you lift things and so on. And
you also know what the weight of something is and you know
what it feels like. I remember years ago saying to a painter, 'Give
me a hand to move this' and he was amazed how heavy it was.
You do get to know the stuff.

*The whole question of how you start. Where does the idea for a piece
come from? How does it develop?*

That's the question one's often asked and it's so hard to answer
because there are so many ways in which it comes. It comes from
thinking about art. It comes from looking at art. It comes from a
conversation you had. It comes from the last work you did. It
comes from what the architects are doing. It comes from paintings
you saw. It comes from seeing two bits of steel on the ground
together or it comes from coming across something and saying,
'That's a start, now wait a minute, what else does it need?' There's

so many possibilities or ways it can come. I think when you start you've got one way of working, but as you get older you've got so many ways of working.

And, presumably, you don't start on a piece and then work through to completion? Are you working on a number of different pieces at one time?

Personally, I start a piece and take it up to a certain stage, quite a long way on, and then I get the people in my studio to make it and I don't want to see it while it's being made. And then I take another look – and that can happen four or five times because each time it's fresh for me. Each time it's like covering it up; I'm not seeing it for a bit. So in that respect, I work on several things. In the old days, when I had a one-car garage when I was making those first things, I could only work on one and that was very tedious. I used to sit and look at it for days and perhaps move something six inches, and that would be a day's work, and that was a very tiresome way to work. Now I can work on more things because I've got a bigger studio and I've got people helping me.

Do you work a long day at making sculpture?

I work a reasonable day at making sculpture. I start late, I start about ten thirty or something.

That's not very late!

It is late, really – and then, unfortunately my time clock is an afternoon clock, not a morning clock, so I don't actually really get going until the afternoon. And then by five o'clock or five thirty, things are going really well and I would love to be able to go on till eleven at night, and cut the mornings out and start later. But you can't with sculpture. For one thing you've got people working for you; for another thing you've got to get different sorts of materials and you make a noise; and there are practical reasons why you can't work into the night. But that would suit me very well; working into the night would be very nice.

Do you splurge on work? Do you have times when you say, 'For the next fortnight I feel dry, I don't have an idea, I'm not going to do anything'? And then suddenly you find that the ideas come back and you work as intensively as you can?

No, I don't work like that. I say, 'I'm going to have a holiday now. I'm going away for two weeks or three weeks.' Before I do that I always try and finish everything off as if I was going to die tomorrow, and then I go on holiday – which is madness. But I do try and keep fairly systematic and fairly regular. I don't want to have these moments and I don't think I know any painters and sculptors that are like that.

There are so many writers who write eight hundred words a day, whether it is a good day, a bad day. So you're part of that discipline, the equivalent discipline?

No. I don't like to think like that. I would hate to think that I was writing eight hundred words a day. But I go into the studio every day, pretty well, and when you get into the studio you can't help it. You start by messing about and in a little while you're enjoying it so much that you're working away. I do think that in a way you get to know yourself, you get to know the way that you can operate – and Pat Cunningham knows it. So if we're looking at small sculptures, let's say, I say, 'Pat, give me an easy one!' So he'll give me one which is nearly right and I'll say, 'That's OK' and then you look at the next one that is nearly right or not quite right, and then you only get to the difficult ones later. But that's rather like you asking me questions! The difficult questions are not the first questions you ask me, not the hardest ones, you know. And I think that if you can work like that in some sort of way, it's quite a good thing. When I'm in my garage at home I put on some music and get the thing sort of moving in the right frame of mind so I get into the frame of mind of the sculptures I'm going to work on.

Now is this an easy one or a difficult one? Does the word 'inspiration' mean anything useful to you? Those of us who aren't artists look at artists and say, 'Ah, yes, this is an inspired work' and so on. Does this mean anything useful to you?

No, I think it's too broad a word. Of course I would hate to make a work which didn't speak to me, which didn't say anything to me.

But do you reject works?

Oh yes. I do think I say, 'That one worked or that one didn't work.' I wouldn't use the word 'inspiration'. I'm very cautious about using any of these overheated words.

The interesting thing is when you talk about your work you're very matter-of-fact. In particular this word that you always use about your raw material: you refer to it as 'stuff'. There you are, surrounded with these piles of steel offcuts and I think the fact that you call it 'stuff' shows how close you are to it.

But also it's because I'm bad at expressing words and I would never say, 'I want a piece of wood that's four foot six long or one and a half metres', or whatever it is. I don't say that. I say, 'I want a bit that long,' holding out my hands, because it is very much to do with the bodily experience, this job.

Once you've made a piece, are you possessive about it, or are you happy to let it go?

No, I'm happy it has to live its own life, like one's children have to live their own lives. To my amazement, I was in New York and my dealer said, 'There's a work of yours in Sotheby's but I think it's wrong. Would you go and look at it?' And somebody had had it in their gate, they'd welded it into their gate, and they'd left a bit of gate on! So that was a mistake and I don't like that to happen. I don't want someone to weld it into their gate! By and large, that's one of the advantages of people paying for the work and paying quite a lot for it. They say they'll take care of it and they take care of it like they'd take care of their car; and they keep it clean and they love it, I hope. That's what I want to happen.

And as for physical location, cityscape, townscape or anything. Do you have particular views about that?

No, I've worked on a fairly intimate scale of one to one, even though they're big, some of them. I don't think many of them are public sculptures. I've made one or two public sculptures and I would like them to be in a suitable place. I don't think I'm a rural sculptor. If I've made a sculpture which could go in the landscape, it's really a counterpoint to the landscape. It isn't part of the landscape; it's like a house would be in a landscape. It's an inappropriate thing, in a way. But you recognise the landscape through it.

But by and large, my stuff up to date has been mostly fairly one to one, fairly intimate.

And you still have a store of pieces which you haven't sold or are waiting to be sold or you've forgotten about, do you?

I'd prefer to forget about what I've made. Yes, I have a store and you put the ones there that you've gone on beyond. And in a way, I don't want to feel terribly affectionate towards one sculpture more than another. I feel affection for them when I'm making them and when I've just finished them. And then they've gone. Show them and they've gone. And they live their lives; I live my life. While we're together we're talking to each other – that's real. Afterwards, it's sentimental, I think, to be caring about old pieces, particularly.

How do you see your relationship as an artist, as a sculptor, to society?

I think it's very important that we have a response. I think that it's very tough on an artist who paints his pictures or makes his sculpture and has no means of showing it and he has no gallery, he doesn't put his work into shows. What's he done? He's just turned it to the wall and I think that is like talking in the dark or talking to yourself. And it's a very unhappy way of going about this thing because in a way we need a response, we need it.

Whatever the responses are?

Not really. Incomprehension isn't much good. But I think that a negative response can be quite useful. Somebody saying, 'I don't like it because of this and this' – and you think to yourself, 'Well, is it really like this and this?' You know?

If people say, 'Why should sculpture be made out of steel? Why doesn't it look like an object? Why doesn't it look like people?', I suppose that is incomprehension but it's also hostility. Does that matter to you?

I think it's got to be intelligent criticism for it to have any effect, really. It's got to be somebody using their eyes and using their heads and then saying something about it that's useful. I have had, though, people saying criticisms which have been, not hostile, but have been very critical and that's made me think sometimes,

'Now wait a minute, are you taking this for granted, is what you're doing right?' I'm a very anxious person, I think; I do listen to other people a lot.

So much of the debate about the role of the arts in society nowadays centres on the idea of accessibility. Where does that fit into your own thoughts about how you make sculpture and how you hope that it is received?

I'm delighted that lots of people are looking at art now – many, many more people than used to, twenty or thirty years ago. That's good, but if it lowers the level just in order to make it more accessible, I'm very against that. And I think that what we have to do is to educate people to such an extent that they can appreciate the best so that there are many, many elitists. In other words, I do believe in excellence and I do not believe in coming down a peg just in order to get more people into the museums or into the art galleries. Now you used to go around American galleries and there'd be some lady doing a spiel about what the artist intended and so on, and I know that English people used to say, 'Oh God, it is so awful.' Actually, it's not awful. It's a good thing. Any way that we can bring people to try and appreciate what the artist is doing is good. And I think there should be an awful lot of visual experience taught in schools, a lot of visual education. And it is getting much, much better than it was, much better.

So it's the educational outreach that is important rather than some sort of false accessibility saying to you, 'Caro, you're too difficult!'

Exactly. Well, if I am, too bad then, you know!

Do you think the state should fund the arts? You personally and a lot of other sculptors have always earned your living. But in general should there be major state subsidies for the arts?

I think anything that helps the arts is good. I was very lucky because my work really took off in America. I had good galleries. There was a tremendous sort of audience for art and people were buying it and people were writing about it, people were liking it. And people were expecting to spend money on having a work in their houses. Now that doesn't happen so much in America now, I don't think; but it never happened here to such an extent because people had a lot of old things. You don't need a new work of art if you've got a Van Dyck on the walls.

Well, you might want to change!

Well, yes, but not many people would make that sort of change! And, of course, also there were new rich people in America – the first thing they would do was to start to get a collection of art in their houses.

But is there not now a much greater openness to contemporary art in Britain than there was when you began thirty or forty years ago?

Oh, much more open; and it's wonderful that this has happened. And I can remember saying, 'Oh, the English are never going to like art because we're a literary nation' and all that stuff. Well, in fact it's not true. We are starting to like it very much and a lot of people are really turning towards art. I think it's wonderful that's happening – and sculpture, in particular, which was always the poor relation of architecture and painting. And I think there is a real, real hunger for it now, which is marvellous. But don't forget that I'm not quite a contemporary artist now because I'm getting old, you know, and people who are a lot younger than me are getting the real experiences of nowadays. Whereas I'm on my own track, rather than being on the track of the nineties.

But, in fact, you have been critical of some of the more sensationally directed young contemporaries whom you regard as being more interested in sensation rather than in working for more serious ends. Do you feel a real gap or any sort of gap between you – who you are, what you're doing – and what the Young Turks of Hoxton are doing?

Of course there's a gap but I'm very interested in what the Young Turks are doing. I think, also, that I'm not so critical of them as critical of the way they've been used by people who went for, with a small 's', sensation rather than going for art. But there are good artists and bad among them, just as there are among any others. But look, the fact is, here you are talking to a man of seventy-six about people of thirty-five or thirty. And you know, you wouldn't really have talked to Degas about Cubism in 1917 when he was seventy-six. And you wouldn't have talked to Monet about Surrealism when he was in his eighties. That would have been silly.

Well, would it? It would be rather interesting, wouldn't it?

No, I think it would have been silly because it's nothing to do with Monet. I think that those people have got to start to move. It's interesting about Monet but it's not really interesting about the art.

Yes, but it's interesting about you!

I think really, you know, Picasso never understood Jackson Pollock and thought it was nonsense, and Matisse did too, and in a way it doesn't say anything about Jackson Pollock. They were on to a new world. But I think in some funny way, actually the young influence me more than I influence them. I think what's happening is interesting. I think that, in fact, what those younger artists have brought about is the idea of bringing our everyday lives in more; the idea of bringing more meat into art. Not letting it be quite so pure and so abstract. I think that's very important; and I think, actually, it's certainly affected what I make.

Some years ago you said, 'The art that I prefer is the art in which intelligence and sensibility are both given rein.' Do they both play out in your work today; or what is the balance between them?

I hope so. I've never rated my brain that high but I do enjoy people who say things that stimulate me. I enjoy them. I enjoy being pressed, in a way, so I think that aspect of intelligence is something that . . . you know, I don't know that I have it but I do get a bang from it! Sensibility: I think you've got to have that if you're an artist.

In series like The Trojan War, The Descent from the Cross, The Last Judgement, *how does the balance between intelligence and sensibility work out? Because one might say, particularly with things like* The Last Judgement, *which was a direct response to events in the Balkans, is there a greater element of sensibility, of passion, than there was before?*

I don't quite know, John; I don't know actually what's happening to me. I just felt that I had to do those and it wasn't what I expected of myself. I started *The Trojan War* by going down to work in the South of France with Hans Spinner, and it so happened that what came out looked like warriors and was really *The Trojan War*. I just felt it was *The Trojan War*, and I started getting very involved in it and reading the *Iliad,* and so on; and trying to actually recognise who these brutal warriors were and who were their gods, and so on. When I made *The Last Judgement* I knew I wanted to make a 'Last Judgement'. I didn't know how, but I knew I wanted to. And then, I think the difference between that and what I was doing before . . . I think it is the same person doing it but I think it was looking out at the world more than looking in at myself.

Well, it's entirely consistent with what you were saying earlier about your terms of reference for creating sculpture. Being aware of what was going on in the Balkans, the outside world, was so pressing that it did something to you internally. You just had to express your feelings as sculpture.

Well, I think so. I mean, just simply watching the television and seeing how much of that is on it, and reading the newspapers, and it was in your face all the time. It might also be something to do with my age and the fact that maybe you do start to get more conscious of these things.

But The Descent from the Cross?

The Descent from the Cross was more like looking at old art, looking at the Rembrandt, looking at the Rubens.

But it wasn't, from your point of view, just an academic study?

It wasn't, but it's not quite as closely related to outside events.

Apart from the Millennium Bridge – that must have been a wonderful new direction to be part of – is there anything particular that you know is bubbling up inside you that you're going to do?

Quite a lot of things are bubbling up inside me but odd things are happening too. I do have some plans to make some art and I don't want to kind of spoil my luck by talking about them too much now. I do have some ideas for making my own things, quite a lot. But also what is happening, which is odd, is that people are asking me, 'Would you be interested to do something' and that's kind of exciting. For example, there's a church in the north of France where the end of it – the choir and the aisles – has been left ever since the war and they're blocked off from the rest of the church. They say, 'Oh, would you like to activate this area?' and I would like to very much. I mean that sort of thing, which would be completely different. Really, it's almost architectural and I think that would be very exciting.

Which takes you back to the very beginning – to your architecture, however skimpy it was.

Yes, it does. But it's not architecture like making houses; it's like making a space work in a new way, in a more emotional way, perhaps.

So there again, perhaps the balance between intelligence and sensibility is tilting in the way that you feel right and maybe it's different. It should be different!

Well, I think that's another example of how you can start: by somebody coming up to you and saying, 'What about doing this; what about doing that?' You know, another thought is working with this engineer who designed the Millennium Bridge. His name's Chris Wise and he's a wonderful young man who's full of go and he said, 'Let's do something together.' We're going to make a tower, a sort of impossible tower, I hope. And that's a challenge too. In the end, you know, I think that there was a period in the seventies where I knew much more where I was, what I was going to do. Now I don't know where I am and I love it, I love it.

Just a final thought. Is there any sculptor today who will say, as you have always said of David Smith, that 'Tony Caro was an important influence on me'. Is there anybody who you see as continuing your work, somebody on whom you have had a considerable influence?

I think I had an influence on Richard Serra and I think that he is a very important sculptor, and I think he's changed the face of sculpture quite a lot. His things are much bigger and much more to do with people, they're much more to do with large amounts of people in public places and so on. And I know he said that he came out of me originally or somewhere out of me, somewhere a long way away.

And if any young, would-be sculptor came to you, as you came to Henry Moore in 1951, and said, 'Could I work with you for a couple of years', what would you say?

I'd have to say – don't I, on this programme? – I'd have to say, 'Go away, I hate you!' Oh, I don't know what I'd say. Probably

'Have a cup of tea' and that's it. But no, I've got some people working for me. They have been sculpture students. They're a delight. I happen to be lucky, I've got really nice people and we talk about all sorts of things in our tea breaks and we look at art together. We look at my art and I say, 'What do you think about this? Perhaps we should change this end. Do you like the colour of it?' I mean, I talk to them like that and it's very open, it's very nice. I don't think I'd accept somebody out of the blue, no. Don't forget, when I went to Henry he was fifty-something and I'm older than that now, and I have to be very careful that I have just the right number of people in my studio and just the right ones. And I'm very lucky at the moment; it's OK, it's good.

ELLIOTT CARTER

'A sense of disastrous confusion'

Elliott Carter is America's leading composer, though, as he insists, he is a composer who happens to be American. Born in 1908, Carter has been increasingly recognised as a master of closely worked, disciplined, often passionate, sometimes violent music which he now composes with a growing facility. His very first opera *What Next?* was written in 1999, a remarkable achievement for a man of his age. Carter has also written and talked very widely about music as a journalist and critic. A figure who spans the century, he has known all the great leaders of contemporary music from Stravinsky to Charles Ives, Edgard Varèse, Aaron Copland, and many others.

In an essay you wrote some fifty years ago, you said that 'everything is a problem for the composer'. Everything from what to write, how to write it, how to make it popular or not, how to deal with publishers, audiences and performers. Fifty years on, have any of these problems gone away?

Some of these problems have gone away. For one thing, fifty years ago, I was talking from the point of view of an American and the situation in America. Even before that time, there were very few composers and there was a difficulty for composers to learn how to write music, to learn the techniques of various kinds. It was my generation, actually, that started the idea of having music taught, of having composition taught, not only in conservatories but also in universities in the United States. We started out maybe with thirty or forty composers at most in America. Now we have twenty thousand – the result of my unfortunate efforts.

You taught a fair number of the twenty thousand – well, a few score of them for sure?

Yes, I taught some, so actually the problem has become a reverse problem, that the publishers can't keep up with us; performers can't keep up with us; too many pieces being written. While in the old days it was quite the opposite, there were pieces written and it was hard for us to get performances; because at that time there was not very much interest in contemporary music except among very small groups of people. Now the composers are fighting to get performances and as a result, the entire moral attitude about composing has changed.

Did you say it's a moral attitude?

Yes. I mean moral in a certain sense, in that in our day, when we first started in the 1930s, composers composed because they loved to compose and then they thought, 'Maybe we can get performances and possibly get publication.' But publishers didn't want to publish much because the works didn't sell, and furthermore we didn't have the glory that you have. We didn't have the Performing Rights Society which was partly organised by myself and Aaron Copland and others, so that the remunerative effort of a composer was nil, except that he got a great deal of pleasure out of writing the music and being interested in it and having a few friends like it.

Are you suggesting that there's less writing for enjoyment now, simply because there is a whole sub-class of composers – twenty thousand people? This is a noticeable sub-section of economic society, isn't it?

That's right, and there are a very large number of composers now writing who are very concerned with reaching the public. This is very new. That was rare in the old days. But it has now become one of the most usual things, which from my point of view is rather disturbing – because I feel that in the end the music that I've always liked, and the music that I admire and the music that I write considers the public as a secondary matter. The reason we write is because we love to write and we think music is a very beautiful thing and we hope that we can do something nice.

Let's just get that relationship right. So you're saying now composers are saying, 'I want my music to speak to the public and that is a prior consideration' rather than 'Am I writing something which comes strongly from me and which is going to be a piece of good music?'. And that's a complete switch from the attitude you had?

That's right. I mean, the attitude I still have, as I say. So it's rather bothersome for me to have this attitude now while before it was a normal thing to have.

But just because you say the audience come second, that's not necessarily wrong? Because if you didn't have the drive to make the music as good as you can, you wouldn't have anything excellent to put to the audience, would you?

That's what I think, yes. The thing that has happened is that young composers will do anything to reach the audience so that they follow the kind of music that, as you probably know, involves very large recordings of music for backgrounds of films. Very often this kind of background film music is not at all concerned with the problem of writing pieces that have any length, that have any development. It's concerned with different kinds of styles and characters. It makes no difference whether the music is, let's say, for a horror film, for which that may be a little twelve-note music, or music for a love story, which will be like, Gershwin, say. All this kind of music is mixed up into one stretch of music which, to my mind, is one of the things I can't stand.

It's a total confusion, though, if the respectable job of being a journeyman composer fulfilling a function such as writing music for films is confused with the person who writes art music, which is music that stands or falls on its own terms and in relation to its own quality.

That's exactly right, and the problem has become that many young composers and even many critics feel that writing something that stands by itself, as I say, is not as important as something that is accessible to the public. Hence very often the music that young people write is, 'We'll have a little bit of Bach and a little bit of Schoenberg and a little bit of Gershwin, all mixed together', and this pleases the public and unfortunately it even pleases many conductors of orchestras nowadays.

Fifty years ago, of course, American minimalism – John Adams, Philip Glass, Steve Reich and their like – didn't exist. They were only just born of course.

Well, we thought we were writing for the small public that we thought were very musically literate. Repetition was something that was not a very interesting thing to do. Now, the public apparently likes to hear the same thing over and over again because they can't understand it until they've heard it ten times.

But you don't dismiss what the Reichs and the Glasses and the Adamses of this world do just because they base a lot of it on conscious, deliberate, patterned repetition?

Well, I don't dismiss it. Let me say, I think anybody should write what they want to write, what they think is important to write and assume the situation they want to. But I myself feel this is really a terrible thing, because in my opinion we have been overwhelmed with the problem of advertising in the whole world. Advertising is a system of repeating the same thing over and over again, true or false, and trying to bulldoze the public into believing what they're saying; and furthermore, we're getting into more horrible and awful situations. We had this in many ways during all of our lives in propaganda. We have not merely had our own propaganda, but much more unfortunately, Hitlerian propaganda. And I find that this repetition thing reminds me of all of that and I don't like it.

That's quite a charge against the minimalists.

I'm not saying that they want to do it. But for me, that reminds me of it. I'm not saying that they're doing it that way; but it bothers me very much that I see in the background this awful thing, which is to beat people down to believing something just because it's repeated over and over again, and this is terrible. In my mind this is a way of destroying intelligence.

What made you first want to be a composer. Did you know that you were going to be a composer rather than a performer or a teacher of music?

What made me want to be a composer is hard to say. It was hearing *The Rite of Spring* played by Pierre Monteux when I was in my twenties. It was a scandal. Everybody walked out of the hall and people were terrified. Maybe that's why I liked it, but in any case I became a fan of modern music in very early adolescence, I think I was twenty-three or twenty-four.

Didn't you take your father to hear The Rite of Spring?

Oh, father hated it. He thought it was awful. But everybody else did too. That wasn't unusual at that time. But I also had a teacher in school who liked this kind of thing and he introduced me to Charles Ives and Edgard Varèse, and all sorts of people who were involved with this group of musicians who were interested in modern music. So I just carried on as a person who liked modern music, which was played in all places.

But let me say another thing, that in that particular period, post First World War, there was a very different economic structure in

America. There was not the income tax system that we have now; therefore very wealthy people supported contemporary music in rather elaborate ways so that in the twenties and early thirties before the Depression, there were very big performances of important works. I heard, for instance, *Wozzeck*; it was given by Leopold Stokowski at the Metropolitan Opera House and this was all paid for by private money. I remember reading that one of the patrons was Mrs Thomas Edison, for instance, and other people, notable people. The sort who were wealthy and who felt modern music should be encouraged. I heard *Glückliche Hand* of Schoenberg also played at the Metropolitan Opera, again by Stokowski who was very active in contemporary music in those years. And also Stokowski played Varèse and all kinds of things.

What sort of audiences did they have for those concerts?

They had a full house. Everybody liked it very much. I realise I'm contradicting myself. What I'm saying is that there wasn't much American music being played of a contemporary kind. But there were these big important European things that were brought over that were very grand and very beautifully performed and very striking to this poor boy that wanted to hear all these things. I sat next to George Gershwin at *Wozzeck*, I remember, rather timidly. I didn't dare say anything to him.

So you don't know what Gershwin thought of Wozzeck?

No, I have no idea. But then, this was also during our awful period of Prohibition when alcoholic liquids were not sold. We all went to what were called 'speakeasys' to drink whatever we drank – and I used to meet Varèse in one of them often in those days and I got to know Varèse. I knew him all through his entire life until he died. And I got to know Charles Ives. He was not a drinker so he didn't go to that kind of thing, but in any case, I got to know him very well as a boy.

And Ives helped you a lot, didn't he? He wrote a letter to Harvard, recommending you and saying you had all the usual virtues and also saying 'He has a fine sense of humour', which seems to me to be true.

That's right. Well, it was nice. It was nice of him to say that. We had a whole group of people who went to contemporary music.

Even Ives went to some contemporary concerts and supported one contemporary music group in New York for quite a long time. In fact, later, when I became an editor of a magazine called *New Music*, I found that Charles Ives had been supporting that for many years with thousands of dollars every year. But then there was also this very wealthy group that followed contemporary music, mostly European, and it was also the same group that started the Museum of Modern Art and all kinds of things in New York City. All that disappeared with the Depression, and then a new income tax system came so that these people no longer supported the arts in the way they had. It became something that only small individuals supported; let's say, symphony orchestras. This has changed the entire character of it because in order for a symphony orchestra in America to persist, they have to raise large amounts of money from not such wealthy people, so that they have to be sure to interest all of these people to come to the concerts, otherwise they won't come. So less contemporary music is played now than it was.

So by broadening the base of the supporters to whom you appeal, you also narrow the range of music that you can perform?

That's exactly what has happened.

Because to many of us Europeans, when we go over to the United States, we go to a gallery, a concert hall, or an opera house, and we're amazed by the long lists of major supporters and we think this is a terrific strength. The way in which this large American middle class supports the arts we regard now as a very real strength.

Well, it's a real strength except that they approach the arts, and in particular, music as if it were entertainment and not as education. While with state support it's assumed that this is more of an educational thing than we consider it.

Let's go back to Charles Ives, because you were so close to him – you wrote many letters to him. I just want to take up the time when you were a young music critic and you were reviewing his Concord *Sonata and you really weren't happy with it.*

Let me talk about that. Ives encouraged me to be a composer very early on in my life. I wrote some little things before I studied music that were settings of James Joyce and other things, and he thought they were quite interesting and I should be encouraged. And it was partly due to that factor that I finally decided to be a composer. Then I realised when I went to Harvard that the music department disliked contemporary music very much and I was very unhappy. I finally studied English Literature and didn't study with the music department at all. Meanwhile, the Boston Symphony Orchestra were playing all the works of Stravinsky and I was very happy to be in Boston because we heard more contemporary music with the Boston Symphony than we would have in New York. And then I felt I had to study and I went to study with Nadia Boulanger and became very much more interested in the sort of neoclassicism of Stravinsky and Poulenc. So that when I heard Charles Ives, I was no longer seeing Ives as I had as a very young person. I was seeing it through the eyes of a neoclassicist. And it seemed to me that that music was excessively Lisztian and extravagant, which was something that at that particular time I didn't like. Now I do.

So then there was a break between you and Ives for a period?

It was largely timidity on my part. I didn't like that I had to say what I thought and it worried me that I might have hurt him. That gradually disappeared over the years and before he died I saw him a good deal. I can't say it was guilt but feeling badly about this whole thing and my feelings also changed. I actually started a group of us when Ives was rather ill and couldn't do very much, getting his scores in shape, because he wrote scores that were very messy and very confused and rewrote them and wrote one thing on top of another. They were terribly confused things and I thought, well, it would be nice if we straighten these scores out and got him to OK them before he died. So I started a whole project which in the end bothered me so much I had to stop, but other people like Lou Harrison and Henry Cowell continued and edited a good many of his works so that they could be played.

But you were very frank with him, weren't you, because in one of your books there's a letter from his wife to you recalling that Ives said to her after one of your visits, 'Carter says people think I'm crazy. I'm really crazy.' That's a very brave thing to have said to Ives; and clearly came as something of a shock. It hadn't occurred to him that his music created that impression on people?

Well it did. When Ives published his *Concord* Sonata, which I think was in 1923, he sent the score – he was a wealthy man, after all, he made a lot of money selling insurance – he sent copies of this to every important organisation in the United States. So that everybody knew what this crazy man was doing. They all thought it was crazy. In fact, when I was a Fellow at the American Academy in Rome there was a copy of the *Concord* Sonata. He'd even sent it to Rome because it was in the library of the Academy, and as a result there was a great deal of negative feeling about Ives because of all of that.

What about now? He's still not an easy composer. He's still radical and shocking and unexpected, isn't he?

The Fourth Symphony is very difficult to play. I got involved with that. I was on the jury of the ISCM – the International Society for Contemporary Music. I was one of the vice presidents in 1955, and we gave a festival in Baden-Baden. And I went up and said, 'You know there's a Fourth Symphony of Charles Ives which is very unusual and very difficult to perform and has all sorts of problems – a lot of it exists only in sketch form. It is something that you people could do,' because Süd-West Funk in Germany had enormous amounts of time to rehearse and research very difficult pieces. And their conductor, Hans Rosbaud, got very excited. It was the effort that German radio made to play this piece that stimulated Leopold Stokowski to play it in America because up to that time he was not interested. But when they felt that the Europeans were going to get there first, they said we're not going to allow that and there was a whole operation about getting the fourth movement into some kind of shape where it could be played.

Let's talk about how you write and the actual disciplines and personal routines of being a composer. Do you find that there is a seed of a particular composition, let us say a string quartet, which suddenly starts to appear? Or do you think, 'I want to write another quartet so I'll now start to think about the thematic subjects' and so forth?

Well, at this stage of my life everything I write is commissioned. On the other hand, I don't accept any commissions for pieces that I don't want to write. So that the focusing on what the commission should be becomes an important matter. But still, you know, string quartets want me to write a quartet or the Berlin Staatsoper wanted me to write an opera. These are all directed things and I decided that I would do each one of them so that I already had the instrumentation and the general type of thing decided for me in collaboration with another group.

But you must have had the idea that you were ready to write a quartet and certainly that you were ready to write an opera?

I wouldn't write a quartet that I didn't want to write. I mean, I was not interested. In fact, I tried throughout my life – I've written now five; I guess that's all I will write – but I've always felt that I shouldn't write another quartet until I had another idea that was different from the previous four. So I've always tried to write the opposite of, or differently from, the previous ones. They aren't that different but I always thought they were at the time.

Where might you find that idea coming from? Is it only when you sit down with the blank music paper that you know you're writing a quartet?

I think about it a great deal before I write it, oh yes. My music always arises from the instruments that are going to play it or the situation of the singers or the orchestra. That's the first thing. The second thing is that there are certain types of things that I like to do and there are other things that I don't like. So that there's a focusing on the particular field of operation that I have been concerned with since 1950 when I wrote my first string quartet. And that idea was that music is played by, or sung by, individual people and I wanted to give the impression in a performance that these individual people exist as individuals and that they're not all sunk in one mass following the orders of one leader, so to speak. They're all living, to a certain extent, to themselves and they contribute in their own way to produce a piece, in a concert. There will be four individuals, let's say in the string quartet – all of them having their own character and they will contribute to produce the piece. When I come to orchestrate music I think of them as groups of teams, or in some pieces like the *Concerto for Orchestra*, it is even down to the point where even the teams have individualities. In the *Concerto for Orchestra*, the double basses have a whole little fight between themselves, so I'm very concerned with individualising the players and or the singers, which means giving contrasts. So that they are sometimes co-operative, sometimes they're not so co-operative, and contrasting the various elements that these different people are contributing.

Does the word 'inspiration' figure in your work or is it something which is not a useful idea to describe what goes on when you compose?

If there is inspiration, it's not something that comes at the beginning of the piece. It comes in the course of writing it. The more I get into the piece the more the inspiration – well, I don't know exactly what inspiration means – but I would see more clearly and with more excitement and more interest new things, and would not be in the process of discarding a great many things I don't want to do. Once I've gotten focused on this thing, let's say the excitement of writing, it becomes more and more important as I write the piece. I think this is the way we would normally behave under other circumstances. If you were writing a letter or a novel, the more you get into the novel, the more clearly you see what you're trying to do, and so forth.

Are you a tidy writer on the paper or are you constantly scratching out? Do your scores look like what you said Charles Ives' scores look like?

Well, there was a time long ago when Stravinsky said, 'You write music with an eraser'. I don't do that quite that way. What I generally do is that I sit down – I don't play the piano very well any more and I never did play it very well – but I would just sit down and write large amounts of the music. I'm writing a cello concerto, for instance, right now and I'm writing the cello part first from beginning to end and then there are two things that happen after that. One is that I begin to go back over it and sometimes play it on the piano and I don't like this or I change that. And the second thing is that I take this particular part to a cellist – a very good one – and he shows me what it is that's awkward. Then I decide whether I really want it to continue being awkward or not and he discusses instrumental problems which may arise. Most of it doesn't but there might be little details and I might change them or I might not. We have a little discussion about the speed, let us say, of certain passages that are maybe too fast to make an effective performance out of them.

Isn't there one of your works where the pianist Charles Rosen has said that towards the end, the only thing for the pianist to do is to ignore the conductor, put his head down, and just get to the end of the score because it is so complex and so fast. That is you setting a major problem for the performer and doing so deliberately?

Yes, that's right. Except I'm not quite like Brian Fernihough. I don't feel I should make a drama out of the difficulty of playing – the excessive difficulty that makes it so hard that you feel that the performer is in a state of frenzy. Now let me say, though, that old cello sonata that I wrote in 1948 was a piece of frenzy for the two performers at the time. It's played now and taught in conservatories, and students play it with ease. But when it was first written it was a horror for the performers. They all sat there and they came out dripping with sweat.

Reading some of your essays, it reminded me of how much we've come on in fifty years. In 1940, I think, you were saying how difficult Stravinsky's Agon *was thought to be. Well we don't regard that as a difficult score now. I suppose that it does take thirty to forty years for music to, as it were, fall into our ears in a way that makes it sound comparatively easy rather than just difficult.*

But you know the other side is, when I was much younger I felt that it took me four or five years before I could hear the music the way I intended it to be played. Because there were all these performers who got so nervous they couldn't get through it and it took a long time before the music sounded the way I hoped it would. When I was very young, I used to change the music so as to try to accommodate the situation; then in the end I always changed it back to the way it was in the first place, because it was a matter of getting the performers not merely to play the notes but to understand what the notes meant and that's sometimes not so easy. Now since I've written so much music and there's a large number of performers that know my music, this doesn't happen so often. My music gets played practically at once the way I intended it to be.

But by no stretch of the imagination is it easy music. I remember when your Concerto for Orchestra *was played by Pierre Boulez and the London Symphony Orchestra, and somebody said, 'Only Boulez under-stands this piece. I've heard it four or five times and it is so complex that I don't understand it.' He was not complaining. Just making an observation. Do you recognise this question of the complexity of your music – that your music, let's say, requires a lot of attention?*

Complexity is a very difficult thing to describe or to mention in music. I mean, there are very, very complex music pieces of Bach – for instance the opening of the B Minor Mass is just about as complicated as anything I've ever written. Now, it doesn't sound that complicated to the audience in one level and that is (a) there are rhythmic patterns that are consistent throughout that are recognisable, and (b) there are vertical harmonies, traditional harmonies, very often ornamented to such a point you can hardly tell what they are but still the audience catches on to this.

When I write something, the vertical harmonic system is not the traditional one, but it is something eventually people will hear if they bother to pay attention to it. I mean, complexity – what is it? There is that enormous canon of Tallis, for example, that is in one sense very complex but when you hear it you don't know that it's even a canon because you just hear the total sound. You could call that very complex, in another way it's very simple. Of course I'm prejudiced, but my music is very simple from the point of view of understanding what the character of the music is. There is a sense of disastrous confusion in moments of my music. I feel this is a way of expressing what I feel about things. It doesn't happen very often, but I'm not trying to present chaos in the way that Haydn did in *The Creation*, but there is something of that element in it.

Did you have any doubt about taking on an opera when the commission came when you were in your eighties?

Daniel Barenboim commissioned and played my *Partita*, which finally became the first movement of a big symphonia, which was recorded by Oliver Knussen later. When he heard that he said to me, 'I'd like you to write an opera for the Staatsoper,' where he was conducting at the time. And I said, 'I've been asked to write operas many times in my life and I never found a libretto that I wanted to write. I would write my own music and I know that in America it would never be played or it would be played so badly I wouldn't want to hear it, because the kind of music I write is not the kind of music that people play in opera houses in America.' And he said, 'Look, we have lots of rehearsals in the Staatsoper, so do it.' And I kept having great doubts. Meanwhile he called me up every month, and then later I had a nearly fatal case of pneumonia. I was breathing oxygen for six weeks in a hospital. Every day I got a telephone call, 'How's that opera going along?' So when I survived my pneumonia Barenboim said, 'Well, what's the subject?' and I said, sort of humorously, 'I'll set *The Bald Prima Donna* of Ionesco.' Then I began to think about it; it's an interesting play but not for an opera because it's about how you speak language and that would be dull. And then I saw that movie of Jacques Tati called *Traffic*, which has a comic automobile accident, and I thought, 'That is where we're going to begin an opera.'

Then you got Paul Griffiths to write the libretto?

And then I told Paul Griffiths and he came up with a libretto. All of it. He invented the characters and all the situations. You see, Paul Griffiths knew my music quite well so he was thinking all the time what kind of music, having these different strands of music, quartets and so on – he figured how that could be put into the opera and he did a very good job of writing a libretto that fitted what I wanted to write.

So you more or less set his libretto. In the constantly wonderful relationship between the composer and the librettist, this was a fairly unusual one?

It was very unusual in the sense that I really didn't intervene in his writing of the libretto hardly at all until we'd got through it. Then there were things that I wanted to change because there were matters of timing, for example. How long something should go on, little details, nothing very important.

But the structure of the opera is the structure that Paul Griffiths delivered to you?

There were two things I changed and they were maybe important. One of them was that since this automobile accident happened and there were all these characters dazed by the situation, they all stayed on stage. In opera people sometimes have to go off the stage because then one person can stay and sing. All operas have an enormous amount of entrances and exits and you don't have anything in this. They're all sitting there like that. So we decided to make everybody go off the stage in the middle of the opera and they all came back again when he tried to motivate them. That was one idea. So the opera then fell into two pieces rather than one, which is easier to compose as a matter of fact.

And the second idea was that one of the characters seemed to be a rather flamboyant character; and I said, 'Why don't we just make her into a singer and what I'd like to do is to have her sing from beginning to end. She will be the one that pays no attention to anyone else. She just sings and sings, and everything else goes on and her music is always in the background of whatever is going on.' And then I thought, 'Well, she's really singing one aria and at the very end of the opera she sings high C and that's it.' So that was the way I thought about it. That was what it turned out to be – I don't mean to be praising myself but it turned out to be a very good idea as an opera. One thing is it is very novel, nobody ever thought of doing that. And the second thing was that it held the whole opera together. You have little scenes and everything, but here's this lady sort of singing little bits, fragments of coloratura all through the whole thing and that was a thread that made the whole opera into one big core. It's like what I do in my string quartets, to tell the truth.

Are you an American composer? An American-European composer? An international composer or in the sense of none of these categories?

I'm a composer. I'm Elliott Carter, the composer. I don't know what country. Let me say, when I was young, after I studied with Nadia Boulanger and came back, and one of my best friends was Aaron Copland and he was very concerned about being an American composer. For a while I wrote a number of pieces that were sort of Americanising pieces. I met Sir William Glock very early on in Britain, and William got a hold of that early Americanising First Symphony of mine and it got played many times on the BBC and I said, 'William, I don't want that played any more. I want you to play what I write now!'

Because that was putting you into a category and it was a category you didn't want?

I left that category more and more from 1945. 1948, my Cello Sonata and then finally the first String Quartet was the change to an entirely different direction and I didn't want that First Symphony to represent me. It's not a bad piece, as a matter of fact, as I look at it now. It's OK for what it was. It has jazz in it and things.

Yes, but do Americans regard you as an American composer in the sense that they say, 'These are American sounds'? These sorts of nationalistic gestures matter.

I don't know what they say. What I say is that I am producing the American sound. I'm making a new sound, it's an American sound. Nationality, as I see it, is something that's being produced by all of us all of the time. Henry James lived in England and he was an American and he wrote American novels and no English person would have written novels of that type although they were all written there in Rye. And even Henry James's novels, many of them are about England and yet they are the view of an American.

In this whole question of what is an American composer, how do you relate to the John Cage type of music?

Now, what I feel about this West Coast thing is this: my particular period of development and interest in music was believing that the musical situation was a static thing that existed. There was a symphony orchestra, there was an opera house, there was a string quartet; these things were a given and I was writing pieces for them, believing that by writing something new and lively we could make the opera house have something that was vivid in a new way, and similarly with a symphony orchestra, a string quartet or whatever, a pianist. Now I understand that there are people that feel that the opera house ought to be destroyed, that it's an old-fashioned thing that really has no meaning. And it would be the same for each of the other things that I've mentioned. I can understand that they're maddening in a certain sense, but I don't believe I want to do it.

But what about the Cage type of music, deconstructing the musical experience, deconstructing the conventional concert hall experience?

Well, this is all part of what I was saying. Cage was deconstructing not merely the concert situation but actually the way music is produced, and I think it's very entertaining and it has an overtone of Zen Buddhism which fascinates certain people. In my opinion all that kind of thing is again going back to this awful domination of a certain group of people over other people. It is a diversion. It's fun, but I don't think it can amount to very much. It has an overtone of seriousness because of its relation to I Ching. But it's not part of our society and Chinese society is a different kind of thing and to import it in this ridiculous way I find embarrassing.

As far as performances are concerned, presumably in the 1960s orchestras didn't play your works at all well, which must have been very frustrating?

Yes, I wrote a piece at the very end of the Second War, *Holiday Overture*, which had its first performance in Germany when the American troops arrived there. It was not played very much. It's now still played occasionally and it was one of the transitional works between the neoclassics and the old Americanising style, if you want to put it that way. I've always had trouble having my music played but now I have the enormous luck of the Chicago Symphony with Daniel Barenboim and Pierre Boulez playing every year. They even play my old Piano Concerto, which was always a nightmare.

Do you fear that there is not going to be a real audience for contemporary art music in the future?

Well, putting it the other way around, if there is an audience at all it will be for that, because I think that the other kinds of music that have been written – less serious kinds – will die just as they always have. It wears itself out. If you write a piece that repeats itself twenty times and you play the piece twenty times it's finally going to have a diminishing audience.

Yes, it may be popular but in the end it gets boring much more quickly than a serious piece of music. I think you've argued that people might have said to a composer in the nineteenth century, 'Why don't you write music like the Strauss family' at the time when people found Brahms difficult. A hundred years later, who had survived?

Well Brahms . . . as you've probably read in one review, when I was a student in Boston it used to be said that the exit sign meant 'this way in case of Brahms'. And it was said by the audience. It was really cruel. Brahms isn't very hard to understand. But I can imagine for a person who is not musical and didn't know it, Brahms is very intricate and quite novel, and there are very unusual things happening, even in the symphonies.

It's said by observers that you are composing with a new fluency and perhaps not just because of the number of works that you are producing. Is that the case? Are you finding composition easier?

Well yes, let's say that there was a long period of my life in which I was developing a musical vocabulary, and finally this vocabulary became something that I didn't have to think about as a thing to be produced. So I can now write more quickly simply because the pre-compositional effort of trying to find just what it is which will produce the kind of music that I want, I already know. For example, if I learn German I could finally write letters in German after I knew it better.

Your own language has become entirely integrated in yourself.

That's right. You know at my age, at the age of ninety-one, there are many things that occupy your efforts that you didn't have to think about when you were younger. And it becomes harder and especially with a wife that is not very well, it becomes harder and harder to find time to do this, and, secondly, it's harder and harder to find energy to do it because you get tired very quickly.

How many hours a day do you find that you can write now?

Well, if there are not many interruptions in the day, I can work from about nine in the morning until about twelve or one, and that's about it. And unfortunately I then have to take my wife out for a walk, I have to answer the telephone, I have to go shopping and all of this is very time-consuming. I think in some sense I've been lucky here in London. I've been able to write in my hotel room. I've been able to continue writing my cello sonata rather quietly – when you're not interviewing!

One final thought. Can you hear in your mind every piece that you've written?

Oh no. That worries me. I recognise them immediately when I hear them. I can remember bits of it but I can't remember the total thing. That frightens me a little bit. I can't remember very much of any musical piece. When I was younger I could remember all the Brahms symphonies, for instance, and most of *Tristan*. But you ask me the question. I don't really make this effort to do it. As far as I know I can't, but it's possible if I started to try and do it, I might do it.

I think it might be a waste of your brain power!

I remember very vividly in the old days when you crossed the Atlantic on a boat and I tried to keep from being seasick by going through the Brahms Fourth Symphony in my head.

MILOŠ FORMAN

'You have to tell the truth without being boring'

America has been a refuge for artists throughout the twentieth century, refugees from political, ideological and racial persecution. Miloš Forman settled there after the Russian invasion of his homeland, Czechoslovakia, in 1968. Then, he was just starting work on his first American film, following the international success of his Czech films *Black Peter*, *Loves of a Blonde* and *Firemen's Ball*. The last two received Oscar nominations. All of them were made under the eyes of, and played games with, Communist censors and bureaucrats. *Taking Off*, that first American film, failed to create such a stir. Holed up in New York's Chelsea Hotel, Forman waited for the chance to create that success. It came with his screen version of Ken Kesey's novel *One Flew over the Cuckoo's Nest*, which starred Jack Nicholson and won five Oscars. Success of that kind eluded Forman for almost another decade until *Amadeus*, adapted by Peter Shaffer from his play and partly filmed back in Forman's native country. That garnered more Academy awards. Since then Forman has worked at his own pace. He's not prolific, just eleven films in all. He's consistently attracted to projects about characters who refuse to conform as America would like them to. Such as the real-life pornographer Larry Flynt in *The People vs Larry Flynt* and the comedian, Andy Kaufmann, the subject of Forman's last film *Man on the Moon*.

When did you first get your hand on a camera of any kind?

When was that? It was 1960, I was working on *Magic Lantern*, the show for Brussels World Fair and the creator of the show was a brilliant man, Alfred Ruddock, who was hated by the Communists because he was a nonconformist and always had very extravagant ideas. And he was very often banned from working in the National Theatre. But for export, right; for Brussels, they let him do the show and I was working with him. Of course, when he brought the show back to Prague, you know, they fired us all.

There wasn't anything political in it as I recall. When Magic Lantern *came over to London, there was nothing political in it; it was just rather folksy and pretty.*

You are right, but that didn't matter. What really mattered, you know, was 'always follow the money'. Because what happened was that after Brussels the show opened in Prague. Because it was a very complicated show, it could not be in repertory, it had to be played every night, every night, every night, and according to the international copyright law we had royalties as authors, right? It was quite substantial money even in a Communist country. And so when we did the show for London, it was obvious again the show would be shown in Prague. Suddenly, you know, there was a political storm, we were all fired, and the next day the programme was shown with different authors. They changed a couple of words here and there because suddenly we were without money and somebody else was taking the royalties! So that was the real reason, you know. Now, being fired I didn't have anything to do. I had a little money so I bought myself a 16mm silent camera. I got a rather noisy East German camera with excellent lenses, Zeiss lenses. And I asked my friend Ivan Passer if he knows somebody how to put a film in it, because I didn't know. And he brought me Miroslav Ondriček and since that time I didn't see the camera because he wouldn't let it go.

And Ondriček has shot most of your films, hasn't he?

Yes. In that time he was only a focus assistant in the Barandov Studio, just a young kid, you know. And I offered friends of mine who were running a very small musical theatre in Prague to do some kind of a home movie about them so that they can look at themselves when they will be old, what kind of crazy things they were doing when they were young. And I started to shoot, in a very amateur way, this film called *Concourse* or *Competition*.

Which was about a singing competition?

Yes, about a singing competition. Girls were trying to be accepted on the stage in this small theatre. And this was very funny thing. I had my own tape recorder, but it was not synchronised with the camera. So, yes, I had a sound and we had a picture.

So how did you synchronise it?

Well, a really brilliant editor, you know; he just put it together, two frames cut out here, one frame here, one frame there; he just put it a little bit, you know, approximately into sync.

This was the film where you have about twenty or thirty girls all singing the same song, and you cut from one to the other as the song goes on?

You know why? Because we asked the girls, 'Okay, sing something', and this was at that time the most popular song, so everybody knew that song, so everybody was singing that song.

And of course that was a sequence which you then repeated in your film Taking Off, *wasn't it?*

Because, as you know, I suffered when I saw how imperfect and technically bad and poor the Czech version was. And so when I was doing my first film in the United States I said, 'Oh, I can do this scene the way I really wanted, you know, beautifully, technically perfect and right.' So that's what I did.

But it's a long way from that particular first movie which in a way anybody can do; we've all had 16mm cameras of our own. When did you think that you were going to become a serious film director?

Well, you know, I graduated from film school as a screenwriter and I wrote a couple of screenplays, as a matter of fact, which were done by different directors. And I'm not saying that these films were better or worse, but they were different. I wrote the screenplay and the film came out different from what my imagination thought it would be, or it should be. So I just decided that I'll try if I will get a chance to direct my own screenplays myself.

Even then, what really appealed to you about the business of directing, getting things on the screen?

Oh, I guess it's something which grows with you through the childhood. It's just a desire to tell stories, to attract the attention of some audience, even if it's one person or a hundred people, you know, listening to you telling a story. And the film was a wonderful, wonderful media to tell the story.

Was there any family background which made you particularly attracted to the telling of the story, or was this just something very deep and instinctive?

Not really, my older brother, he's a painter, he's an artist. But that's the only art, as far as I know; artistically sort of working person.

I suppose the most important experience for you had been the murder of your parents in concentration camps. What effect did that have? Because to the ordinary viewer, you are not a person who is replaying that personal family tragedy in your films. So what effect did it have on you?

Well, I was . . . you know, I don't know if I should say lucky, because it's sort of ironic to say that. But I was lucky that it happened when I was a child, because you don't really realise what's happening. First of all it was during the war when they were arrested by the Nazis. I was eight years old and so I was told, 'Yes, your parents are taken to the concentration camp.' But nobody would tell me what, how they are suffering horrors and everything. The opposite is true: they said, 'Oh, they will be back, don't worry, everything will be all right!' The only camps I knew were scout camps, so I didn't have any imagination of what was happening. And they would be back. Fine, fine. One year goes by, two years go by, and they are not there, and suddenly somebody comes and says, 'We're not sure if your mother died.' Well, nothing changed in my life, she was not there already for two years. Probably if she died at home I would feel something very strongly. But this way, nothing changes. And I'll tell you, the child doesn't really comprehend the death, the finality of life, it's something abstract. So it really hit me after the war when I was at the age of puberty when you would suddenly start to think a little bit more philosophically about your doings and the life around you.

But it's not something which played itself out in any of your films?

No, no, no. As a matter of fact, I was offered subjects, and for some reasons, you know, I don't want to touch it because . . . I don't know what it is, I don't want to touch the subjects from this period of my life.

But you don't feel that you are repressing it?

No, no, no. I don't feel that. I'm at peace with it, you know. And I feel a great respect for the legacy of my parents, yes; but I'm not repressing it.

Are you at peace with the people who murdered them?

Yes, yes, because in those times I didn't understand why it happened. And now these people are gone already and the fact that my parents are just two people out of millions and millions, you know, it wasn't their fault, it was the fault of some ideologies running amok. I guess it influenced my look at certain aspects of life, you know, in a sort of quasi-philosophical way – then I asked myself, yes freedom of expression is very important.

Are you a more accepting person because of this experience? You had no choice but to accept that your parents were murdered, and therefore you had learned the lesson of how important it is to accept when you can do nothing about a particular event?

Oh yes, you learn one thing: that you take very seriously things which you can influence. But you can't, and you must not, take too seriously things where you don't have any influence on.

So you had the experience of living under Nazism, and then from 1948 onwards the experience of living under Communism. I think as time goes by people forget what the experience of living under Communism was. How would you convey the essence of living in that sort of regime to somebody who didn't live in that way?

Simply said: it's living in fear, which is boring. Because you are afraid to lose the chance to go to school, to have a job, to do things. So you have to censor yourself: what you say, what you do, how you behave. It's not an exciting kind of rebellion, I guess any totalitarian system is basically very, very boring.

You said that the problem is that self-censorship – which you have just described – 'bends the spine'.

Self-censorship of course enters your life, you know. You are watching very carefully what you say, how you say it, to whom you say it, and it's not fun.

What about the people who actually ran the Party, the bureaucrats. What sort of people were they?

Well, I guess they are people who their only pleasure in life is power; nothing spiritual, just power. I don't even know if they believed in it or not. They just did it to keep themselves in power and keep everybody away who could disturb their power.

So how did you deal with this when you started making movies which were going to be main movies?

Well, my situation was sort of lucky because I really started at the right moment; there was a certain kind of a relaxation of this strict totalitarian, ideological control, in late sixty-seven, early sixty-eight. And after Khrushchev, you know, denouncing Stalin and telling them, 'Comrades you have to give confidence to young people' and like that. So that was a little more relaxed period. Fortunately for us – because as much as the Communists had condemned the West, it was falling apart and very soon would disappear from the planet. So because our first films were fortunately successful and brought some hard currency, so they started to tolerate us.

But you were always looking very carefully at what you were saying so that you didn't overstep the boundaries of what they would regard as politically acceptable?

Oh, of course. With this little relaxation, of course, everybody who had a little freer way of thinking was pushing the boundaries, right? And the authorities became very sensitive. But it was the time when it was not very popular to ban films, for example, in an administrative way. So what they were doing is that usually when they saw a film and they didn't like it and they thought that it should be banned, they arranged a screening for working people. And they always planned it, you know. One or two people there who would say, 'OK, comrades, let's have a discussion about the film.' And now they attacked the film and finally the result was the people rejected the film! And this was supposed to happen to my film, *The Firemen's Ball,* and it's kind of a comedy, you know.

Kind of a comedy? It's the best satire against the Communist regime!

And I was told that when the President and the First Secretary of the Party and his cohorts saw the film, that he climbed the walls, you know!

So he wasn't that stupid, Novotný, that he couldn't see exactly what was going on in that film. He wasn't so stupid?

Oh no, he knew exactly, right away, right away. And he immediately ordered this kind of screening. And they decided, 'Now listen, he is making fun of these firemen,' because the whole film was shot in the small town with real people. There was not one professional actor, all the people are from the town and mostly they are the real firemen from that town. So the President said, 'We'll show that film there, and then these people will see how this film is mocking them, making fun of them, making them look ridiculous. They will tell the film makers what kind of a dirty job they did!' So they arranged the screening in that little town, everybody was there, everybody who was in the film was there.

Except you?

I was advised not to go there because I might be attacked, you know, by the enraged mob of very angry firemen; they could beat me up. I didn't go, but I was told what happened. The film ended and, of course, immediately the planted man, you know, got up and said, 'Well, comrades, I think this film is a disgrace, full of lies about our heroic firemen who are fighting to keep our lives and our properties intact from fires! And look what they did and they are making fun, and these lies.' Like that. So he'd finished and then one of the firemen, a local fireman, had got up and said, 'Well, comrade, I don't know why are you saying it's a lie. Do you remember when the shack of this old man was burning and we couldn't get there because Loisa was drunk and we couldn't get the car out of the garage.' You know, my God! And people started to applaud and laugh, because what the Communist organisers of this screening didn't realise was that they are not showing this to local people. They are showing it to the actors, to people who were immortalised on the screen. They were proud to see themselves on the screen. And I think that they understood that the film is a comedy, is a satire, that they didn't take it personally. So the screening was a total fiasco. But they banned the film anyway!

In 1968 you left Czechoslovakia as it then was, you went to Hollywood and in a very short time you found yourself facing commercial pressures. So you had the ideological pressures in Czechoslovakia and then in Hollywood you ran into the commercial pressures, or shall we say the subjective pressures of the studio. You really faced this when you had made Taking Off, *which was your film about the sixties generation and the panic of American parents. Tell me about that.*

Well, I'll tell you: if you asked me to choose between ideological censorship or commercial censorship, I prefer commercial censorship rather than Zhdanov, the ideological one. And with commercial pressure you are at the mercy of the audience and I prefer that. But the problem was that I was trying to make my first film in the United States the same way I did in Czechoslovakia. I tried to make a Czech film in the United States, and I found out that that doesn't work. It doesn't work the same as if the Czechs are trying to make American movies in Czechoslovakia. It's probably a little snobbish also. Today I see it as a little European snobbism. It's the style of the narrative, you know, with the open endings and you leave the audience to guess what you really meant.

And Hollywood likes an ending?

And Hollywood wants to know who is good guy, who is the bad guy, and who won. And that's it.

In the case of Taking Off, *the reaction from the studio was a very subjective and personal one, wasn't it?*

Well, that was because of one scene or two scenes in the film which were offensive to the wife of the president of the studio. Actually that's what I was told.

Anyway, both Firemen's Ball *and* Taking Off *are still there and are classics of their kind. Going back to 1968 for a moment, can you remember what you felt and what you thought when the Red Army marched into Czechoslovakia in the autumn of 1968?*

Well, at that moment I was in Paris working on the script for *Taking Off*. And well, I'll tell you. For me the biggest shock was my brother, twelve years older than me who was, who is, a home body. He lived in a small, tiny little place, a village far from Prague. And for him to travel to Prague, that was big undertaking, you know. And now the Russians came to invade Czechoslovakia. I'm in Paris, I don't know what to do. I am trying to find my brother. I find how he's on his way to Australia. And I reach him and said, 'What are you doing?' And he said, 'Look, I remember when in 1938 a friend of our parents came to our father and said, 'Listen, I am leaving for England, as a matter fact, and if you want I can arrange for you to leave too.' And I remember our father who said, 'No, no, no, no! I have a clean conscience here, nothing will happen to us.' And they both paid for this decision of our father with their lives, our father and mother. And who knows what will happen now with the Russians? And I will not take the responsibility if something bad would happen!' That for me was, 'OK, this must be serious!' My brother, the home body, is now on his way to Australia, the only country where he had some friends. That was something.

Did you even consider going back and saying, 'There will be some kind of political resistance and I will be part of that political resistance'?

No, I was in a very particular situation because I was outside legally. So I didn't really have to consider defection yet, because the contract to let me make a film in the United States – which was *Taking Off* – was signed by the previous Dubček Communist regime during the liberalisation. If the new Communist regime wouldn't honour the contract, they could be sued for a lot of money by Universal, right, who they've got the contract with. So I finished the film outside of Czechoslovakia legally, but then I was asked to come back. And I knew that the moment I come back – because I learned that *The Firemen's Ball* was banned for ever – I would not be able to work in the cinema. So I asked for extending my exit visa and they fired me, and that's how they made the decision for me.

You said something about Czech films and American films, and I just want to clear this up. Is there a difference between how you worked as a Czech director and then, when you got to Hollywood you suddenly became an American director? Is there any difference in the way you make the films?

Well, I want to believe that there is not. I am sure there is for certain because just knowledge of the language is different, you know. In Czech language I can understand every word I overhear in the pub. Here today I don't; in the United States especially when you go to Harlem, for example. I realised one thing: that I can't function any more as a screenwriter. My knowledge of language and the way people talk and the characterisation of people by the way they talk, these nuances I don't have. So the only change I am aware of is that after *Taking Off,* I stopped working on my own screenplays and I turned to adapt materials which were written originally by English-speaking writers.

Sticking with the Czech language for a moment: do you still hear the Czech language in your ears? Do you still dream in Czech?

Yes. I'll tell you the most important distinction which is your real mother language is the language in which you appreciate poetry; that's the big difference. I can really appreciate poetry in Czech language. I really can't fully appreciate poetry in the English language.

You were a screenwriter; you're very sensitive about scripts and about the verbal content of your films. You've always had very strong cameramen to work with; no doubt, editors to edit. Where do you as the director really have your impact?

Well, I'll tell you. Director is a little bit of everything, a little bit of the writer, a little bit of an actor, little bit of an editor, little bit of a costume designer. A good director is a director who chooses for this profession people who are better than he is! Yes, I can write, but I have to have a writer who is a better writer than I am; I have to have actors who are better actors than I am, I have to have sound engineers who are better sound engineers than I am. Then it's a strange profession, you know – the fact is that visually it's your vision!

Even working through a cameraman, when you have a cameraman like Ondriček, what do you have to say to him? In a way you don't have to say anything to him, do you, about the way he composes?

No, you are the only person who really has the whole film in your mind. How to pace the film and the rhythm you give it, the speed of actions and things like that. And that influences everything. You have decisions about the camera angles and lenses and camera movements and motion. So the camera, yes you have to influence that if you want to see on the screen what you dreamed about at the table.

Which is the critical action? Is it shooting, or can you recover things that go wrong when you edit?

Well, the critical thing, the most important, is editing. Because there is no other opportunity to do the film. When you work on the script and you know that it's not the right idea: 'Well, during the shooting we'll improve it.' When you are shooting you feel that this is not still entirely right. 'Well, we'll fix it in the editing.' But now you are editing, and that's it – there is no other step when you can fix it! So that's when you start to panic.

Have you ever panicked? Was there one of your films where when you came to the editing you thought, 'I'm never going to recover this'?

Well, I wouldn't call it panic in a threatening way. But you always panic, because you never know if what you are doing will work. You never know even when it's finished until you show it to an anonymous audience, because friends never tell you the truth either. You never know if it will work or not, because the curse of a film maker is the film maker never sees his own film; never. For one simple reason: that every moment I know what's coming next.

But if something is wrong? Surely you are hypersensitive about a change of shot that irritates you? Do you say, 'Every time I see that it jars me; that must be wrong'?

Well, you know, but it's not wrong because it's wrong. What bothers me is when I see immediately that it's not true – if a performance doesn't ring true, for example, or a moment of storytelling. Suddenly you realise, 'No, no, I wouldn't believe that if I saw this in a film.' You know what I mean? But otherwise, the moment of surprise, discovering, suspense, is so important for the perception of the movie by the audience, which a film maker never has, because they know what's coming next. So I don't know if it works or not. I know if it rings true or not; yes, that I know.

So once you feel that it rings true, even if the audience says, 'We didn't like it' or 'We didn't think it was funny enough', then you have to say, 'For me it's true. It's a pity you didn't like it'?

Yes. It's whose stupidity is it, mine or theirs? I don't want it to be mine.

But the question of truth: how do you get this truth out of actors? You have this reputation for allowing actors to improvise, but how much do you allow them to improvise?

Well, it depends on the scene. Some scenes have to be done exactly as they are written in the scripts because otherwise the pace would suffer. But then there are scenes which allow a space for improvisation and then I like to encourage improvisation. But you have to always have an exact script because ninety per cent of improvisation is usually very boring, unusable. But the ten per cent or even less, even if you have one per cent, you can get such a gem of unrepeatable moment of films that it's worth it to try to improvise. But if improvisation doesn't work you have to have a solid script to go back to.

Everybody quotes the scene in The People vs Larry Flynt *where Woody Harrelson and Courtney Love are in the sauna and they discuss love and marriage, and that is largely improvised, I think. That one really worked.*

Yes, they had a point, you know, to touch; they knew that exactly. But I encouraged them: 'Listen, you don't have to slavishly stick to every word. But say the same thoughts, say the same things, but you can use your own words and go at it' and they did and it was just a wonderful firework show.

What made you choose Courtney Love, although I gather you didn't realise what her reputation was when you cast her? You cast her as Larry Flynt's wife on the basis of the screen test?

And then subsequently the readings and the screen test, yes. Because, you know, I think she's a brilliant, brilliant lady, actress; wonderful, raw, vulnerable, fragile. But she can't say a lie. She can't tell a lie. Even in her own life she's always putting herself in trouble, you know, when she opens her mouth. But she had a big problem when I met her. I didn't know that she was such a big deal in rock and roll. But from the first moment I saw her I knew that she is on something, you know.

And then people asked, 'Do you realise what you're taking on?'

And then studio said, 'No way, Courtney Love, no way; we can't insure her' and that's very serious because if you can't insure a main protagonist, you can't use that person because if something happens it costs an enormous amount of money.

So how did you get her insured?

Through a friend of mine here in London, I found an insurance company. But it was very, very expensive, it cost a lost of money.

And the studio said, 'No, we are not going to pay this money for insurance.' And then I realised that I was right betting on Courtney, because everybody was so impressed. Woody Harrelson, Oliver Stone who was the producer, Michael Hausman who was co-producer, myself and Courtney, we put down $1 million to pay for her insurance.

That she would complete the film; that was the insurance?

The insurance was that if something happens, she's insured. If suddenly in the middle of the shooting she overdoses or whatever, insurance would pay, so it cost a lot of money. And I went to Courtney and I said, 'Courtney, I'll fight for you if you give me your word that you will not betray me.' And she looked me in the eye and said that she would not betray me, in such a way that I trusted her. And she kept her word.

But did she find it difficult?

The first three weeks were a nightmare for her. Because she was shooting the scenes when Althea is still a normal girl, a nice girl, a together girl. And I found her several times, you know, shivering in the bathroom because of the withdrawal. That was tough for her, but she did it and she's clean as a whistle till today.

This film still pursues you in a sense. People said, 'There is Forman, who seems a pretty decent sort of chap, making a film, glorifying Larry Flynt, publisher of the most raunchy pornographic magazine, The Hustler, *and Forman raises it to be a matter of freedom of speech.' Now just how do you reconcile what others see as a contradiction?*

Would you consider *Romeo and Juliet* glorifying in suicide? And you know how many young people die with *Romeo and Juliet* in their hands, committing suicide? But that's not what the play is about. It happens, yes, but you can't blame art for extreme cases of imitation. The same way people know *Larry Flynt* is not about pornography. It's about freedom of the speech, it's about freedom of expression, it's about much more important things.

Even freedom of expression of things which, you, me, none of us actually value as expression?

That's why it's important to show how important freedom of speech is. Because if I made a film about that, somebody is free to tell you, 'You scumbag'. So what? Who cares about that? The most important freedom is not for those who are saying agreeable things to us. Freedom is important that you are free to say things which nobody likes!

You have this record of heroes who are active counter-heroes. Larry Flynt is certainly one, McMurphy in Cuckoo's Nest *is another. Were you aware that you were producing this extraordinary canon of heroes who stand up to oppressive society, or was it just instinctive as it emerged?*

Well, I would like to say that, yes, I am showing the world the conflict between an individual and an institution. But in fact, I think I just glorify this rebel because I am myself a coward. I would like to be a hero but I don't have the courage to do that. But on the other hand, this is the eternal conflict between the individual and the institution, because we create institutions to help us live. We pay them our taxes, and we end up very often being dictated by them how to live.

And the last scene in Cuckoo's Nest: *I believe that you see the end when McMurphy's friend, the Indian, picks up this huge safe, throws it through the windows of the mental institution and suddenly they are all out in the countryside, free – that's not, as far as you're concerned, just about America?*

No, no. That was the dream, I would say, of 99 per cent of the young people in Communist countries, you know. Because we were not allowed to travel, we were in a cage like in the zoo, and we all dreamed about one day to take that thing and throw it through the barbed-wire fences and go and run to see the world.

So that was a universal gesture both about the oppressions of capitalist societies and Communist societies as well?

Any kind of oppressive society, yes.

What was Jack Nicholson like to work with, as an actor?

Wonderful, wonderful. He is an enormously talented man. To be honest I don't know till today if he's crazy or not himself, you know. But very professional, very helpful to other actors, never refusing anything to help even the other. He's smart: he knows that if the other people are better, then even he comes across better on the screen.

But was he dangerous as an actor? Was he difficult to handle?

No, no, no. It was also interesting, we had only one blow-up during the shooting, and it was, you know why? Because it was late afternoon, the light was going down and we had only two takes. And I thought it was perfect and he just suddenly said, 'No, I can do it better, I want to do it again.' 'It was good, Jack, it was perfect. Let's see, you know, we need to do two more shots before the dark comes.' 'No, no, no, no, I was bad, I was bad.' That was the only blow-up he had, you know. And finally I won. It was interesting at the beginning of the shooting, for the first two days or three days he went to see the rushes – I wouldn't tell him not to, you know. And then he stopped going to see the rushes; fine, fine. But in this case he went to see the rushes and he said, 'Yes, it's good, good, that was all right!'

You said that you make these films about heroes, people who rebel against society, because you're not heroic yourself. The question which is almost always asked of a Czech sooner or later, and so I apologise for putting it to you, but because our national archetype is Svejk, the ultimate evasive anti-hero, do you feel there is something of Svejk inside you?

Oh, very much so, very much so, yes. You know it's this kind of humour that made the Czech nation survive centuries. Because, you know, it's Bohemia, it's Moravia, a small entity in the middle of Europe surrounded by very powerful neighbours who are always through the last two thousand years trying to dominate this part of Europe. And this small entity can't protect itself through power. It's survived through humour, otherwise we would be dead.

Is that how you deal with studios as well? Do you use Svejkian tactics to get your own way when it comes to making films?

Well, I was sort of lucky. I made only one film or two films through the studio, otherwise I was working always for the independent. It depends who you are dealing with in the studio. Because behind every door is a different type of person, and if you open the right door and meet the right person, you need to play Svejk.

But you have fought for principles; you won the John Huston award for standing up for the moral rights of film makers against studios. Now what was behind that?

What was behind that was that one day I had in my contract that when the studio want to sell the musical *Hair* through the network, they have to have my consent what they do with it. But they didn't have this. So what they did, they didn't sell it to the network, they sold it to a syndicated television where I didn't have that right. The film played on one hundred and fifteen syndicated stations practically all over the United States, and it's a musical. Out of twenty-two musical numbers, eleven musical numbers were cut out from the film, and yet it was still presented as 'A Miloš Forman film, *Hair*'. It was totally incomprehensible, gibberish, butchered beyond belief. I thought: can we do something? No – because this is such an irony . . . Let me ask you a question: who is, according to American law, legally the author of Larry Olivier's *Hamlet*?

The director, the studio?

Well, it's not Shakespeare, nor Larry Olivier; it's MGM. MGM is legally the author. According to American law, who owns the copyright is the author, legally, and can do with the work whatever he or she wants – which I think is such absurdity, you know.

But you fought that and you won it?

No, we are fighting it. Already every couple of years I go to the Congress together with other people. Once I was there, for example, with Jimmy Stewart and Ginger Rogers, you know, and George Lucas. But it will take another twenty years the way that the studios lobby the American Congress.

Why in the end do you think that film, as such, matters to society?

Not as much as we would like to think, but not as little as they would like to think.

Who are they?

Who are the 'they'? Whoever, whoever. The culture policemen. Look, the most powerful anti-war film was shot in the thirties you know: *La Grande Illusion*. It didn't stop the war.

By Jean Renoir?

Yes, yes. And we have a little bit of tendency to overestimate importance, I think. Every film is very powerful, very powerful over an individual during this two hours you are sitting in the cinema. But once the film is over and you go out, the film becomes just one little part of all your life experience. It enriches you, if it is the case of the film. But let's not overestimate its power.

But with a really strong film (and certainly One Flew over the Cuckoo's Nest *is that) and last night when you were doing a screen talk, and the cinema was filled with people mainly under thirty who'd clearly seen the film, and for them the film was an experience which has lasted them for over twenty years – this is quite something.*

Oh yes. A film or literature or theatre can be very inspiring, especially for young people. But, if you say how important it is, then you will have to admit that you must censor a lot of films because then young people imitate them. And you start to blame these shoot-outs at the schools in the United States on culture, on movies. And you start to call for censorship and then this and then that, and that's wrong.

Do you believe that there is a copycat element in people watching violence on the screen and then doing something violent?

Yes, but that shouldn't matter at all, because you always find one person, crazy person, who can copycat anything. But that's not the reason to ban that thing for the tens of millions who saw the same thing and didn't do anything to imitate the bad things, violence or whatever.

But you wouldn't want film just to be written off as 'well, it's entertainment, it's something which fills up the videos, it's something which fills up the digital channels'?

Oh, I think that it's primarily entertainment, and should be primarily entertainment. But if it gives you some nourishment to your brain and your heart and mind, that's even better, it's the icing on the cake. But you know the only thing I'm saying is: if you want to make a respected film, and also a commercially successful film, you have to tell the truth without being boring. And I'll tell you something: that's very difficult, very difficult because truth is usually very boring, because it's the truth.

You haven't made a lot of films by the standards of many directors; you make about one every two to three years. Does that disappoint you? Do you have a feeling there are half a dozen films that you really wanted to have made and that it would be nice if they had filled in the gaps between the films that you actually did make?

No, not really, you know. I'm not saying this is a better way or a worse way, but that's not my cup of tea, you know, I have to get hungry to work.

And what do you do in between films? You have this reputation of becoming slightly reclusive. Are you happy just to become fallow for a time?

Oh no, I don't feel that I stop working between films. I'm reading scripts, I'm reading books, you know, and I am meeting friends and I like to travel. And now I'd like to spend the time with my family – and that's work, family; that's work.

Do you have a favourite film of your own?

I don't really have a favourite film; I must say it's sort of artificial or superficial kind of attitude. I favour or I feel tender towards the films which were molested by critics or feminists or people, you know, because I've some kind of a protective instinct. *Cuckoo's Nest* and *Amadeus*: they can survive by themselves; they don't need my protection.

Fireman's Ball, *that was attacked. Now that can look after itself?*

That's a film I can feel very tender about!

And what is your favourite film made by somebody else?

I like a lot of films, but for me the hero is American silent comedy: Buster Keaton, Charlie Chaplin, Harold Lloyd, Laurel and Hardy, Ben Turpin, you name them all. Because they made me laugh and moved me at the same time when I started seeing films, which was only when I was thirteen years old after the war. Before the war I saw only two films as a child. I saw *Snow White*; my parents took me. And then I saw – this is totally absurd – it was in 1937 or 1938, but I saw a silent version of the most popular Czech opera, *The Bartered Bride*.

A silent version!

It was an experience I will never forget in my life, and the weirdest experience ever. Because, of course, in those times, in the small town where we lived, my father took a tie and a white shirt, and I'd go in my best suit, and we went to the movies in the afternoon on Sunday. And now it's the darkness and the curtain on the screen and the silence of the curtain. In front of the curtain the orchestra starts to play, you don't hear anything of course. And then the curtain goes up and then the opera starts with some choirs singing a song, and suddenly the whole theatre started to sing the songs, because everybody in Czechoslovakia knew these songs, knew the opera. So you had the sound better than you have the sound today because it was live, it was so strange and weird.

You thought it was weird at the time?

Well, I thought it was normal! Next time I went to the movies and people didn't sing, I thought this was wrong. Then during the war, of course, nobody would give you money to see the Nazi films. So the next films I saw were after the war; that's when I discovered American silent comedy.

Have you ever wanted to direct an opera? Because it seemed to me the scenes in Amadeus *of* The Magic Flute *are so brilliant that I thought, 'Why can't we have a production of* Magic Flute *like this?'*

I'll tell you, practically every major opera house in the world, after *Amadeus*, invited me to direct an opera. And I know I can't do that because – this is terrible to say but it's true – most of the operas except for two or three arias, I find very artificial and boring. For the film, then, you can pick only the plums, the gems of the opera, the most beautiful arias, the most dramatic moment; that's something else. But to do the whole of *Don Giovanni* . . . I wouldn't do that, I wouldn't be able to do that. I am not really good musically, I can't play an instrument, my ear is not perfect, so I wouldn't do it for the love for music because I was not born with this talent.

But given how you direct actors and how you love working with actors, why haven't you directed on the stage?

I did, once, first time in my life I directed on Broadway, *Only in America*. I enjoyed doing it, but I realise theatre needs a different imagination than film. How many people do I know . . . One or two – Ingmar Bergman, Mike Nichols – who can do as great work on the stage and on the screen. Otherwise, I don't know. It's a different kind of imagination.

Do you count yourself lucky that having started life under two dictatorships, you've then ended up with most of your life in a free society, however peculiar, however imperfect?

Oh, now, I consider my life not as boring as my movies.

NICHOLAS GRIMSHAW

'You apply rigour to everything'

Nicholas Grimshaw is the quiet man of modern British architecture. He is of the generation of Foster, Rogers and Hopkins – yet he is probably less well known in a publicity sense than his other contemporaries. Which is odd. Many people know great landmarks such as Rogers's Dome, Foster's British Museum Great Court, Hopkins's Parliamentary building – and the controversy surrounding them. And yet Grimshaw's Eurostar Terminal at Waterloo may have touched many more people than any of those three; and his vast Eden Centre in a disused clay pit in Cornwall may become the Millennium Dome that we all remember – and visit.

Grimshaw has always built for people and for everyday activities. His Sainsbury's in Camden Town in London, his Homebase on the road to Heathrow, the Oxford ice rink, the *Western Morning News* building outside Plymouth, the forecourt at Paddington station – all these show an engagement with people and with work that is at the heart of his approach to architecture.

And by the time he has finished converting the disused, upturned, rotting molar hulk of Battersea Power Station on the Thames into a vast entertainment and leisure complex, he too will be on the roll-call of architects who have created a new London landmark.

You have been called professionally reticent, and you have said you believe that your buildings should do the talking. But you lecture, you write, you explain. Does putting things into words help you in designing your buildings?

I think that it is true that buildings should stand on their own and speak for themselves. I am quite keen to explain in lectures, though, what my philosophy is and to talk about the way I think people should get great pleasure out of looking at details; and quoting other buildings and bridges and so on, and focusing on details of them and saying, 'I think people like to see this and this is the sort of thing we are trying to do in our building.' So the lectures are illustrating the philosophy rather than necessarily specifically talking about an individual building from start to finish.

What people say about you in general is that you're against landmark buildings, you're against the sort of flashy architects' style. Justify what you mean by being 'against a landmark building'. After all, it is not as though you put up buildings which people don't notice!

I don't think I said I am against landmark buildings. What I am rather against is buildings which are highly stylised, which I think won't stand the test of time. I talk a lot about what I call 'wallpaper architecture', where it is a kind of street façade that you're looking at without understanding the bones and the thinking behind the building.

When you say 'highly stylised', would you include architects like Frank Gehry and the Bilbao Guggenheim, or Daniel Libeskind and his proposed building for the V and A? They couldn't be more different from the sort of buildings you put up.

Well, I think both Frank Gehry and Daniel Libeskind are sculptors, actually. They are three-dimensional thinkers who do pieces of sculpture, which stand up in their own right and don't necessarily pay any attention at all to what's around them.

But what about internally? To call them three-dimensional pieces of sculpture is to avoid the question as to whether they are good pieces of architecture.

Well, I haven't been inside a Daniel Libeskind building. I have been to the Bilbao Guggenheim building, and I do think it is rather marvellous both inside and outside. You're right in a sense that it stands for a lot of things which . . . Well, it doesn't address many of the things I think about all the time. I know Frank Gehry, and sort of tongue in cheek slightly, he says to me, 'Look, Nick, you know I don't give a damn about details.' Of course, it's not entirely true. For instance, if you go into that building, you cannot see any relationship between the inside and the outside. It is shaped completely differently and there is a very complicated web of structure between, which actually is completely ad hoc; it is not a structural form at all.

It just makes these external sculptural shapes work as a building. He makes it stand up.

It holds the outside skin and it holds the inside skin but it is not a structure as such and it could be scaffolding. And Frank Gehry would be the first to say so.

Does that annoy you because, as you say, it couldn't be more different from your approach to the essence of the building being its structure, its skeleton? I mean, that's one of your fundamental positions, isn't it?

I think you have to go back to site in this situation. The Bilbao stands as a piece of sculpture on a site and it is a three-dimensional object. Very often one's looking at buildings which are in a street scene or facing one way or seen in a particular kind of way which is different to that. Also the functions come into it in a big way. I mean, if you are doing a railway station you wouldn't make it look like Bilbao, for instance. Most people would see that as totally illogical. But with an art gallery, which is holding all kinds of disparate shapes of art and pictures and sculptures, then you can obviously reflect it in a more fluid kind of way.

The faint implication of what you are saying is that if you designed a building which was in as free-standing, three-dimensional a site as the Guggenheim Bilbao, you might do something that was closer to Frank Gehry. But even on a three-dimensional site, your buildings don't come out like Frank Gehry's; they come out like Grimshaws where skeleton, sculpture, and your words 'structure, order, detail, flexibility' apply. Those are the four words by which you act as an architect, are they not?

Yes. And if, for instance, I had a concert hall to design – which is something I have never done and I'd love to do, something you know quite a lot about – I would start by trying to understand it acoustically and the way people relate to the playing area. And then spend hours and hours and weeks and weeks on that kind of shape and the feel of that interior. And then move to the circulation systems and then gradually see what the impact of all that on the outside was, bearing in mind that you always have to have a strong acoustic protection from the outside, which would affect what you built it out of. So it wouldn't be a piece of sculpture with the concert hall shoved into the middle of it; it would grow from an understanding of the process. And I think that would produce some kind of regular structure of some sort, or at least an understandable structure.

And do you think that is what the public likes about buildings, that we like to see some kind of coherence and logic in a building, without absolutely saying that we can see every single bit of the plumbing? That part of the recognition of a building is that we can see how it stands up, what actually makes it stand up?

Well, I believe so and I think you can't always immediately take in the way a building is working but, even if it is at a subliminal level, people do take it in in some way. And if they are in a heroic railway station and they see the arches coming down to the ground in pin joints – like at St Pancras or Paddington – you get a satisfaction out of seeing that detail. You feel you're in the presence of something rather grand and a great piece of engineering and architecture in its own right. But if you ask the average person to say how St Pancras works, I am not sure whether they would be able to draw it for you and I am not sure they even know how big the span was or how many trains you could get underneath it.

What do you want people to take from your buildings? You've mentioned railway stations; you've adapted and you're continuing to adapt Paddington Station. Apart from it being an easier place to get around, what do you want the using public to feel about the building by the time you have finished it?

Well, Paddington is a restoration job. Our work there has been to try and restore the Brunel structure to as near its original as we can, and to make it work in today's much more intensified travellers' world, if you like. It was designed as a kind of cathedral-like structure, with a small span, a big span and a small span. Very much a tripartite idea, and it had another span added on in 1917, which we're actually working on a scheme to replace with a whole new transportation arrangement, which will make the station work much better.

There will be a few cries of 'You cannot destroy this masterpiece of a building', presumably? You have to face the fake conservationists as well as the real conservationists.

Well, actually, I think the general view is that if what you replace this extension with is good enough, then people won't fight for it too hard. I think that's the right attitude. I think there is no point in tearing something down and replacing it with something inferior. It's a challenge.

Let's go back to your earlier days when you were at the Architectural Association and see what light that throws on your work today. There's a quote from one of your tutors, Maxwell Fry, when he examined your thesis about grid planning in Greek cities and he warned you against being 'mechanistic at the expense of architectural features'. Was that a fair warning and was it one that you took heed of?

Well, yes. I am not quite sure what he was driving at there because he was a pretty precise kind of architect himself. This was a fascination on the historical side with the grid which I had at that time when I wrote my history thesis on Hippodamus of Miletus who was the great Greek grid planner. And I translated that into a modern-day three-dimensional grid structure which covered most of Covent Garden which at that time, interestingly, had a hoarding around a lot of it and was going to be demolished by the GLC. And it was just before conservation came into its own and in the end the hoardings came down and almost the whole of it was preserved.

Are you glad that your grid system wasn't imposed on Covent Garden?

Well, it was a very open flexible system which could have been infilled with all kinds of fascinating things and I don't think London would have suffered too much!

But what I read into it was that Max Fry was warning you against being too logical, too systematic, just too devoted to mechanistic solutions – as it were, the numerical side of design and architecture, rather than the softer inspirational side?

Yes, I think that in some ways was quite perceptive. I mean, take a piece of music, take Bach or something. Everybody loves the intricacy of the phrasing and the way it fits together – the detail, in fact, the perfection in the detail, if you like. But of course, there is also a marvellous shape to the whole thing, a marvellous sweep and creative shape to the piece as a whole. And what one tries to do is to do both. But perhaps the reason I talk about detail so much is that so many buildings fall down on the detail, and the materials and the way they're used.

But you talk about both detail and structure, to be fair to yourself. If you were only a detail man then you wouldn't have the reputation for logic and system in your buildings that you do.

Yes, absolutely. I think the interesting thing is when you apply the reverse, and I think you might find a quote which I use quite often, that it is very difficult to find a really good building anywhere which actually doesn't have a good structure and isn't well-detailed. And it may be that Frank Gehry has given the lie to that, but up to that point that was true I think.

I say, 'Part of the black-and-white view of you comes from this sense that maybe you are too logical and mechanistic.' And they say, 'Ah, yes, Grimshaw, you know, admires Brunel, admires Paxton, the strong engineering tradition.' What do you take from the work of Brunel and Paddington and the Great Western Railway and the Crystal Palace and so on? What of their work matters to you?

That's a very difficult question to ask. I suppose I admire them for their thinking, for their daring and for their logic when faced with the pretty major issues of the time. I mean, one has to always think of the time people did things. And Paxton's effort with Crystal Palace was an absolutely inspired thing, partly because of the time it was done in. I mean the period it was done in, but also the time it took to do it – and I believe it still holds the record for the most amount of space covered in the shortest period of time. It was an incredible feat of imagination to put that together and one admires that enormously. Similarly with Brunel, his great kind of pioneering inspirational spirit. And if you read biographies of Brunel, you actually see not an absolutely straightforward logical engineer at all – you see an absolutely impassioned creative person surging away underneath, determined to get these things done, and not a kind of clinical mathematician at all.

I think you've said about both of them that you admire the clarity of their path from concept to final building. I think 'clarity' is a very interesting word. It doesn't imply that it's a straight path or it is a path without problems, but that they know where they have to go and they get there. You also mention logic in the context of Paxton and Brunel. So what do we have? A sort of overriding logic and a clarity about where they want to end up, and then flexibility and creativity as they get there?

Yes, I think it is a very interesting issue. What you want, I think, to see is clarity of concept carrying through. And what annoys me most when walking around a building which I don't like: it's if you suddenly see a break in what's going on, in the clarity of the way the concepts are working. And you think, 'Why the hell did they do that, and what is the logic, what is the point?' If you start to see pointless gestures, angled pieces of wall which actually don't do anything for anybody, then it starts to really annoy you. And I think no amount of hot air in terms of description can let people escape from buildings which actually don't really work.

Were Paxton, Brunel and of course Buckminster Fuller of the Geodesic Dome, were they leaning over your shoulder symbolically when you designed the Eden Centre down in Cornwall, which I suppose is in the great line of the English greenhouse tradition?

Well, in a way! It's using a very much twentieth- or possibly twenty-first-century structural system and cladding system, and it's also – and I think this is quite interesting – relating to the whole idea of order on the one hand and the grand sweep of a building on the other. We've used a very formal structural system to create an extremely organic and flowing shape, which comes directly out of the landscape and out of the contours in which we're dealing.

And would you be able to say of that building as well that the structure and the skeleton is the essence of it?

In many ways it is, and the placing of it in its landscape. It is very important that it is placed exactly where it is and it is leaning on the piece of cliff that it is leaning on. It has been a very, very carefully constructed arrangement.

So even on what is a very restricted site, which is an old disused quarry, the precise bit of that space that you use and that you don't use is an important part of designing the building?

Absolutely, yes, and that is really always the case in siting and everything, but particularly important there. But what you say about the bones is right. I mean, I do see, over the years, that building could be reclad with even more wonderful materials than we've got – materials that breathe and materials that change colour and so on as technology moves on. But the bones will remain, as I see it.

What strikes me is the human, animal, biomorphic language that you use about your buildings: 'skeleton', of course. One of your buildings, I think in Berlin, has been compared to an armadillo. You've written that your buildings must be able to 'shed their skin'. Your drawings for the Waterloo Eurostar Terminal are, as you say yourself, an arched hand. So it's a very interesting interplay between these human and animal images and the strictness of your engineering.

Yes, well, that's of course the wonderful thing that nature does – because it has wonderful structures within it, nearly always. And from the hexagonal structure of a fly's eye to the way a tree stands up and it doesn't fall over! They are perfectly calculated structures and yet there is nothing mathematical about them in a way, any more than there is about the human frame. You can describe it mathematically, but every person is different and they can vary in shape and size enormously. And I think that is the fascination of nature, really: even though it is based on very strong mathematical principles, it has a marvellous living and organic side to it.

Can you remember at what stage you saw what the Eden Centre was going to look like? Between envisaging the final results and the final result itself emerging from all sorts of other considerations and calculations, what is the interplay between those processes when you think of a building, when you conceive it?

It's very, very difficult to pin down an exact moment in a design process and of course we work (I should emphasise this very strongly) as a team. I have always said that my favourite way of designing is to sit round the table well into the night if we have to, and throw ideas on to the table and fight for them. A thing does emerge as a team. But I think the site was a terrifically strong influence at Eden. When I first saw it, we came to the rim of this crater and it was completely like a lost world. You couldn't see it from anywhere else because it's a crater on top of a hill. You can't see into it. It was almost as if nobody knew it was there. It had enormous impact and somehow this idea of the thing, like a row of bubbles clinging to the side of it, exactly like some sort of cocoon which you might have found in nature, had a great appeal – to make that wave and go up and down with the ground, and go in and out of the cliff, to devise a structure that could do that, instead of having something rather rigid which was just sort of in a sense dumped there, I think was the kernel of the idea really.

But there must be many times when you think you have got a strongish image of what the building might be, but when you come to work it out you have to say, 'That would have made a marvellous building, but I cannot actually deliver it with the structural logic and coherence that I demand, and therefore I have to junk it'?

Well, I don't give up easily. I don't think any of us do. And we get round the table with those ideas meetings that I was talking about. It is not just architects; it is engineers very often there as well. And there is an interplay between the idea and what's possible. So you push structural ideas around in relation to the architecture that you want to achieve. And basically all of our designs are very closely interlocked with engineering and engineering ideas. And we are not at all the kind of architect who says, 'This is what I want, can you work out a way of holding it up for me?'

And of course you design where necessary the structural components which are necessary to create a particular building. That's not very common in other architectural practices, is it?

Well, you work with the engineer on these connections. You have to be very well aware of the structural logic and an engineer will not let you do decorative structures! They will only let you do things that really work as structures, and so the interplay is there.. The thing has got to be structurally correct before a decent engineer anyway will accept it.

The average age of your practice is, I think, thirty-one?

That's right.

That's pretty remarkable. How do you handle these Young Turks straight out of the architectural schools who presumably – as you do at twenty-eight or twenty-nine – know everything about architecture?

Well, bear in mind that is an average. There are plenty of steady guys of forty and forty-five to hold everything down. But we believe very strongly in bringing in young blood and bright young people directly from colleges. And the office in many ways is a kind of training place where they go through working on small parts of jobs and then work their way up, and not many people leave us. Sometimes they leave us to set up on their own, but a lot of people work their way all through the office and have a very strong feeling of how we like to do things.

Yes, but do you learn from them as well? Because I know one large and distinguished British practice which says just that: 'When young architects come to us, the first thing they must do is to learn how we work.' If your own practice is – as somebody has said – 'a place of innovation, imagination and invention', that suggests that you are far more ready to listen to what the young newcomers have to say and have to offer.

Yes, that is absolutely true. And it takes me back to this idea of designing around the table and in that situation there is a great deal of equality, I think. The engineers that we work with and the young project architects and so on, we all sit round the table together and I think it is open to anyone to speak and argue their case, and it does work. Sometimes it is quite interesting because a new young architect might come up with an idea that actually has been done in the past and we have to slap him down! And sometimes he will come up with something completely new and we will say, 'Really, really fantastic, let's pursue that for a bit and see how it goes!'

So the process of innovation and renovation takes place by having this young age structure to the practice?

Yes, and we also learn a lot from the people we work with: the other consultants, the other engineers, the services engineers doing the mechanical and electrical side of life. There is innovation going on in all those fields too.

But who holds it all together? Because, after all, the services have one set of imperatives, and there are all the health and safety imperatives, structural imperatives, the imperatives driven by materials and so on. At some stage somebody has to say, 'Look, this has got to be a building which is beautiful, which is elegant, which is structurally sound, and which works.' Is that one of your key roles: to bring these sometimes divergent disciplines together into a unified logical solution?

Well, I suppose the great thing about being an architect is that you have all these different roles you can play. I mean, you can play in the orchestra and you can stand up and conduct which is quite nice; and you can play many of the different instruments in the orchestra and you can also be the person who collects the fee for the orchestra and deals with the legal complaints if you fail to turn up! So you have to be all kinds of people; all things to all men, in a way. But in the end the architect is the person who has to stand up and speak for the concept and say, 'That won't work with the basic concept we are driving forward, you know.' And usually if you are informed, if you're listening to the others, to the structural guys and services guys and so on, they are subscribing to the idea by that time anyway. I mean, it is not often where they will say, 'This doesn't work, I am not going to be a party to it.' They have to be with you, otherwise you are nowhere.

So you are a sort of collective chairman as well as all the other things?

Well, sort of, yes. I remember, for instance, with the British Pavilion in Seville, which was very much driven by energy savings, where that was a kind of, if you like, mechanical, electrical services idea. Seville was the hottest city in Europe and we felt that rather than just throw air-conditioning at the thing for six months and then hope for the best, it would be fascinating to make the building a demonstration of how you could save energy, even using modern materials and modern construction and even temporary construction. And everybody subscribed to that. Everybody, you know, all the engineers, everyone who was involved, was driving that concept forward and it was really the driver for the whole building.

And that is a building that was also designed to be dismantled and packed away, and perhaps reconstructed somewhere else?

Well, the original idea was that the components could be used in the Third World. The pumps and the water tanks and so on could form little nuclei for the water supply for thirty villages in the Third World. That was part of the original concept. But it didn't happen.

In fact, it is now going to be reconstructed, isn't it?

Well, it is still lying in component form somewhere on the North Circular Road by the canal in London. The hope is that it will form the centre of a new complex, and it will be used for huge large-scale entertainments, and for Asian weddings attended by thousands of people.

I know that doesn't worry you because you are well known for saying that the point about buildings is that they are going to be used for many different purposes, and you design them so that they can be used for many different purposes. It strikes me that it shows a considerable lack of vanity about your building, that you are probably just as interested in what the second and third uses of a building are as what the first use is.

Absolutely. And I think if a building is worth having, it will go on and there are many, many examples from the past about buildings being used for other things. For instance, if Sainsbury's in Camden Town turned into an ice rink, I would be perfectly happy and, in fact, I think it would be rather thrilling, it wouldn't worry me at all. Because so much time went into the structural idea of creating a clear span which in some way was expressed on the street. And any kind of use which required a wide span would go in it very well.

I wonder whether you mind what has become of it now? I speak feelingly about this place because I often shop there, and in the early years it was clear Grimshaw inside – neat, cool, clear, logical. It has now become a sort of hideous multicoloured bazaar. Is your attitude to that, that's their business?

Well, it was always designed in a way as a kind of market hall. As far as I know, it is the only Sainsbury's that hasn't got a flat roof, it has a gentle arch to it which gives it more of a market hall feel. I think that one has to accept that shopping has its own mores. And in fact we were rather fascinated learning about it at the time: the way that the aisles had to be laid out and how more popular things need bigger space in front of them, and so on and so forth. There is an absolute iron logic to shopping, which probably has its variations and changes regularly over time, but basically I think very much you have to accept that.

But you also accept that you can't be a perpetual style and design

*policeman over what goes on inside your buildings, years after you have
had them signed off?*

Absolutely. I think you have to be strong enough to stand up to
almost anything people can throw at them, really.

*You've also said that the important thing about buildings is that they
have to be democratic, or your impulse towards them is a democratic
impulse. What do you mean by that?*

I like the idea that people can manipulate their surroundings
and they can have an effect on the place they're in. And I think it
is quite important. If you feel a building is so rigid that it is just
imposing itself on you and you can't change it, all you can do is
live your life as the building tells you to. I think there is something
very, very overbearing and difficult about that situation for me.

*But there is the image – and maybe it is cultivated by some architects
– 'I'm the architect; you the client have given me an idea of what you
want; I will now tell you what the solution is and you'd better follow it!'*

Well, that's not the way that I would see things and, since we've
turned to the issue of clients, I don't think you get a good building
unless the client is really with you on what you're doing. I think a
solution imposed is never really a happy one, and probably one
that won't last.

*I'm told though that there were some very senior people at the top of
Sainsbury's who didn't think your Camden Town shop was really at all
what they wanted from Sainsbury's stores!*

Well, I think the people we were working with were pretty well
behind the design. And of course, getting the planning permission
was a bit of a coup in the first place, because Camden had turned
down four or five previous solutions to building a supermarket on
that site and we got it through in breakneck speed first time
around. So there was a certain amount of satisfaction about that
whole side of things.

*I think the planners said to you that they wanted a 'good strong
modern building'. Planners are often decried for things that they do, but
the message was a very uncompromising one, wasn't it?*

Yes, I thought it was a wonderful message to get as an architect.
And the other thing, of course, is that the building has been pretty

damn successful. I think it has one of the highest turnovers in the country of any Sainsbury's, so it doesn't seem to put anyone off.

You've been quoted as saying that you hate 'contrived folksiness, monument making and forced regionalism'. If those are on your pet hate list, what other architectural hates do you have? Upturned matchboxes and concrete towers?

Well, I am strongly of the belief that one always ought to try to design in the age you live, with the materials of the age you live in. If you actually look at the average High Street, when planning authorities (which are often pretty retrogressive) say they want a building to fit in, what do they mean? The buildings normally span about five hundred years in the average High Street. So what do they expect you to fit in with? Up to the early part of this century, there were no controls on fitting in. People just simply did the best thing they could with the materials of their age – that's why I think the buildings have a certain kind of credibility and people accept them for being good buildings. I think that's what we ought to be trying to do. And to look back down a High Street and try and pick out a style which might appeal to a planning authority, it is frankly an appalling thing to do.

Yes, these parody styles. I think they were named in connection with the Camden Town planning application – Sainsbury's had previously tried LEB Georgian, Bypass Tudor, Surrey Farmhouse and Hi-Tech Pastiche. I suppose these are just those categories which we all know and recognise as being the blight on British architecture for fifty, a hundred years?

Probably since the war, the last fifty years anyway. After a brief period after the war, when there was a sort of monumental Corbusien type of architecture, there has been a gradual sinking back to this pastiche and copying, particularly in the area of housing, which is slightly depressing. I think that good modern architects haven't really turned their attention to housing, particularly individual housing, in this country at all – haven't been asked to, is probably a better way of putting it.

Yes, would you like it if Barratt's came to you and said, 'Will you design us a series of buildings with which we can build estates and from which also we can make money?'

Well, if they said, 'We want to give you – as long as they work properly as houses – a creative free hand,' I would be very interested. But I wouldn't be subject to what they consider to be normal kind of formal regulations!

But they would say, 'People want the pitched roof and all the other characteristics that you have on most housing estates; that is what people want. They don't want glass and metal and so forth.' Do you think that's right and if it is, why do we still want these rather cutesy traditional buildings?

I don't think people have really been offered the choice. And so, therefore, I don't think they know what possibilities there are. I think the real answer to that question would be to build a small pioneering group of houses and see what happened, and allow people to actually have a choice and see if they were excited and see if they sold.

Wouldn't it be said (and it must have been said to you), 'I can't afford to hire an architect, it's not just his fees, but they always produce expensive solutions.' This is one of the mythical milestones hanging around the architectural profession's neck, isn't it?

Well, to a degree, I suppose. But certainly it is not something that I believe in. In some ways we've built much of our reputation on doing good design and producing quite economic buildings. I think that often, having an absolutely fixed or tight budget is a very, very interesting discipline to work with, and sometimes calls forth some rather good solutions. There is nothing wrong with fixing a budget, particularly if that is controlled in some way by market conditions or what people have paid for the land or what offices will rent for. You have to respect these reality factors. And I don't think any architect is asking to be given an unreal situation. What a good modern architect likes to do is to be given the reality of the situation, but involved in the situation, of being able to design within that reality and with discussion with the client. So that you can talk about priorities and you can talk about alternatives that you can have underneath that overall ceiling.

How much of your time do you spend going in for competitions? Is that something that you don't have to do now – because it must be very time-consuming, very expensive and often pretty frustrating?

Well, competitions are a very interesting issue. We do quite a few a year and people find them particularly exciting to work on because there are areas where you can push the boat out to a degree. And funnily enough, the very big building that you mentioned earlier in Berlin, that was an international competition that we won. I think that was an interesting solution because basically we didn't think that we stood a chance of winning!

When you look at the architects who built the stations on the Jubilee Line extension – and it is pretty much a roll-call of the great and the good of contemporary British architecture – Nicholas Grimshaw Partners are not there. Did you not go in for it deliberately?

Well, we had an enormous amount of work on at that time and the conditions imposed by London Transport were some of the toughest I've ever seen in terms of programme, working often in a design-and-build situation, and also on fees. We thought we'd leave it alone and I think every single one of those architects who worked on it had a very, very tough time, actually.

On the other hand the Jubilee Line stations are great British architectural sites. I wonder whether you sometimes think 'I wish I were on that string of architectural pearls because I damn well ought to be'?

Well, we had some nice projects ourselves at that time. I was actually a judge on the Royal Fine Art Commission Awards and was very, very keen on the Jubilee Line Stations being given the award earlier on this year, and I am a great admirer of the whole chain of stations, as you say. And also of London Transport for doing it, because it in some ways throws down the gauntlet as to what the whole system should be like. I don't know whether anyone has worked out what it would cost to do the rest of the tube system like that, but I think we should. We always do things in bits and pieces in this country. And I think that the new chief of London Transport, that's the first thing that he should do. If it costs £500 billion over twenty-five years – well, it should be divided up year by year and it should be done.

In a recent book about your partnership, it is said that the practice is not complacent, you're still explorers, you're still reaching out. What sort of directions are you reaching out in?

Well, there are still buildings I'd love to do, like the concert hall I mentioned earlier or a theatre, for that matter. There are buildings in the arts which would be lovely to have a go at. So there are new building types and I think somehow we've got to a point where we are very trained at pouncing on a new subject and really enjoying it, and enjoying the dialogue that you have with a new client. And I think if you meet a new client who is enthusiastic about what they want to do and what they want to achieve, it is one of the most inspiring things. You get together and you toss ideas to and fro, and you spark off each other, and you can't achieve a good building without that sort of relationship. But there are plenty of people out there who are seeing the value that they can get out of a building. And a lot of our clients have used their buildings almost like trademarks or in some way as part of their identity.

Part of the brand, as we have to say nowadays!

I hate the word 'brand'. But a building that expresses their identity is very important to people and they can use it. But it won't emerge unless there has been a proper dialogue with them during the design.

Years ago, as a student, you wrote that 'technology could improve efficiency but it should transform the world morally'. Do you believe that it has achieved any moral transformation?

I don't remember ever saying that. I think that possibly, thinking in the Buckminster Fuller mode, where he was enormously influential in talking about the haves and have-nots, as he put it. And of course, technology can do an enormous amount for the Third World and the nations which are deprived and it is not used nearly enough for them. It is used far too much for the rich nations to get their cars to go faster or to do things that work perfectly well a little bit more slickly. And a huge amount of investment and technology goes into making our world even better than it really is. And I feel very strongly that a lot of that technological input should be diverted to improving the lot of the people who don't have so much.

Which goes back to your feelings about architecture as an instrument for democracy!

Well, I think so; and, I think, of economy too. And the diversion of funds to help the rest of the world is not actually anything like the sort of scale of problem that people think it is. And in fact, I think the right sort of interventions at the right sort of intellectual level could make an enormous difference to people's lives.

Are we frightened of technology?

I think there used to be an inherent criticism of technology in that it was seen as the exact opposite to creativity, in a way. And it was a sort of damper on creativity. I think now, with everybody's connection to the computer age and so on, almost the reverse has happened. In lots of ways people think that you can't be creative without understanding technology. I think that is a very, very important switch that has possibly happened over the last fifty years. It goes right across the arts, sculpture, film making and everything else. There is a strong feeling now that technology is there to be used to help you be creative.

Every day you walk to work (three miles, I think) and you say that you calculated that by doing so, this will save three hundred trees at least. Now that is clearly you as an individual doing it, but is that also you as an architect doing it?

Well, of course it keeps you healthy, but there is a kind of philosophical bent behind it all. What I am saying is that if I drove my car on that journey every day, there and back, the pollution it would cause would need three hundred trees to counteract it. So, in a way I suppose you could go out and plant three hundred trees and then drive your car. But I think it is a much more creative thing to do not to drive the car. In fact, in the same article I said maybe the car tax should be in some way gauged in terms of people planting trees, and that as a licence to drive your car, you should plant the necessary trees to counteract the pollution it was going to produce!

But again, that sort of thinking is part of your philosophy as an architect and the buildings that you put up. In other words, the building is not just in the environment, it is concerned with the environment?

Yes. And you mentioned the youth in the office, and that is something which is very much subscribed to by the young in the office. We have been accredited as the first architectural practice to have full-scale green credentials. And we have a very rigorous programme: every building we look at is assessed technically and rated on its green potential, right from the materials it uses. For instance, we got a bus route altered so it stopped outside the building. That kind of thing we take very, very seriously.

How far do you think you are recognisably the same architect as the one who set out at the Architectural Association and was chided by Maxwell Fry for possibly being too systematic and rigorous. Can you recognise yourself as the young man you then were?

I think very much so. It is difficult to put your finger on the core of what your practice is, but I do think I stuck to those principles. I think that rigour is something you have to apply to everything. Whether you're doing an abstract painting, a building or whatever, you've got to be able to justify the concept you're working with, so that it is not completely thrown on the table: 'Well, there you are; that's what I wanted to do at the time.' And I don't accept that as a way of proceeding. I don't think any really serious building, or work of art come to that, can escape having that kind of rigour behind it.

TONY HARRISON

'Darkness is a familiar friend but
I'm not afraid of it'

Tony Harrison writes for the theatre, the opera house, television, the cinema and, of course, the printed page. But first and foremost he's a poet, a person who decided years ago that he would earn his living the hard way by writing poetry. His uncompromising approach to his work comes from a belief that it's possible to use a contemporary style, alliteration and rhyme to handle the ordinary themes of everyday life and the great themes of classical tragedy in an accessible way. Driving these beliefs is Harrison's own background. His father was a baker. He is the archetypical Leeds working-class boy who was seized by the grammar school scholarship system and turned into a classically trained intellectual. Upward mobility? Yes. Meritocracy? If you want. Painful uprooting? Certainly, a theme that recurs in his work like a nagging tooth. And this tension, dichotomy, antithesis, haunts him and his work with highly productive results.

His years teaching in Nigeria and Czechoslovakia in the 1960s found their way into his first major collection of poems, *The Loiners*, a name for Leeds people. His first job at the National Theatre was to make a verse translation for John Dexter's production of Molière's *Le Misanthrope*. It was modernised, updated, savagely funny. Further adaptations followed, including the *Oresteia* of Aeschylus, and then the celebrated version of the *York Mysteries*, which he reclaimed into their native Yorkshire tongue and vowels. God creating the world with a Yorkshire accent? Whoever heard of such a thing?

Harrison is political and personal as a poet. Personal – sometimes daringly so, since much of his poetry is about the people who matter most to him; parents, wives, lovers, children. Political in his television films on subjects such as the Gulf War, Alzheimer's Disease, blasphemy, the fall of Communism. He's been called the Poet Laureate of the Left. As for the laureateship itself, he thinks it should not have continued to exist after Ted Hughes.

Tony Harrison sees all of this seemingly wide-ranging output as poetry. 'Poetry is all I write,' he said. 'whether for books or readings; or for the National Theatre or for the opera house and concert hall; or even for television. All these activities are part of the same quest for a public poetry. Though in that word "public", I would never want to exclude inwardness.'

What is your definition of public poetry?

I think that the move for me towards public poetry came from some of the dilemmas I had when, having left a working-class background and started learning Latin and Greek at grammar school, I wanted to write a poetry which did some kind of honour to what I was learning, but also would reach people like my parents, and use what I think of as a common language. And it seemed to me that the common language was used in the theatre. It has to be in the theatre, the common bond of the theatre, especially in Greek theatre where the audience and the actor were lit by the common light of the sun. These were the ideal conditions to create a common language. And out of that need, I was moved into theatre. And in theatre I was able to find a language which I hoped would address more than the kind of people I found read poetry and books.

But it's certainly not anything to do with filling an establishment position and writing special poems for special public national events?

Ah, no. I've written about public events. Certainly. I've written about the Gulf War for the *Guardian*. I went to Bosnia for the *Guardian* and wrote poems from the war there. I'm not against addressing difficult public issues or engaging in political controversy even, writing occasional poetry of invective and satire, which is another wing of poetry which one should occasionally resort to.

It must be quite a relief, I would have thought, to let the feelings out in that sort of way.

It is, it certainly is, and I've often done it. What I found when I grew up wanting to be a poet, seemed to me a poetry that restricted itself to a lyrical norm or an adventurous epic norm, as in the case of Pound, which had virtually lost the struggle with comprehensibility. I wanted something that would have all the range of the poetry of the past, when poets – from the Greeks through Shakespeare, through the Jacobeans, Molière, Racine, Brecht, Lorca – these were poets who wrote directly for the theatre. They engaged in the theatre.

Do you think it is increasingly difficult for the poet to be heard above the sheer noise and volume of communication of the technological world?

There's too much of a noise about for that quiet act of concentration you need both to write and to read the poetry on the page. But you can gather people together in a special place, whether it's the National Theatre or the Barbican or a theatre anywhere.

It's hardly mass communication, though, is it?

It's hardly mass communication, and I think I'm aware of that, that it's not mass communication. And I think that one of the things I've always tried to build into the way I either take on a former classic, or do a play, or write a poem or make a film of my own, is to realise that somewhere there's a privilege of participation involved. And there are people outside this privileged participation. If I'm not able to bring them into the theatre, I can make those who are participating in the privilege aware that the theatre has glass walls so they see those who are not participating.

Have you got a website of your own; for your own poetry?

No. I don't.

Have you considered that, and shouldn't you? Isn't that a way of getting through to a mass audience?

It is, but I think I've tried rather to shift my energy towards the public into readings, which I find better; much more personal. It's the best way of finding your audiences. And I've read everywhere. Everywhere in the British Isles and almost everywhere in the world.

Let's go back to the beginning. You got on well with your parents, from everything that you have written about them.

Very well. Until I started publishing poetry!

You also had two uncles; one who stammered and one who was dumb.

One was deaf and dumb, and one had the most terrible stammer I think I ever encountered.

What effect do you think that had on your wish to be as articulate as you could be?

These things only become clear in retrospect. I was aware of a hunger for articulation. And I think, in retrospect, it came not only from the fact that I had an uncle who was deaf and dumb, and one who stammered, but a father who was reticent, shy, unable to express himself. And the idea of articulation, expression, became for me absolutely vital to existence. I wrote a poem called 'Heredity', because everybody used to ask me, and my mother even used to say to me, 'Well, I don't know where it comes from, our Tony. There's been no artist in our family.' And hearing someone when I first did *The Misanthrope* at the National Theatre, at the interval, I sensed it was going really well. I heard a woman say, 'He has such a command over language, but they say he comes from Sheffield!' It's actually Leeds, but you get the idea. So I wrote this poem about heredity, which goes to answer both my mother and people like this condescending woman. And it goes, 'How you became a poet's a mystery. / Wherever did you get your talent from? / I say, I had two uncles, Joe and Harry. / One was a stammerer, the other dumb.' So, as much as the books I devoured and the languages I learned, they were important presences.

And then you became the grammar school boy on the scholarship, and education and learning, and that really created a terrible tormented gap between you and your father. He assumed, rightly in some ways, that you were completely different? You weren't going to be 'our Tony' as they knew you?

What happens is that there's an inability to share what you're learning, which was for me hugely frustrating. And I think that my work gets a certain energy from retrospectively trying to inter- pret, like the ancient theatre, to people like my parents. It's still going on, and the last film I did, *Prometheus*, is taking an ancient dramatic theme and dropping it into the Yorkshire of my child- hood, and seeing how the two get on. But it did create a division. I was hungering for all forms of articulation. I was lapping up Latin and Greek and French, and also beginning to write poetry.

I wonder whether the tension between you and your family over education is a very English thing? I mean English, and I'll tell you why. I heard an interview with John Hume, the great Northern Ireland politician. And he, like you, came from a very ordinary background, and he got scholarships, and the interviewer said to him, 'Wasn't all that a problem with your parents?' John Hume didn't understand the question. He said, 'They wanted me to get on. That's the only way that a working-class boy could get on.' And that seems to me to be instinctive to the Irish, and the Welsh, and the Scots probably. Do you think it is a particularly English thing?

I think it is English. I think that they did want me to get on, but they wanted me to get on so far. My mother, particularly, was more ambitious for me than my father. She would make the effort to bridge whatever the gap was and try to understand what I was grappling with at school. But I think they didn't want me to go that far. They wanted me to be a teacher in the local school, something of that kind.

Something that people would recognise?

They could recognise as getting on better than they had, but still in the same area.

But then it's not as if at school everybody said, 'Tony, come on in. You're now part of us, a different intellectual world.' You've many times told the story about the teacher who rejected your accent.

Well, it's again a source of the sort of retrospective aggro I built into the reclamation of the *Mysteries*. The reason is that an English teacher I had at Leeds grammar school, as soon as I opened my mouth to read a poem, would always stop me because I had a thick urban Leeds accent. And I had none of the knowledge then to know that Keats was a cockney, that Wordsworth was often considered incomprehensible when he came to London because he had a Cumbrian accent. I hadn't got that information. I didn't know then that the idea of received pronunciation was simply based on the speech of the southern public schools, that culture had been dubbed into that voice. Even things like the *Mystery Plays*. I saw them in the fifties in York; and they're written in an earlier medieval form of the accent I ended up speaking. And God was terribly posh, and Jesus was terribly posh, and only the comic parts were allowed to be Yorkshire. And even then I was irritated by that. So that when I worked at the National Theatre, I thought,

'Now is my chance to reclaim Northern classics for the voice they were written in.'

So, just to round off on this: the teacher particularly hated the way you said 'uz.'

That's right, 'uz, uz, uz'. Yeah. It's in a poem of mine called 'Them And Uz'. 'It's not "uz, uz", it's "us, us".' And of course 'uz' is the pronoun of solidarity, of family feeling, of inclusivity.

But this has been useful for you, hasn't it. It's been like the grit in the oyster, hasn't it? You don't worry away at it in a sort of neurotic way – or does it really hurt when you think of the times when he used to say, 'you mustn't speak like that'.

No, I've got over all that. But I think it gave me a kind of creative background, which is in the poem. I think part of the poem says, 'Right, you buggers, then, we'll occupy this lousy old poetry'. And it gave me the energy to say 'I'm going to do poetry as well as I can, so well that you're going to have to look at it. But it's going to be in my own voice, and you're never going to be able to dub it into this pseudo-cultural voice that everybody thought poetry should be read in, and that everybody felt Shakespeare should be played in, and it still lingers in English theatre.'

And did you feel when your first book of poems was printed, The Loiners, *that that was expressing both your experience, and your background and the tone of voice that you've just described?*

I think from this distance it looks a little bit like showing off to me! A lot of it is showing off, showing that I could manage the forms with my hands tied behind my back. And also I not only took on classical forms, I also wrote about politics and sex. Certainly sex was never discussed at home, and it's one of those subjects over which there was an enormous pall of silence.

Your mother thought that the book was rather mucky?

Yes, it was mucky. I have a line in a poem which quotes her, 'You weren't brought up to write such mucky books,' she says. And I wasn't brought up to write mucky books, but I went on to write them. Interestingly, in that poem, that line, if you scan it properly and not like academics tend to scan poetry, is iambic pentameter. And you find iambic pentameter on the lips of people the whole time. And I love listening on trains to people speaking unconsciously in a metre that's natural to English speech.

But you just accepted with regret and with sorrow that you'd upset your parents, but there was no way that this could affect what you were going to write?

No. It didn't. It wasn't like D. H. Lawrence giving his first book to his mother and being proud of her having it in her hands and so on. I didn't actually give my parents a copy of *The Loiners* because I knew they would be offended by it. But someone, a cousin, found it in the library and said, 'Look what I've found in the library!'

But that led to your commission to translate, or to render, Molière's Misanthrope.

Yes, I think the apprenticeship and discipline of learning classical metres, rhyming couplets and quatrains and so on, that I put myself through attracted the attention of John Dexter when he was looking for a poet to translate Molière.

Is translation quite the word? It's a completely new version, apart from the fact that it's updated. Not only is it updated, but you render it completely afresh.

You look for another context in order to look more clearly at the original and make its tensions clearer. In this case I spent many months simply getting the right tension between absolutely acceptable colloquial language in a very strict classical metrical form. And that I did, and I was very careful to keep all my imagery within the boundaries of 1666 when the play was first written. But when I gave my first draft to John Dexter and Laurence Olivier, they were both first of all impressed by the colloquial energies. It sounded very modern. And John Dexter said, 'I think we should do it in modern dress. I'll ask Christian Dior to design it.' And I said, 'Wait a minute. If you do that, you are going to maroon these images.' English needs to concretise more than French. I concretised the images, but they were still historical. I said, 'I have to rethink the language.' So I took it away and because the occasion of the production was the tercentenary of the death of Molière, I suddenly had the idea of taking a three-hundred-year circle and putting it in 1966.

So you did two versions of it?

Oh, there were more. I do millions of versions of everything I do. The notebooks are enormously fat. And one of the mediations was that in *Le Canard Enchaîné*, the satirical newspaper of France, they always used to depict de Gaulle as 'Le Roi' after Louis XIV. And they talked about the court and so on. So I thought, 'Ah, that's a way of looking at the piece', and also the imminence of the events of 1968 was a way of measuring the political engagement and sincerity of Alceste. So the whole thing then took life from that.

It does have fantastic energy. I know you don't like reading lines that you've written for other people.

I like to read my poetry in my own voice, and I rarely like actors reading my own poetry, but it's a liberation to write for other voices. That's one of the reasons that takes me into theatre, because I don't have to be obsessed with my own preoccupations.

You mentioned all the notebooks. Let's talk about how you work. Are you a regular disciplined worker when you write?

Hugely disciplined. My whole existence is hugely disciplined in that way. All my life I always spend a lot of time every day working. I don't always write anything, but I'm working around finding the occasion when the writing becomes possible. Sometimes I have very lean periods. I have periods of darkness, of depression almost, when I can't create. But I can prepare for when it lifts and the creative mood comes back. I begin things constantly in notebooks, and then I often have periods, sometimes lasting months, which are kind of manic finishing periods. And sometimes these are dictated by the fact I've got a deadline.

Do you think the deadline actually produces the necessary creative energy?

It helps, yes, it's good. I like the discipline of a deadline. I think Paul Valéry, the French poet, said that a poem was ready when an editor asked for it. Meaning that if nobody asked for it you'd go on and on tinkering and tinkering.

Is it true?

It's true. For me it's true. It's very good for me to spend time alone writing and then go into the life of the theatre and write often quickly. And this has changed since I worked with other directors. And now that I direct my own pieces, when you get in a rehearsal situation and a scene doesn't work, and it's not the actors and the director can't see a way round, then I say, 'Hm, well, maybe I should rewrite this . . . and I think, if he says this . . .' and I go away. I don't mind to throw away anything. I think that you haven't to mind!

You can't be precious about it?

You can't have a holy text in theatre until it's there. Until it's there. And getting there, it goes through rehearsal. I have to withdraw, go to my special room that I used to have and write, type it out, bring it back, copy it, bring it back on paper. But if I'm directing myself, I just learned to say, 'Oh, say, ladidadidaladidala . . .' And somebody else writes it down. And this is wonderfully liberating for people who are, you know, inward and grudging with their creativity.

But when you're writing free-standing poems, how does the idea for that come to you? Do you sit down and say, 'It's time I wrote some poems'? Presumably the idea for a poem must force itself to your attention, mustn't it?

It does. It's sometimes in a phrase or an image. I always have a notebook with me and I still work in notebooks rather than on a computer, although I use that to update text when I work in the theatre. I still work with pen, and then I type, then I correct on the typescript and I stick it in, and I stick in another one on top of it, and . . . and so on. It's a very layered thing, which comes out of often months of putting down phrases which I'm sure will lead somewhere, but I'm not sure where. And actually to find out what the context of that phrase is, is finding the poem.

The phrase will find a home somewhere?

It will find a home somewhere. But I don't know often with my notebooks nowadays whether it is going to be a poem, a short poem, a series of poems, a play, or a film. They all begin in the same way, in the same notebooks. And there are pictures, and there are little drawings, and there are collages, and there are visual stimuli as well.

So they are image-driven and word-driven, and also feeling-driven?

Oh, sure, sure. Absolutely feeling-driven.

Dreams?

I never dream. I never dream.

Come on, everybody dreams!

I don't dream. I dream all day, I think that's why. I've just come back from America; I dream when I change countries. That's about all. Because I haven't been sitting daydreaming, if that's what you can call poetry. I don't dream.

Do you play word games with yourself just, as it were, for the exercise, because you like words?

One of my favourite poets is the Latin poet Lucretius, who wrote this great scientific poem 'De Rerum Natura', which is about the teachings of Epicurus and the early atomic theory. But there's a wonderful passage in there where he talks about 'elementa', meaning these atoms. And he says, 'It is like the same sounds appear in my verses, but they're always reassembled into new forms.' And this gives you a wonderful insight. I don't know if all poets do it, I'm sure they probably do: you're continually monitoring or radaring for the combinations of words, not simply for what they mean but the way they feel in the mouth, the way they attract each other in alliteration or they attract each other in rhyme, which have no real sense to them but are part of the power and energy of poetry.

Do you always check what they sound like? Given how powerfully your poems lift off the page, it's as if you need to check when you've written it, 'How does that sound?'

Well, if I'm writing for the theatre, the only criterion is how does it sound when it's performed. I think it's different with the poem on the page, although I do monitor everything for sound. And I read my poems aloud, and poems that you know you're going to read aloud may have a different form than those that you want people to take away with a private light and read in bed. They're slightly different. But this constant monitoring of words for their sense and sound; my mind's like that all the time, not only thinking what I'm saying, but what are the relationships of tastes of the sounds, the assonances, the consonantal repetitions, the voice and voiceless counterparts that Welsh poets made a great deal of.

Let's talk about how this applies to the classics. You learned Greek and Latin at school. You have made some significant translations, reworkings of the Oresteia *in particular. But the deeper question is about the Greek myths and why they still remain relevant to us. Because the standard thing that people say is, 'Why bother to teach the classics; what do they mean to the young?' But to you, they are burningly relevant and real still?*

They are. I think my interest chiefly is not so much the myths as the invention of drama, especially tragedy. I'm not a religious person and I think in some ways the monotheistic religions were a kind of disaster after things like the culture of Greece with its essential role for drama and for tragedy. It seems to me that it was one of the human resources that was an incredible invention for grappling with, coming to terms, sometimes even celebrating, the darker parts of experience. And it seems to me that the darker parts of experience are the ones we need most help with. We can all cope with our joys, I think, alone, or in the company in which we have the joy. There's not much really good poetry which is joyful or happy. So for me, art is the deepest thing we have to grapple with the realities of existence and one of the best arts that did that was Greek tragedy. And it seemed to me that we needed that kind of art which was open-eyed about savagery and darkness and blood, and yet refused, as Nietzsche said, 'to be turned to stone by the experience'. And tragedy has that pre-eminently, it seems to me. And we needed exactly those resources for the experiences of the twentieth century.

But in that case, why do schools say that classics are irrelevant to the young? Is it another case of the difficult being badly taught?

I think so. I think there are people who do classics in translation, which can be also a very interesting course, but fewer people doing Greek, as I did.

Recently, when Deborah Warner directed Medea *in the West End with Fiona Shaw, the cast talked about what it was that was producing the intense response from the audience. And they all got the very strong feeling that what was churning the audience up was that it was about something that they may well have experienced – the break-up of a relationship.*

The interesting thing for me is that the resources are not those of naturalistic drama. It seems the cliché of today that film and theatre are naturalistic. I think that if we want to force ourselves to look at, not only the horrors of the last century, which in some ways cancel out what seem to be the acclaimed achievements of culture, then we need other resources than naturalism, because the end of naturalism is to scream. It's an inarticulate cry, or it's a covering of the eyes. For me Greek drama is emblemised by the mask, which is created with open eyes and an open mouth, that it must see everything and it must sing about it. It must speak about it. And I can think of one Greek play where the messenger's speech is often the great speech. We can do any kind of mutilation and violent death very graphically. The Greeks didn't do that. They reported it. And the messenger comes on stage and says, 'I have seen something I can't speak about.' And then for three hundred lines he speaks about it. It's been filtered through the reporting human heart and the reporting voice, which I think is an essential one.

In our films, our cinema, our television, we behave as if you have to show the ultimate in the real, the so-called real.

But then we don't attend to it, you know. Our instinct is to turn away. You turn away your face. You can't look at it. The great thing about the Greek tragedy is that it is always witnessed and then spoken about, and somewhere you get the ear to go into the close-up that the eye somehow refuses. So I go back not just out of antiquarian interest – I'm not interested in antiquarian repro-duction – but to go and find stylistic resources for our own times.

You've also done a lot of work on television. The particular piece that I want to talk about is the television film about your poem, 'V', which for those who haven't read it is a poem about the fact that your parents' grave was desecrated by vandals and four-letter words were spread all over it. And you're then shown reading this poem with many four-letter words in it. That was a television programme and much outcry it caused. What is amazing is the outcry that there was at the time.

Well, like all these things, it was all stirred up by the *Daily Mail*. They phoned around people who've never read the poem and don't know me from Adam, and they shoot off their mouth, and they're happy to be quoted, condemning something they know nothing about. That's how it started.

But for you, was there a dual sense of pain? Pain at the desecration of your parents' grave, but also a sense of pain at the thought of the deprivations of life that led to the football hooligans to do what they did?

Well, there are all kinds of things behind the poem. One is, you would go to any city area like the one I grew up in, and look at the graveyard, and once it was a fairly settled community with people who were butchers, and then their son was a butcher, and so on and so on. You can see this in the graves; the graves are quite high, and they leave space for other people to come on. My own family grave is like that. And of course everybody goes away. People leave, because economically they go somewhere else to find work, and so on. So the families, who belong to the dead that were there, have moved away. I've moved away. I go to the grave, as I say in the poem, for an odd ten minutes when I'm changing trains or something. That's a social difference and the people who live round there don't have the settled continuity of jobs as they're represented on the graves. It's a shortcut to Leeds United, and as they go through they spray 'United', which has all kinds of other associations. It's also an expression you find chiselled on graves when a wife joins her husband, or children join their mother and father in death.

Don't the graffiti writers know that?

No. They don't, and they weren't aware of that. But I'm the sort of person who notices those sorts of things, so that appears in the poem. And it was also at the time of the miners' strike and the closing of pits, and one of the reasons was that some of them were being worked out. Well, underneath this particular grave was also a hollowed-out pit, which made the graves lean a little. So all that's part of the theme. And I then encounter the sort of person I probably would have ended up being had I not had the opportunities I had from the 1944 Education Act, going to Leeds Grammar School and so on.

Because you couldn't express yourself in any other way?

Because I couldn't express myself. And so the poem is a debate between me and the skinhead who graffitis the grave.

You obviously have a very strong and a very useful journeyman streak to you. Words are there to be crafted.

Oh, absolutely. I always remember, when I was very young on a train in Ireland going to Galway, an old woman said, 'What do you do? What are you? What do you do?' I said, 'I'm a poet.' She said, 'Well, that's a grand trade to be in.' I've always loved that expression. You've got to learn, you know, the mechanics of the theatre, the film, and sound, filming, all the techniques. I like all that, as I did like to learn, originally, all the technicalities of poetry itself.

Somebody wrote of the tension in you between 'the allegiance to the diction of poetry and to the four-letter rage and dark sarcasm of the scorned and excluded'.

Both of those are in there. A lot of people, those who looked at the poem, were irritated that all these tensions and this debate, which uses the language of the street, is in the rhymed quatrains of Gray's 'Elegy in a Country Churchyard', deliberately. This is a rage in an urban churchyard, but I'm using the metre of Gray's 'Elegy'; and some people like certain things uncorrupted, unpolluted, kept sacrosanct. I think they found it hard to cope with. If it had been a rambling sort of poem, a free verse, I don't think they would have been quite so offended.

The Times said that you're the first genuine working-class poet of the century. Does that mean anything to you?

Not much. I don't quite understand it, to be honest. I think what it might mean also is that there is a kind of English journey through what I call in a play the 'Ladder of Aspiration', meaning learning to pronounce your 'H's as much as anything else. That you go up this ladder and then you kick it away. Whereas I still even now keep returning the immense acquisitions I've had culturally in literature and so on back to the background, and keep measuring the one against the other. And this is more than simply measuring the resources of one class against another. It's to do with trying to find what the value of the work I'm engaged in is about.

It's clear, of course, where your loyalties lie. There are a couple of lines, 'The dumb go down in history and disappear / and not one gentleman's being brought to book; / the tongueless man gets his land took.'

There are historians now, like E. P. Thompson, who are correcting these biases. But if you look in the written records of the history of any culture, you find mostly the writing of the privileged. You find the words – I've used it in another poem – of working-class people and unprivileged people only when they're written down before they're going to be hung or before their execution. So that if you're looking for vocal bearings, you don't find any. If you feel that these are the waves and the currents on which you are carried, and these are also represented by those uncles and father I had who were unable to express themselves, if these are the currents that carry you, it's very hard to find where they come from, because they're not recorded.

In that poem, 'V', 'Versus', in the football sense, there are so many things that reflect the tensions in yourself – left versus right, nature versus nurture, school versus home, north versus south. Are they things that you can wholly reconcile, or is there also an element of confrontation in your working out of these 'versuses' in your life?

I think the 'versuses' are very important to creating the verse! This rather awful pun in that title, I think I need that dialectic to create. It's part of my way of looking at things.

The tension at the heart of your poetry, you've said, lies 'between the pessimistic intellect and the celebratory heart'.

Yes. I would say that in many ways I have a pessimistic view of human history, but from day to day I have a sensual sense of the celebratory richness of existence. And sometimes it's very hard to bring the one to the other, although sometimes you find that darkness is the best burnisher of light in so many ways.

But you've always found that the celebratory aspect has triumphed over the pessimistic intellect, even when the pessimism has driven you close to depression?

It's an ongoing struggle. It has to be fought all the time. I think it was worse when I was younger because I understood it less. Now, darkness is a familiar friend; I'm not afraid of it. I say, 'Oh, come in. Sit down,' you know. 'Come and join me in my study.' I'm not trying to drive it away.

But you don't know that it will go away, do you?

No. You never know it will go away, and probably it doesn't, but you have to let it in. I'm afraid it's a co-producer of my creative work.

Let's hear your thoughts on Keats and the kumquat, which I think expresses what we're talking about ?

The kumquat fruit, you know, is a small, cherry-sized citrus. And I wanted to discuss it with John Keats, who is our most orally sensual poet in English. Because there's a line I thought that was going to come about, 'Life is a skin of death that keeps its zest', which I might have on my grave. My poem to Keats!

> For however many kumquats that I eat,
> I'm not sure if it's flesh or rind that's sweet.
> And being a man of doubt at life's midway,
> I'd offer Keats some kumquats and I'd say,
> 'You'll find that one part's sweet and one part's tart.
> Say where the sweetness or the sourness start.
> I find I can't.' As if one couldn't say
> Exactly where the night begins the day.
> Which makes for me, the kumquat taken whole,
> Best fruit in metaphor to fit the soul
> Of one in Florida at forty-two.

Is one of the things that you're representing, a concern for a culture which has a memory of its past; facing a contemporary culture which tends only to be aware of the present?

I think in some ways I've always thought that poetry is a kind of an art near to extinction. I've written, in a series of poems called *Art in Extinction*, that probably animals which are near to extinction show the beauty of the natural existence almost more than at any other time. So that I have that belief in it. But in order to give myself help from day to day in feeling like this and giving most of my life's energy to poetry, I need also to connect to the past where poets were more ambitious and more central to cultural and social life. I think there's something about it which carries some of the truest meanings of our culture, even though it can be neglected. And I feel it's also my role: by trying to keep alive the energy of poetry, you are also allowing the stream of past poetry to keep entering into the culture.

I'll risk summing you up, because I must have a chance to read a few of your words, with your attack on the poet laureateship:

> *I'd rather be a free man with no buts,*
> *Free not to have to puff some prince's wedding,*
> *Free to say 'Up yours' to Tony Blair,*
> *To write an ode on Charles I's beheading*
> *And regret the restoration of his heir,*
> *Free to scatter scorn on Number 10,*
> *Free to blast and bollock Blairite Britain.*

Is that the true you?

It's a great deal of the true me, sure. Certainly in regard to a ridiculous institution like the laureateship, and the monarchy, I might say, I've always been a great republican. I enjoyed writing it a great deal. I think it came off the pen quite fluently.

HOWARD HODGKIN

'The memory comes back in another form'

Howard Hodgkin has described his paintings in apparently very direct terms. 'My subject matter,' he has written, 'is simple and straightforward. It ranges from views through windows, landscapes, occasional still lifes, to memories of holidays, encounters with interiors and art collections, other people, other bodies, love affairs, sexual encounters and emotional situations of all kinds, even including eating.' Well, the simplicity of that statement is only an apparent one.

Using strong colours in bold sweeps, dots, curves, hooks, his pictures have very direct titles, things like *Girl By a Window*, *Mrs Acton in Delhi*, *Coming Up From the Beach*, and many more like that. Memory, the recapture of memory, is his subject, and he paints it with energy and passion and single-mindedness.

Howard Hodgkin was born in 1932, represented Britain at the 1984 Venice Biennale, was knighted in 1992 and has had major retrospective exhibitions in London, New York and around the world. By his own definition, he paints representational pictures of emotional situations.

Here you are, I hope, committing some of these thoughts and ideas to words. In fact, you've been very generous in talking about your work with many people. Do you find that useful? Do you find it easy?

I don't find it easy, as you will probably discover. I think that words are often extraneous to what I do, but I work in a country where words seem to be paramount as a form of communication and I think that if I didn't talk about my work at all, people might not even bother to look at it.

Really?

I think it's as serious as that. In other countries, in New York, for example, when I had a very large exhibition at the Metropolitan Museum, there was no need for verbal communication, as far as I could make out. People would come and talk to me about my pictures, but they understood exactly what they were all about. They would tell me about the feelings that they evoked in them.

Would you get the equivalent response, for example, at the great Hayward Gallery retrospective? Would the British audience come up to you and say, 'Mr Hodgkin, what I see in that painting is this'?

Yes, by that time they did, but I felt that it was because of all the things that had been said previously. I may be completely wrong about this.

Would you be much happier in having what you put on wood – not canvas – speak for itself? Would you want us to take a risk in saying, 'What I feel from this picture is such and such'?

Yes. In fact, you're quite right to pull me up about the Hayward exhibition because I asked that the labels should be put as far away from the pictures as possible, so they were put on the edge of the floor. And several people said to me they always knew exactly what the picture was about and then they'd look at the title to check. Nevertheless, I think that words in this country are paramount, where the visual arts are concerned.

Is that why conceptual art is so popular?

I think it might well be. And most successful and most visible artists at the moment – and this is of course a crude generalisation – are artists whose work, in many cases, depends considerably on words.

Would you rather we described our feelings as we look at your paintings: if I come and say that what I see in this picture is such and such, would you say, 'No, you've totally missed the point'? Or would you say, 'My emotion when I painted it was something different, but if that's what you see in it, that's all right by me'?

I would feel that was perfectly all right, because the feeling in any work of art, if the work of art succeeds, gets through and the label on it is perhaps not terribly important.

Sticking with words for a moment more. You have kept diaries at certain times of your life. Do you keep a diary the whole time?

No, I don't. I hope one day I will write something about my life – simply because the older I get, I'm appalled at the inaccuracy in biographies of friends and people I know, or knew.

But I think you've said that you find keeping the dates of your own life as something that doesn't greatly bother you and that you find rather difficult. Critics say such and such a thing happened in such and such a year and you say, 'Well, if that's what you tell me, that's all right but I don't terribly remember myself.'

No, I don't terribly remember. But I do remember events: I don't remember chronology.

Would you remember, say, a love affair or even a dinner party over thirty or forty years, one that had been strong enough to make you paint about it?

Yes, I would. And almost the only skill I have, a measurable skill I would say, is a strong visual memory, and I can remember what things looked like from very long ago.

How many of your pictures can you recall?

The pictures themselves yes, certainly I can recall most of them. And I think the source material for nearly all of them as well.

So if you wrote, that would be the basis from which you would write. That is your own personal mental card index, your reference library?

Indeed. I could look at the list of my paintings and that, I suppose, would be a kind of chronology.

I'm going to try to draw you a bit on the business of painting and how you go about it. Tell me a little bit about your routine. Are you a regular worker in the studio?

Yes, I am a very regular worker in the studio. But I often sit in my studio, apparently doing nothing at all. Because sitting with what I'm working on – and particularly with age, I find that is one of the few things that's really changed – by sitting looking at a painting for a very long time rather than keeping it away from me and then returning to it, I can work on it more quickly.

How many paintings do you work on at the same time?

It varies. It varies considerably. At the moment in my studio I should think I've got about twelve unfinished paintings. But sometimes I've had as many as twice that number.

When you go into the studio in the morning, do you have some idea which is the one that is going to call out to you, and say, 'I know how to move on to the next stage with this one'?

It is more disciplined than that. I've decided as I walk to my studio – or no – I probably decided beforehand, which picture I'm going to look at and which picture I'll work on.

Is it physically hard?

Yes, well, it varies again. It's physically very difficult with very large pictures because the necessity of making the kinds of marks I do and the necessary technique for making them, requires considerable stamina.

You say marks, not brush strokes?

I say 'marks' deliberately. Because a brush stroke suggests something that is sort of free fall, and of course it's not. It's made with a lot of deliberation, which I cannot describe. They're made to look like a very free gesture, but it very rarely is.

And of course you work layer upon layer until you have got the necessary results. The process of painting is to add layers until you have the right surface, texture or whatever?

That's absolutely right. I work and work and work until the picture's finished, but I always work on top of what went before. When I began, I used to occasionally wipe it all off, but I don't do that any more.

Is it an important part of what the finished painting is, the fact that there's a lot underneath the surface?

No, not particularly. I mean, some of my pictures are very thinly painted, some are very thickly painted. I don't think it affects the physical object very much. But for me, emotionally or even intellectually, one thing leads to another, so that – as I did once or twice, many years ago – if I try obliterating it by removing it, one thing doesn't lead to another. You have to start totally afresh.

You said, some years ago, that you began with a quasi-realistic sketch – whether on wood or on paper – and then started to paint. Do you still do that or have you moved way beyond it?

I've moved far beyond that. Though where I moved beyond that is still related to it, in that I always begin with a very firm – or rather, very exact – visual memory. But I wouldn't now feel it necessary to put it all down. I might put down just a part of it.

Visual memory, emotional memory or both at the same time?

Both at the same time. But of course, it has to be visual, somehow.

And I know in a correspondence that you had with an art critic, he raised the question as to whether what you are doing is the deliberate veiling of the objects and the emotion. That is to say that you start with something fairly explicit in your own mind and then you make it – not more obscure – but 'veiling' was the word that he used. Whether, as you paint, you reveal the full nature of the memory, even to yourself.

I think the second. I think I reveal it to myself – well, I'm quite certain about that. The picture is finished when, as I have said – and it sounds very glib but I can't think of any other way of putting it – when the memory comes back in another form. So it's becoming more and more intense as the picture gets finished.

But when you come into the studio in the morning and you're going to work on a particular painting and it looks at you and you look at it and you think, 'That's right', is that the only way in which you can judge when the process of painting is finished?

It isn't quite as random as that sounds. It's when a great many things are being taken into account and settled. So, the moment a picture is finished is very precise and usually anticipated. I wish it was as you describe. Life would be simpler and better if it was.

Let me quote from one of the painters you most admire, Matisse, quoting Chardin, who said, 'I apply colour until there is a resemblance.' Does that strike a chord?

Absolutely.

Let us move on to a very different part of your life, the art scene in which you live. How strong is the British art scene today?

I think it's very strong indeed, but the reasons for that are quite complex. When I began as an artist, there was hardly any art world, as we know it now. There were very few dealers and for living artists, it was very difficult to – I choose the word deliberately – get a hearing. Now, of course, that's completely changed. But it hasn't changed abruptly. It's changed gradually over the last twenty years. But at the moment, I would think that to be a young artist in this country, there has never been a more hopeful moment.

Does that mean that the potential for achievement in the art scene has never been richer than today?

The opportunities, as I was trying to say, have never been greater. Whether everything will work out remains to be seen. The first great movement – and it was at the time a great movement that I, as ever, was not actually involved in – was Pop Art. I have always been an outsider. I appeared once in a book on Pop Art. In the index it just said, 'He was not one.' It came and it went, very quickly. All art movements, I should say, quickly throw up a lot of people, a lot of artists at once who seem to be working in harmony, and then out of them come the one or two that remain, who go their own way and are not sort of washed up on the shore. But they begin as being part of a group. And Pop Art was of course a very powerful group and there were some remarkable artists among them. But it faded very quickly and I remember wondering whether in any other country it would have faded quite so fast. And the reason I'm suggesting it's never been better here than now (though I personally – and it's probably through old age and perhaps seeing a different kind of art – I can't see a coherent movement) but it's obviously never been a better time in terms of public response and public support.

Yes. Because the days when people said, 'I don't know what all this modern art stuff is about', when you look at the attendances for contemporary art of all kinds – the more avant-garde, the more unexpected the better – this is a quite extraordinary reversal?

It's a complete change and the reason that it's such an extra-ordinary moment now is mainly because museums and public institutions take a much more active role than they ever did before. The pattern – this is very crudely put – but the pattern used to be that artists' work was promoted in all sorts of different ways, in as far as it could be, by dealers. This has changed to such an extent that it's often promoted by museums and this is, of course, very much a worldwide phenomenon. But in England, it's been perhaps more powerfully the case because there weren't many great promoting dealers. But now, we have three or four dealers of international class. This is quite new in London. We have Charles Saatchi, whose role in the English art world could never be overrated, who is immensely important. And then we have Nick Serota, whose passion for contemporary art is like that of the founder of a new religion. I mean, it is so total, dedicated, selfless and successful.

And audiences follow. We're ready to look afresh at things that we wouldn't have looked at a couple of years ago?

Well I think it's because when there is great passion about anything, it does draw an audience, it does pull an audience, and

Charles Saatchi started it with his extraordinary personal museum and people went to it. But one shouldn't forget the artists themselves, who have made their own careers in a way that never existed before, when there was a sort of passivity among artists who sort of waited to be chosen, waited to be promoted, waited for people to come and sell their work. Now, all those things are done by the artists themselves, far more successfully perhaps than any dealer could.

But presumably that starts with the art schools and the quality of art education, opening up young artists to the possibility of expressing themselves in a whole range of ways, which changes and develops every five years?

Well, I wouldn't agree entirely with the changing every five years. I think now, as always, with any situation of this sort, it begins to sort of academicise, if I can invent a horrible word. Arteries harden very, very quickly. But the other name I should have mentioned is Michael Craig-Martin, whose work at Goldsmiths' was extraordinary, in that it broke the mould of teaching in English art schools, which was almost non-existent. But it was particularly almost non-existent because nobody was taught anything about being a professional artist.

What were you supposed to do? Were you just expressing yourself on canvas or on paper . . . ?

Yes, exactly. Or not even doing that, just looking in a lackadaisical way at a model and then sort of doing a little copy of what you thought you saw.

But when you say 'the business of being an artist', do you mean that they weren't taught about what the rough world of making your living as an artist is?

Or being in the rough world. In the days when I was a teacher – which is a very long time ago – I remember trying desperately to tell my students that working alone in a room by yourself with the world outside was quite different – in fact, totally different – from working in the entirely protected confines of an art school, or of any academic institution. And they just didn't want to know, naturally enough. But Michael Craig-Martin did manage – and some other people as well, of course; these things always seem to happen by some curious osmosis. It's not just that he particularly was a teacher of stars. He simply had an attitude, which was totally different.

You mentioned the loneliness of painting, of any creative work. What are your own props against this necessary loneliness? What support mechanisms do you have to break out of that essential loneliness?

Very few, I'm afraid. And the older I get and the longer I work, I sometimes think I'm dragging behind me an enormous weight, a sort of bag full of all the loneliness I'd felt in the past. It can become very oppressive and I envy, quite literally, the kind of artists who do not do their work themselves. There are many. They have assistants who do their work and they talk to them and they say, 'No, do it like this, do it like that.' And actually I only have that when I'm making prints. I do have assistants, because I work on wood and there's a lot of work like that to be done, lots of carpentry and woodwork, but I don't really have a proper support system. I try and see people in the evening. I go out and have endless cups of coffee in cafés, and look at the people walking past and read too many newspapers. But there's no cure.

But music? I see you a lot at concerts and opera.

Oh, I often try and think about what I'm going to do in the evening, but it doesn't really work like that. It sounds appallingly self-pitying to say so, but the pain of working is incurable.

Do you ever take a long rest? Apart from holidays, because you travel and that. But do you ever say, 'I'm now not going to do anything for two or three weeks'? Or is that actually impossible; the pressure of re-creating your memories in your paintings is so great, that you are constantly having to do it?

I find it almost impossible to stop working. My friend Patrick Caulfield said, 'Painters are always working'. And in a curious way, it's true. When I was very young, I thought one year I will take off a complete year, but I never have. And I suppose, now that I've grown so old, I think there's no time. Because there is a moment when one thinks there's endless time and then, of course, there isn't.

It just occurred to me, as we were mentioning music, I don't think you have ever done a painting which is based on a night at the opera or a night listening to music?

No, not yet.

Why is that?

I said not yet!

Yes. Given what you say about the necessity of capturing the intensity of your memories, the glib conclusion would be that the memories you get from music and opera are not so strong that you have to capture them in a painting.

I don't think that's completely wrong. I have painted pictures about a very few pictures, which are meant to evoke the work of other painters. But I think to simply paint a picture about a work of art as such, I can't imagine painting a concert unless something happened at it or there was someone I went with.

Going back to politics. What do you feel about the role of government in supporting the visual arts, apart from supporting museums which I suppose one takes as a given?

Well, it certainly isn't a given. There was a period in my life when I was a trustee of the Tate and the National Gallery, and was also involved briefly with the National Art Collections Fund and the Arts Council. It's a period which seems to be very distant now. One thing, however, was very clear then and is unfortunately still true: the government provides less and less support. It doesn't look like it, at the moment, but the purchase grants are cut and cut and cut and cut. Nobody knows any more because it's not a sexy subject to get talked about.

Well, we're all told to stop whingeing, aren't we?

Yes, yes. And I think that what has happened is in many ways tragic. The extraordinary enterprise of the two Tates in fact conceals what has happened and the tremendous fight there was to get money to pay for the running costs. And even then, it's not quite enough. And to me it's terrible. I must be very old-fashioned in my view of government, but I once said to Mrs Thatcher (but of course she didn't understand the source of what I was saying) that it seemed to me terrible that the National Gallery should depend on 'the kindness of strangers' (a quotation she naturally didn't recognise, perhaps fortunately) in order to mend the roof.

I have a feeling that the government would say that the combination of sources of funding that the Tate has found actually represents a stronger position, because it has drawn in private money, lottery money and individuals. Collectively, this is a more secure base, because it's a more complex one than if the government had just said, 'This is the kind of modern museum we want, here is the money.' Isn't there something in it?

Well, I'm not quite sure I know what they would say. But I imagine that they would say, 'Well, we're giving you as little money as possible, but this is the kind of museum we want, this is the sort of museum you should make'. They become more and more dictatorial. I would like to go on for a moment, with the question of government support for the arts, because it's marvellous what is happening, but the fragility is something that is kept completely secret. Like, you must make money from your shop, your café and so on, in order to keep open. I don't, myself, think that's very healthy. I don't think it's healthy at all. And great museums, as we know, like the V and A, have been virtually smashed to pieces through a variety of circumstances – but they do not include having enough money from the government.

Do you have any hope that that might change? Or are we just way past that period, that post-war period, still a rather collectivist period?

I don't think even then we'll ever see it again because museums increasingly are meant to be not places where you go to be surprised, delighted and pleased by something you don't know about. It's supposed to be pushed further and further within a familiar experience, before you even get there.

Back to something more personal to you: the artists that you admire, but you've always been very careful to say they're not necessarily influences. Matisse, who we mentioned briefly earlier, Vuillard and the Intimists. I think you have said how close you feel to Vuillard's concern with interiors, with patterns, and with figures as they emerge from these patterns in quite a veiled way. Does he still matter to you?

Yes, I enormously admire him. But it's become academic to say it because nobody ever sees his paintings.

I saw a wonderful retrospective in Washington about ten years ago.

Exactly – ten years ago. There's been talk of a huge Vuillard retrospective in England ever since I can remember, but it never happened. I think there certainly should be one, partly because people are becoming interested in painting again. Very slightly, but they seem to be.

Is the concern with interiors and with the experience of people sitting, often working, in those interiors, what draws you to him?

Yes, certainly in part. But I think what really draws me to Vuillard is his extraordinarily radical ideas of representation, which, of course, people have from time to time pointed out are extraordinarily radical. It didn't last long. He became a much more conventional painter quite quickly, as so many radical artists do. But he painted three haunting self-portraits where he showed that before a picture is a battlefield or a landscape or a bunch of flowers (I can't remember the exact words), before that, it is a series of coloured marks on a flat surface. And he painted himself like that. And he painted the world he knew like that. And he painted his emotions like that. They owe nothing to light coming from one side on a three-dimensional object. They were simply marks, of different colours, on a flat surface. They're far more radical than anything that Matisse ever painted. It doesn't mean they're better, but they were far more radical. And it's a direction which somehow disappeared, and painting has never followed that line since, but it soon turned into decoration and triviality and so on.

What about Seurat? I was very surprised when somebody mentioned you and him in the same context, because while there are dots, points, in Seurat, in your case they are rather bigger and bolder marks. And you're using them for a very different purpose; you're not concerned about the sort of theories of light behind Seurat. So, isn't the connection with him rather superficial?

Well, I've just finished painting a life-size picture of Seurat's *Bathers*, for the exhibition which is going to be put on in the National Gallery in the summer. No, I've always felt a tremendous affinity with Seurat, not because of his theories, which I was, in fact, taught about – Chevreul's colour theory, which he adopted absolutely sort of hook, line and sinker. But Seurat is a great classical painter and someone who represented life in the way that he did . . . Seurat's drawings, I think, are among the most extraordinary – it's very difficult not to sound pompous – they're the most extraordinary depictions of humanity that exist in the history of art. I think they're amazing. His paintings are more variable in their success. I don't think he's a truly great painter. They don't have the total authority that his drawings have.

The word 'classical' comes up a number of times in what you say about yourself. You were talking about Degas at one stage and you say, 'He's classical and that is what I aspire to be.' Now, I don't quite understand what the classical element in your paintings is.

Well, I try to make pictures, which are sort of inviolable physical objects. They stand up by themselves, they absolutely can't be changed, they're unambiguous. Few people would agree with that. And they are containers for very strong emotions. When I look at a painting by Poussin, for example, I see just that. When I look at a painting by Seurat, I see just that. They're monuments which defy time.

And part of that process of defying is that they are captured in this space; and sometimes a space within a space within a space. And at the heart of it is the object, the emotion, that you are releasing?

I think that's brilliantly put, yes.

A word about your own periods of development. I know you hate talking about chronology, but art critics put your life into a number of periods. Do you recognise that some time in the 1970s there was a sort of resolution in whatever tensions there were, and that from the mid-1970s onwards you painted with a more complete sense of yourself? Do you recognise there was some great change in you in the 1970s?

No, I don't, and I think one of the reasons perhaps that this has been suggested is because the only retrospective exhibitions I've ever had started about then. And I have always had mixed feelings about retrospectives because they are, in a way for many artists, a kind of death. And what do you do afterwards? But I do now begin to want to have a real retrospective because I know if I had one, I think it would be possible to see quite clearly that that catalogue, for example, does not go back very early, and it is all a very continuous process.

We're talking about the catalogue of the Dallas Fort Worth and then the Hayward exhibition in 1995?

Yes, that only covered the last twenty years.

Which goes back to the very beginning. What sort of process of development would we see, if we saw your paintings over fifty years?

I think you'd see not much change, and as a friend of mine once said – who bought one of my earliest pictures, which would have fitted in perfectly happily into my last exhibition at Anthony D'Offay – he said, 'Just one damn thing after another and not much change.' But I like people to be able to see that.

Do you sense any change? People noted with that last exhibition at the D'Offay Gallery that 'Hodgkin is now painting much more quickly'. Is that true?

No. It's not true, but I got so fed up with all the problems of doubly, trebly dating pictures and sometimes they'd taken so long and they didn't look as if they'd taken a long time, I thought to hell with it and I just put a date in. So I lied about their age from time to time, sometimes making it much shorter. This time I thought I'd just start. And for the new millennium, I'm just going to put the year that I finished.

So people said you're painting much more quickly and you'd just changed the dating on the paintings! Is there any lessening of your need to paint?

No, it's increasing. When I finished this Seurat copy, the cataloguer of this exhibition at the National Gallery (he's a man who's very exact about all things that I'm not, Richard Morfet, who used to work for the Tate) said, 'This is the largest picture you've ever painted.' Because it's the same size approximately as the original. And that surprised me. I thought, 'No, no, no, I've painted other pictures as big as this.' But that shows, I think, that my pictures are organically getting bigger and bigger and bigger.

But otherwise, the drive behind them, the need to recapture emotion

*in memory – not always recollected in tranquillity either – I mean there
are a lot of very painful paintings . . .*

Oh indeed. Painful and angry and so on. No, the need becomes
greater, but I think that's age.

*Do they provide a reconciliation for you, when there was something
which was painful or which made you angry, and you had to turn it into
a painting? At the end of that, has the anger and the pain of what you
are recollecting been purged and eased?*

No, I don't think it has. But I think it's put it in another place.
It's as if it was now in a cupboard and you could open the door and
look at it. But then it all comes back.

*So it's not an obvious release, the release of talking about something,
of coming to reconciliation, realising that anger is something useless to
carry around? You've displaced it, but not altogether got rid of it?*

Unfortunately not. Yes, I suppose it is a terrible burden, but the
fruit is the picture.

*But that also seems unfair: that having produced the fruit you should
be unable to get rid of the emotion?*

Yes, I agree, I think it is unfair, but then I think being an artist is
a rather unfair situation to be in.

*What advice would you give to a young would-be artist starting out
today?*

Don't.

Come on!

No, I would. I'm not being flippant when I say that. The reason
I'd say 'don't' is because the strains of being an artist are not
something I would wish on anybody.

But the satisfactions?

They are always sort of just around the corner. They're like the
pot of gold at the end of the rainbow. Perhaps saying 'don't' is
being much too negative. Nevertheless, if you say that to somebody and then they pay no attention . . . well, then that's a good
sign already.

*And if somebody had said that to you fifty years ago, you would have
paid no attention to them.*

Oh, they did say it. Oh yes. And the sort of background I came from, it was probably – I don't say this with any retrospective self-pity at all – but it was probably about the least fertile or useful background for any kind of artist to come from.

So you really had to kick against it?

Oh, desperately! I had a great friend at the first art school I went to, who came from an extremely impoverished background – I mean, the kind that no longer exists, it was so bad – but who had been saved by being an evacuee with two spinster ladies, and he'd come out the other end and he became an art student. But it was he who said to me how wonderful his life was because he was given the front room at home to paint in and nobody cared a damn what he did. Nobody was interested.

But despite everything, despite the pain, despite the loneliness – and I know you've said painting is the only thing you can do – if you had followed the advice of people fifty years ago and not gone into painting, now you would be a very, very frustrated and probably bitter person, wouldn't you? Certainly unfulfilled?

Yes, yes. Probably much bitterer than I am. I don't really feel bitter at all. But I saw the other day an old friend, we'd been at school together and he had had a hard time. He didn't escape. He's been painting patiently for years and years and years, but he had nobody like . . . he needed a Michael Craig-Martin.

GYÖRGY LIGETI

'The cogs have to mesh, exactly'

György Ligeti is one of the seminal figures in contemporary music. A composer who has been at the forefront of the avant-garde for over forty years, he escaped to Vienna after the Hungarian revolution of 1956 and became closely involved with some of the leading experimental figures like Boulez, Stockhausen and Eimert. But then as now, Ligeti resisted becoming drawn into the rigid rules of any movement. In the 1960s he began writing a series of textural orchestral works and choral works such as the *Requiem* and *Lux Aeterna*, pieces which brought him to a wider audience. His musical terms of reference are incredibly broad – from Renaissance polyphony to American individualists such as Nancarrow and Harry Partch.

For himself, Ligeti says he composes because he has to – yet his music speaks to a large and admiring audience. Now in his late seventies, Ligeti remains busy with new projects. In the last decade they've included an ongoing series of *Etudes*, one of the most important additions to the piano repertoire, which has now reached a Third Book. Most recently he has written a Horn Concerto and a piece for a typically novel combination: for solo voice and four percussionists, called *With Pipes, Drums and Fiddles*. The latter is lyrical and sensuous; the Horn Concerto lean and epigrammatic.

As examples of current work, these two are fascinatingly different. They were written at more or less the same time, weren't they?

No, the Horn Concerto is older. I wrote it late 1998 and early 1999, so it's ready since long time. And the *Seven Hungarian Poems* I made last year.

These poems are written by a Hungarian poet whom you hugely admire, Sándor Weöres. What is it about his work that has such a strong attraction for you?

Well, to say that he was one of the greatest poets in Hungarian literature, for all times, it's of course a very subjective judgement. I also am influenced by the fact that I knew him very well. I set three of his poems for song and piano without knowing him in the year 1946. And in the year 1947, I met him. He was interested to listen to these pieces. And he is one of my deep favourites both as a poet and as a person. It's very difficult to judge his poetry from the small verses which I used in my pieces. Both in wartime Hungary and on several times, I came back to him, because his great poetry, which is absolutely known and adored in Hungarian intellectual circles, is very different. He created new kind of worlds, mythologies, whole descriptions of non-existent universes, more like Borges, but in poetry. And in the introduction for this performance, I wrote he was Hungary's Mozart, in a way of extreme virtuosity. Nobody used, in the whole history of Hungarian literature, this kind of virtuosity.

Does the fact that the Horn Concerto is terse, epigrammatic and is then followed by this lyrical style of the Seven Poems, reflect a distinct progression on your part, or at least a development?

I don't think so. You see, the Horn Concerto was something special because I was very much interested in a new kind of harmonic spectra, a new kind of sound combination using overtones, partials in a non-harmonic way. So it's more or less an experiment for myself. Whether the experiment was a success, it's not for me to judge. When I finish a piece, I always have new ideas. And it's very similar like work in science: when you solve the problem, there are a hundred new problems. So when I finish the piece, especially when I could listen to the piece, then I have a lot of new ideas for the next piece. But this was not in this case, because the Horn Concerto was premièred a couple of months after the *Seven Songs*.

What have you learned from the fact that you have now heard both the Concerto and the Seven Songs in fairly close proximity to one another? What ideas has it given you about the next direction to go in?

There are more practical questions. I am just now writing a next piano study, *Etude Eighteen*, which will be premièred in May by Pierre-Laurent Aimard, my favourite pianist. This has nothing to do either with the *Songs* or with the Horn Concerto.

Is it important that you have a good response at a première or from an audience?

For me, the most important thing is to have good players and singers. Then the moment when the performers are high quality, the audience is always responding. So the whole idea about new music which cannot be understood is because there is no time to rehearse, or there are not good enough performers. Becoming an old composer, as I am today, I can have the luxury, the possibility, to choose between really good performers. And in this case, in both pieces, in the *Songs* and Horn Concerto, they were excellent performers.

Well, a great conductor of modern music, Hans Rosbaud, always used to say, 'Modern music isn't difficult, it's just badly played.' He said that thirty or forty years ago and I suppose the situation still applies?

The same. By the way, you mentioned Rosbaud. I'm very happy, because my second orchestral piece, *Atmosphères*, was premièred by him and I met him very, very shortly – just in the general rehearsal. I never met him before. I knew that he is a great, great conductor. In the general rehearsal he performed the piece, but he had no understanding, because in *Atmosphères* it's important that it is one form. It has no sections. But if you don't know this kind of requirement of the composer, there will be sections. I was totally astonished how intelligent Rosbaud was. A wonderful musician and wonderful thinking person. I just told him, 'Would you please do it again and no cuts in it? One piece.' And he spoke about ten minutes with the orchestra, what he told I have no idea, and then he played it again and it was perfect.

You were born in Hungary. People think of you, misleadingly, as a Hungarian composer, though you are a European composer, a world composer. But what does the Hungarian element mean in your musical compositions?

The language. Think of Bartók. For Bartók, folk songs meant so very much. But basically, both in Bartók and Janáček – Janáček is the Czech language in Moravian dialect – it is the language, not so much the folk music. And for me, also, Hungarian language, which is my language when I was a child; I even didn't know that other languages exist. Then I became aware that there is Romanian, which is different, because I cannot understand it when I heard it from policemen and soldiers. I am deeply connected with this way of thinking in the Hungarian language.

Do you think that affects your approach to rhythm? That the innate rhythms of the Hungarian language then show through?

Yes. Hungarian language is extremely practical for poetry,

because you can use the rhythmic, metrical structure in different ways.

But do you think this affects the sounds of your music, even when you're not setting Hungarian words?

Yes, I think, yes.

I want to go back to your earliest beginnings. Your parents were middle-class, Jewish. There was very amateur music – I mean, not what we'd call a real musical background – in your family. And your father didn't even want you to learn the violin, did he?

No, no. He didn't permit me. I should be a scientist. We had in the family a very famous musician who was Leopold Auer, a famous violin teacher. He was in St Petersburg, Tchaikovsky dedicated him his Violin Concerto and Auer said this is not good music; he refused and Tchaikovsky became furious and dedicated it to somebody else. But I never met Auer. He died in the thirties when I was still small; but he died in Dresden, in Germany.

But this was never part of the family background? Nobody said 'my boy, you must remember that you come from a family which has Leopold Auer in it'?

My father always taught it was the uncle of my father, so the brother of my grandfather, coming from a small town in Hungary, near Lake Balaton and the whole family of my father comes from this area. But we had no instrument at home. The only instrument was a gramophone player and so my background in music is that it was absolutely bad to be a musician and it was wonderful to be a scientist. And in fact, I wanted to study physics and mathematics, and I wanted to find out about life, which is more a question of physics than of biology. I'm still extremely interested in sciences, not only natural science but very much in history and politics, and if I have a hobby outside of music, this is mathematics. But I don't use mathematics in my composition. However, I am very close friend with Benoit Mandelbrod, and someone else who work in fractal-geometry and this is part of mathematics where I'm very deeply attracted.

Just going back, though, to your very earliest origins: you heard a lot of opera, didn't you?

Because I was born in a very small town, there were absolutely no concerts. There was a cinema. This was the only cultural centre. And when I was six years old, my parents, together with me and my brother, we moved to Cluj, which is the main city of Transylvania with university, opera house, theatre and symphonic concerts. The first opera I heard was *Boris Godunov*.

Is it still one of your favourites?

One of my favourites. Mr Tusa, you have a Czech or Slovak name?

Czech!

Czech. So you should know that beside Bartók and Stravinsky, my favourite composer is Leoš Janáček, from Brno!

Quite right. What excellent judgement! When did you become aware that you were part of the Hungarian musical tradition – Bartók, Kodály and their intimate links with Hungarian folk music. Was that something that was almost instinctive from the moment you started to be interested in music?

I'm not aware that I was especially interested in music in childhood. I always imagined music, but I thought every child is doing the same. In the small town, everybody spoke Hungarian, and we were part of Romania but the population were Hungarian-speaking, mainly. And I heard a lot of Hungarian folk songs, where peasant ladies who came in the small town to work in the kitchens and do housework, they just sang folk tunes. And then I heard a lot of also Romanian folk tunes; there were some Romanian villages nearby. And then in this small town were a lot of gypsies, so they played gypsy music. Of course, gypsy music is not gypsy music; this is a special music for Hungarian small aristocrats, gentry, which the gypsies did to serve their marriages and funerals and so on and so on. So the home was full with gypsy music, and I didn't like gypsy music.

What didn't you like about it? What worried you about it?

It's very difficult to analyse. I don't know. I heard on gramophone records, for instance, operettas, like Lehár. I hated it instinctively. And I heard Mozart and Beethoven and Wagner and I adored. So, I don't think that I had a judgement as a child.

But you must have had a judgement, because clearly nobody taught you to hate Lehár and to feel uncomfortable with the gypsy music?

No, nobody taught me. It's instinctive. Something in this kind of serving the aristocrats: there is something subdued, something which is dishonest.

Servile?

Servile. And I'm very, very sensitive both against domination and servility.

Let's move forward to this dreadful, appalling period of the wartime. You and your family ended up in concentration camps; your father and brother were murdered, your mother survived. You escaped from labour camp. How much is that a time and a period that you think about constantly?

All the time, I think. I cannot accept that my brother was killed. He was five years younger than me. He lived exactly seventeen years. I saw him for the last time when he was sixteen. Then I was in the Hungarian army in labour service which was very, very difficult, but not as difficult as concentration camp. So, by chance I survived. The hate against the Hitler regime and the Hungarian regime which was allied with Hitler is . . . I cannot forget it and it never diminished. Emotions, with time which is going on, these emotions of hate and disgust become stronger.

So the idea of forgiveness and reconciliation with that regime and those years is impossible?

Impossible. I think it will only happen that people who survived this horrible time of the early forties will die, me too, and then there'll be nobody there with the emotions of hate. Or we don't know the future. Think of Africa today, the Tutsi/Hutu murders were very similar.

You have said that the experience of extreme terror doesn't lead to the creation of art. Have the experiences of the Second World War had any place in your music?

Maybe, yes, but I'm not aware. You have to look at this in the following way. I survived Hitler terror and then came the next terror, the Stalin terror, when I was in Budapest as a student. And we just slipped from one dictatorship into the next. The two gangsters of the twentieth century, Stalin and Hitler, they were allied against the rest of the world, against England.

The period from 1945 to 1948 must have been a period of extraordinary optimism, when you thought fascism is defeated – now there is freedom, liberation!

The Soviet army conquered the eastern part of Europe, but we had no information about Communist Soviet Union; this was some abstract faraway country. And the first three years, until 1947, the beginning of 1948, it was not a dictatorship. It was a free government, elected government, in Hungary. It was hard time. We didn't know that secretly the police became already part of the Communist dictatorship which was in the making.

So the depression you felt when the Communist dictatorship came and you realised that you'd had three years of illusory freedom and now there was another dictatorship, this is impossible to imagine?

It was total desperation. And this happened very quickly. So the installation, what the Germans called *Gleichschaltung* – 'to follow the rulers, to obey' – was very gradual in the Hitler time, because Hungary was not totally Nazi, but it became Nazi. But with the Soviet occupation, the change from a democratic regime to the total Communist dictatorship was extremely quick in late summer 1948. And in a couple of months, the industry and commerce was destroyed; no more shops.

The state controlled everything?

Everything. Imagine concrete things: there was no shoe repair, no repair of water supplies. Nothing. The bureaucracy didn't function. Nothing functioned. So it was a very dramatic change. So I left Hungary in December 1956 – that meant in winter we had to survive somehow in several layers of coats.

The other appalling thing, in that time up to 1956, was that you didn't know what was happening in the West. Now, as a musician – because you were at the Liszt Academy by then – by 1956 had you any idea of the Second Viennese School?

Very little. I would say, until 1955, very little; and then there were smuggled some books and scores. I could see the *Lyric Suite* of Alban Berg. But I could not hear the music, I just saw it.

You only knew the six Bartók Quartets by the time you left Hungary in 1956?

Not the six. Numbers three and four were strictly prohibited. Also number five, but number five I could hear it once.

And you only heard Stockhausen in 1956 as the Hungarian uprising was destroyed by the Red Army?

No, no, no: at the moment when the uprising was still not destroyed. In the Communist time, the Western radio stations were jammed, all the German, American, British, French. It was possible to listen to radio, but you could not understand. And also the music was jammed. So I had a very vague impression. I knew that every Thursday, eleven o'clock, there is one hour of new music on West Deutsche Rundfunk from Cologne. So I had some information about electronic music, but I couldn't really hear. But the Stockhausen *Gesang der Jünglinge* and *Kontra-Punkte*, for instance, I could clearly hear on 7 November 1956, because during the Revolution and immediately after, the jamming station did not work.

And it was to Stockhausen that you went in Cologne, and to the studios of West Deutsche Rundfunk when you fled from Hungary?

But the day before I had no idea that I would be in Cologne!

Of course. So there's this extraordinary process of discovery for two to three years in and around Cologne and Darmstadt, with Stockhausen, with Boulez, with all the other great names of the twentieth century. What did you learn there?

I learned that there is a total different music – this was the music of Messiaen, Boulez, Stockhausen and a couple of other composers, but I think that Boulez and Stockhausen were most important for me – that there is a way which is so different. And I was influenced. However, not totally influenced, because I rejected this idea to write serial music. I am a constructivist, but not a dogmatic person.

What was it about serial music that you found alien to the sort of music you wanted to write?

I was extremely interested in a piece which is not orthodox serialism, which is *Le Marteau sans Maître*. Everybody was deeply impressed by this piece of Boulez. Today, I also think this is a masterpiece. And in Cologne I could see the score and I wanted to analyse it, but I couldn't understand how it's made. And then I chose *Structures 1A*, because this is very simple to understand and I made (I wonder whether this is known) I made a very, very deep-going analysis to describe everything – like a police researcher who goes to the scene of a crime. So, in fact, I analysed everything. I didn't know Boulez at the time; I just knew the score and heard the piece. And Boulez was not happy, knowing about it.

That you had analysed it so deeply?

Yes, and I discovered some mistakes and Boulez didn't like that somebody saw that he did some errors. In this kind of con-structivity, you always have errors, because . . .

Who could be that consistent? Even within the terms of their own system!

Nobody, nobody!

And in the process of doing that, did you decide 'I don't want to write music like this' or 'this is not true to me'?

No, I decided nothing. I'm extremely curious in many, many things. I want to know so many things and this was one; I wanted to see how this would work. It does not mean that I decided to do it similarly or not to do it, neither, nor. Just like I am interested in 'what is life?'

But you finally fell out with the whole of that school, Stockhausen etc., because first of all, you said it was too dogmatic and you weren't interested in dogma; and second, there was a huge amount of factional in-fighting; you either had to be pro-somebody or against somebody?

Yes, this was difficult in Cologne. I lived more or less three years in Cologne, working in electronic studio, and there was a lot of political fighting because different people, like Stockhausen, like Kagel, wanted to be first. And I, personally, have no ambition to be first or to be important. I'm not totally honest; if I would say I'm totally honest, then I would lie. But I'm not interested in these power struggles. I'm not interested in power at all.

Each one of them wanted you to be part of their school, part of their team? Was that it?

Stockhausen wanted it. With Boulez I didn't speak about this question. By the way, today and since the seventies, Boulez is deeply friendly towards me. He conducts a lot of my music. And the fact that I became quite well-known in France is due to Boulez. He was nicer to me than I was to him.

Why were you unpleasant to him? Because you were critical of his work?

Yes. I criticised *Structures 1A*. I thought this was serial music; of course, it was a stupid, naïve mistake because this is not the typical Boulez music. It was just one moment in his work.

But you've never made friends again with Stockhausen?

I never was a 'non-friend' of Stockhausen; also today I have nothing against him.

But you don't have anything in common?

Not any more.

So, having broken with this most influential, most powerful of Western schools, you then had to make your own way?

No, but things are not like this. I never declared that I break with it. There were journalists who pretended that I broke and I'm reading those stories. But it does not happen this way. It was a company of more or less good friends with a lot of intrigues inside, of rivalry, power games, which never interested me. But I still was good friend with Stockhausen, with Kagel, and very, very close friend with Bruno Maderna, whom as a human being I liked. Everybody liked Maderna.

I accept that that is what happened, but you then chose your own path in your own way, which would be the path of György Ligeti rather than the path of any particular musical or intellectual school?

That's true, but I never thought in this way. I'm not thinking in general philosophical or ideological methods or patterns or strategies. I have no strategy at all. It's about writing a composition and then I am concentrating on a composition and I have certain constructive ideas. It's not only naïve, it has to be consistent – not consistent as mathematics, consistent as a natural language. And this applies for a certain piece and then I am ready with the piece, and then comes the next piece where I revise my working method. I'm not thinking in party politics.

I'm glad you raised composition, because it's time we spoke about how you compose. Do you start with a sound in your inner ear and then find ways of translating that sound into symbols on the page?

Yes, but this is an oversimplification. I can explain it more historically. When I was a child without learning music, I had a kind of game which I played. Going to school took less than twenty minutes on foot, and I always imagined some Beethoven symphony or Schumann that I heard from the radio. Of course, Beethoven was the centre. And I always imagined I was listening to a concert, I imagined this music naïvely and I heard it. And from this kind of listening to inner fantasy, which was not original, which was full with influences, I very gradually developed a kind of possibility not only to imagine music, but to compose it on paper, on the page. It was very late when my father accepted that I can have piano lessons: I was fourteen, pretty late, so I'm a very bad pianist, technically. And then I just went in a shop, bought music paper, had a pencil and rubber and began to write a piece when I could play a little bit piano. And it was in Grieg's style, because I played some simple Valse or Lyric Pieces of Grieg, so this was my first attempt to compose.

You said that you could only explain this process historically; how does that compositional process occur now?

In a similar way. I take the music paper and I write. Not always music paper. For instance, in my pieces *Aventures*, and *Nouvelles Aventures*, there is no music paper because there are a lot of spoken words and sound. Then, I had to make like a picture of the score. Or I have an organ piece, *Volumina*, which is not in music. It is music, but I had to develop a special notation, but this was the early sixties, this was the time of musical graphic. I thought musical graphic, as such, is a quite stupid idea.

But you went through the period?

I went through the period. I tried all crazy, stupid things. I even wrote a piece without knowing the Cage piece *4 minutes 33 seconds*, a piece which consisted of one sound and then nothing, silence. I should know better John Cage, then I would not have done it.

You said you take a pencil – do you still write in pencil? Are your manuscripts tidy or is there an enormous amount of crossing out?

Enormous amount of crossing out. For my piano concerto there are many hundred first pages.

You had twenty attempts to start it, is that right?

Much more. Much more. Maybe more than a hundred. I never counted, I am not aware. It takes time until – it's something which I cannot explain, because it's just a feeling. There is a screw which has to be adjusted very exactly. The cogs have to mesh, exactly. There is a description by Yeats, in English, about a puzzle which you try, you try, and at a certain moment you succeed. And I think this is a wonderful image for this kind of work. It's not only the free fantasy of the composer or of the artist in general. There is something where things have to have a certain consistency, but don't ask me what this consistency is. In a mathematical deduction, I can exactly show what is consistency. In art there is no such consistency.

But do you have that sense that you have reached the point when it fits, when it meshes?

Yes. So, I'm so slow in composing, revising all the time and rewriting pieces, until I have the feeling that it's like a mathematical structure – but it's never a mathematical structure, in fact.

A sense of the mathematical may validate it, but it doesn't drive it in the first instance?

Yes. And it's an emotional validation, not an intellectual one; and when I imagine music, it's naïve first. But then I am very interested to have a challenge – like in a school where the teacher gives you a certain problem, 'solve this problem'!

But that does make it sound an intellectually driven process, and of course in a way it is. But it's clearly much more than that.

I think that emotion and intellect are not separate. If you make intelligent, intellectual judgements, it's also emotion. The judges who put people in prison, or even condemn them to death, they are not rational, totally.

They say they are administering the law, but they are driven by emotion?

By hate or by complaint. I think to do artwork is very similar. Also to do science is similar, because it's not true that science is without emotions.

Yes, we are fed this completely mendacious dichotomy between emotion and intellect!

Yes, which is false; this dichotomy does not exist. There are many naïve people saying, 'We don't understand modern music because it's so intellectual.' This is simply not true.

I thought, when I was listening to Aventures and Nouvelles Aventures recently, that the audience should be laughing more. It's extremely witty. But we sit there as if we're in some temple listening to something where humour couldn't be part of it if it was a serious piece of music.

Well, two days ago I heard in Hamburg *Aventures* and *Nouvelles Aventures*; very, very good performance and people laughed.

But not enough!

I cannot propose to people, 'Please, to push a button; now you have to laugh'. No, there is a tradition that so-called high-culture music concert is a serious something. I personally deeply like Charlie Chaplin films and Marx Brothers – more Marx Brothers than Karl Marx. And this black humour: British films with Alec Guinness, a lot of people – Agatha Christie. All this: murder and funny at the same time.

I want to talk a bit about the past and your connection with the past, because you say, 'I like all good music' – Gesualdo, Monteverdi, of course, one of your great loves: the First Viennese School. Now there are many composers who say they're not interested in the past, they're only interested in what is being written now; indeed, they would be happy if there were no knowledge of the past. What is your reaction to that?

I think this is an extremely egocentrical idea – the self-importance and thinking in the future. Wagner began this foolish way of thinking that he's the most important composer. He accepted Beethoven's Ninth Symphony, but now he will create a music of the future. What he created was a contribution to the Nazi Germany, in fact. I'm against it. And also Schoenberg, who taught with the method of twelve-tone row: 'I made sure the domination of German music for the next hundred years.' Well, this is extremely pretentious and stupid.

But the point is that your engagement with the past, your living in the great musical tradition, it hasn't prevented you from writing the most contemporary, the most personal music?

You say this, but I have no judgement about myself. Anyway, I am deeply linked to tradition. I think we don't discover new styles from a zero point. We are always continuing, whether we want to or not.

We've all lived through the totalitarian ideology of Nazism and of Communism; they're both dead, gone, swept away. What 'ism' do we live in now? Maybe consumerism? And if so, what is it like for a composer living in the world scene that we have now? Clearly you're not dictated to by ideology; you live in a world almost of perfect freedom, don't you?

Almost, but somehow we live in this total communication, 'too much information world' with Internet, where everybody is connected to everybody. I think it's not very good for art. We are in a structure of the big capitalist. I'm an anti-Communist, but also anti-capitalist, because look what happens just in these days in Congo; manipulated by international companies who want diamonds and all this business. Business, to a certain amount, is important because we cannot produce all products. Adam and Eve, in paradise, did not need different kinds of production systems. But since humanity is producing tools and products, which is different from animal life, industry and commerce are needed. But when industry and commerce become a huge bureaucratic system and everything is based on money and power, this is very bad for science and arts.

But an advocate of the market system would say to you that it is only because the market creates a surplus that there is any money for art and the money to commission your compositions.

If I look in this way, I have to agree with this sentence. But, at the same time, the pressure of the market competition is not very benevolent for art, because the corruption of artists to do Hollywood-style music is very, very heavy. I have nothing against high-level popular music; I very much appreciate it. But to be in a hurry and to produce something which will please managers, I'm against.

How do you justify, though, if one of these managers said to you, 'What does your music contribute to the good of society?'

Nobody asks this question.

That's probably because you don't talk to these people. That is what they would say to you.

I met a lot of agents and managing people. They are interested to sell their artists or their products. There are benevolent ones.

Yes, but supposing the head of a steel firm comes to you, or an electronics company comes to you and says, 'Out of my taxation and out of the wealth that I create, you, György Ligeti, are allowed to write music. What does your music contribute to society?'

I don't ask myself this question. It has no function. People who make no compromise, who don't write symphony for global companies, they write what they want. I write what I want. If they give me a commission and pay something, it's OK, I have to live. But I never will adjust my output to what agents or industry wants.

But would it be right, looking at your extraordinary, complex, political and composition life, to say that what you do is you pursue an individual path? You've always said that you're not a guru and not an evangelist; but if you are an example, it is as a person who is prepared to take individual responsibility for their actions?

Yes. I have an idea. My father was a very honest, straightforward man and of course, I'm very deeply influenced by the attitudes and character of my father. I want to be as honest as possible. I cannot always afford to be totally honest, because sometimes people ask certain questions or there are conversations where everybody sometimes has to hide something. But I hate to lie. And this is maybe now a very prestigious sentence: in all my life, I try to be as honest as circumstances allowed. I was dishonest with the Communist dictatorship, for instance, I went illegally through the border of Hungary to Austria, which was considered criminal. Because my feeling for personal liberty was much more important than obeying the law. My hero, by chance he was British, is Winston Churchill. In the very critical days of end of May 1940 when Lord Halifax and other people from British government and establishment made pressure on Churchill to make arrangement with Hitler, if Churchill would not insist in his famous speech, 'We don't give in. We destroy Hitler', then today the world would be very different. And in any case, we would not have this conversation here today.

All our lives would be different.

So, it was better. And I'm extremely, extremely thankful for this funny person – Churchill.

PAULA REGO

'You've opened a corridor into the darkness'

There's no problem with being a successful woman on the British art scene today. Forty years ago it was far more difficult for women artists to get noticed – ask Paula Rego. Born in Lisbon in 1935, she came to London in the early 1950s and soon after began studying at the Slade School of Art. There she met Victor Willing, a fellow student who later became her husband and the love of her life. Living variously in Portugal and England, they raised three children together and painted separately. Things changed in 1966. First her father died, then Victor Willing was diagnosed with early signs of multiple sclerosis, and then his father died. Back in Portugal, Victor ran the Rego family business and Paula continued to paint, relying heavily on her husband's advice. This phase of their lives ended with the downfall of the Salazar regime and the seizure of the business. Paula Rego returned to London with her husband and children, and both of them resumed their painting. It was to be another ten years, though, after Vic Willing's death, before Paula Rego began to get the acknowledgement she deserved. Unusually among twentieth-century artists, she glories in being a narrative painter and a figurative one. Some of her series of paintings – *Dog Woman*, the *Red Monkey* series – have created unforgettable images that no one else could have painted. The constants in her work are the female form, the Portuguese woman, stocky and muscular, that she was brought up with, and toys and animals often in disturbingly humanoid forms. And time and again there are references to childhood experiences but always seen through a subversive, remembered eye.

Paula Rego, what were your relationships like with the different members of your family?

A bit strict, with few rules. I was an only child and I stayed a lot in my room, but I loved my father, and my mother as well. I was very, very spoilt and very well looked after.

And there was a lot of storytelling in the house, wasn't there; or you had stories told to you?

Yeah, my aunt Egeria, she spent all afternoon telling me stories. She used to come and stay with us sometimes; and she told the stories I wanted to hear. I'd give her the subject matter; and then she'd go on and on and on, for a day, sometimes two days. And I also had my mother's old nanny, who used to come and stay with us; and she sat by my bed. Because I was afraid of the dark she would sit there till I fell asleep. And during that time she would tell me stories from her native village she came from, about animals and, you know, magic animals, all that.

When your aunt told you stories that you wanted to hear, can you remember the sort of subjects that you suggested to her?

Well, it was always about the king who had a daughter, and then terrible things happened to her, and she had tribulations – going out into the world, leaving her home and travelling, and coming across all sorts of evil things. And then she would be saved in the end and marry the prince. The usual kind of fairy tales. It was a fairy tale I wanted to hear.

Can you remember feeling reassured about them?

Oh, I thrilled to them, thrilled to them. But I was also a little frightened at times, which is part of it. You should be; that was part of it.

You also liked going to the cinema, I think. You were taken to see a lot of Disney films, Snow White, Pinocchio, and so on. What sort of images do you remember from those films which stirred you at the time?

In *Snow White* the stepmother was very frightening, and every child I've known has been really afraid when the stepmother changes into the witch in the mirror. That was terrifying. But otherwise it was a world of mystery and enchantment. It was just like the real world.

Did your parents ever say to you, 'Paula, you live too much alone; we need to get friends for you, you need to go out and behave like a healthy ten-year-old and take some exercise and so on'. Did they ever say that?

Oh, they used to bring in kids for me to play with sometimes. I was forced to play with children and I hated it. I didn't like the games they played, you see; and I didn't feel very comfortable with them. There was a little English boy who used to go out in the garden and cook tomatoes and make me eat them, and that was forbidden. And then there was a little refugee kid that wanted to take out my eyes – and she had me up against the wall – 'Now I'm going to take out your eyes' – and I didn't like that at all. And then the other girls always wanted to play at having babies, and they used to stuff your skirt with cushions and then pretend to be having babies, and I didn't really like that either. So I had not much fun with children at all.

And was that at school as well? Did you find the same sort of problems about not sharing in the games that other children wanted to play?

On the contrary, I loved it at school; I loved it. There were more secrets. You could share a secret at school because there were other people around, there wasn't just two of you. If you're going to have a secret you have to have other people, not just two people, otherwise it doesn't count. It was a school just for girls, and we spent all our time just dancing and acting; we never did any learning at all. And that's why they took me out and had a teacher at home to teach me reading and writing.

And when did you start drawing? When did they realise that you were spending a lot of your time drawing and that you were rather good at it?

Well, I always drew, ever since I was really small, as children do. They just scribble away, and I did that. I loved drawing, you see, because drawing is incantatory, and it also brings you peace, because you rock backwards and forward when you're drawing, and there's something sexual about drawing. And there's a great deal of comfort in it as well. And not just that, but I could do pictures of people and so on. I started very young. I must have been about five, I remember, or even less.

Create for me the picture of what you were like as a young girl at home and physically drawing.

I'd sit on the floor; I'd have a piece of paper and coloured pencils. But actually the colours never mattered a lot, it was just the point of the pencil. And when the point of the pencil scratched on the paper, it was utterly thrilling; and then I'd make a noise, I'd go 'uuunnn'. That's how it was incantatory, you see, the 'uuunnnnn'. And I went into a kind of, not a dream, but somewhere else. And I became completely absorbed in what I was doing. I'd sit on the floor and draw hour after hour.

When did your teachers say to you and to your parents, 'Look, Paula isn't just an averagely talented girl who spends a lot of her time drawing. She can really draw'?

When I went to St Julian's English school, they encouraged me there, because they believed in drawing. My Portuguese teacher, at home, she used to tell me I couldn't draw at all, because we had to do cups, you see, and I couldn't get one side of the cup like the other one. And she said, 'Look at this person, she can't draw, and she wants to be an artist!' I already wanted to be an artist you know, I was only nine. But in the English school they encouraged me.

And then your English teachers really encouraged you. And did they say to you, 'If you work you'll get into the Slade'?

No. Not at all. They were so clever that one punishment I had from the headmaster was to do a huge mural. That was the punishment, because I used to skip school sometimes, you know. And so I was on my knees doing this huge thing on paper, then they hung it up on the wall. So you see, they were clever.

And all this time, the input you were getting visually was very strong; you were also getting all this input of stories from reading? Have you always been a great reader?

I read a lot; and then when I was about thirteen or fourteen, I loved poetry. I wrote stories myself, you see, and illustrated them. About runaway children, curiously enough; I don't know why.

I suppose the more happy the home you have, the more you dream of the supposed liberation of running away, don't you?

I just thought it was an adventure, you know; but I never got very far. I mean, even if I did run away I never got very far.

Oh, so you did actually try?

Well, I once dressed up as somebody really poor and went out begging; but you see, I didn't get very far because I was too ashamed, and I came back home.

Ashamed of what?

Ashamed of pretending, ashamed of being found out, ashamed! So I came back home quickly. So I didn't venture very far.

Let's talk about another aspect of the atmosphere of your younger years. These were the years of the Salazar dictatorship. What impression do you retain of the sort of impact that the dictatorship had on people?

Well, you couldn't speak your mind; nobody even spoke about things, actually. They stopped knowing what to say. People who got arrested presumably talked to their friends, but there was just a general feeling that you couldn't talk about things.

And they couldn't create things either?

No. They talked about football; that stood in for everything else. How do you mean they couldn't create things?

Well, if people can't talk about things, doesn't that limit the extent to which they can be creative? Doesn't the oppression extend to the creative world as well?

Well, there's always secrecy and subversion, which is very powerful, that; but even that didn't seem to go very far, really. It was always in certain limitations. And the ignorance! One of the first things that Salazar did was to shut all the teacher training colleges, so there weren't any proper teachers. People had very, very short training, and schools were appalling, really.

So there was a general clamping-down on everything that was of the mind, everything that was intellectual?

Yes. And also physical. You couldn't go places, you couldn't cross the street, you always had to dress properly. You used to have to wear socks and gloves and stuff, you know, you had to dress properly; and you could never be a tease. I was always being watched and everything. Horrible, really.

And what about the other kind of oppression which you have mentioned, and that is the social oppression that society placed on all women in Portugal?

Nobody had the vote, really. Not just women; nobody really voted. But women had no right to get a passport, for instance, without their father's permission or their husband's permission. For a long time they couldn't have a bank account of their own. You couldn't leave the country without permission. There was divorce, but there weren't lots of other things. And women were supposed to be servants, really.

But upper-class women, middle-class women; what was expected of them?

Middle-class women were supposed to play canasta and have

tea, and manicures and things. That's a form of prison as well. And they had to conform within their own very narrow worlds.

And working-class women?

Working-class women worked like donkeys. They had to look after their children, their husbands. There had to be thousands of children because there wasn't any form of birth control, which was forbidden. Abortion was forbidden. Everything was forbidden. So they had very difficult lives.

Was it a huge relief when you came to London, to the Slade, at the age of seventeen? Was just getting out into a free society a very important part of that experience?

Well, I tell you, when I flew over London and I saw the lights, I thought this was a fairground. I thought, wow, this is really it! And as I landed it was just marvellous, although London was still very bleak after the war. And because it was 1951 when I first came here, you see, it was bombed a lot. And there was still rationing, and there was powdered eggs, which were disgusting. In fact, even that seemed marvellous. There was lots of ice cream, and I could eat as much ice cream as I wanted. I could go to the movies as often as I wanted, which I did.

And what did you learn from the Slade? Did they help you start to become the artist you finally became?

I learned not very much there. I learned from the people I met there. But it was very restricted at the Slade. Coldstream was really rather a good professor, a very good professor, actually, and he recognised that I had to use things from my head. I couldn't just draw, like measuring everything over and over again, because I got desperately, desperately bored. So he liked what I did, he encouraged me always. And we had tutors like L. S. Lowry. He came to see me, for instance. Lowry was despised, he was considered not good at all; and he came to see me, and we got on really well. He liked what I did, he understood; I've always liked what he did. And they had oddballs like that in the Slade. In fact, the Slade was full of oddballs, all different kinds. Some measured everything very carefully, some did pseudo-naïve pictures, some did portraits of their mothers and so on, but it was full of oddballs.

So what did I learn? Always do something that you know about; that's what they told me. Because when I first went there, I did Rome burning, and the slaves escaping, and, you know, melodramatic stuff like David. And they said, 'This is all very well, Paula, but you should really do something you know about, not all this stuff!' So I tried to.

Now, I suppose the most important thing at the Slade was that you met your husband, Vic Willing, an artist, a very good artist later. And was he the most important influence on your life as a painter?

Yes, without doubt. The biggest influence, possibly the only influence. I mean, not copying-wise; I didn't want to do pictures like him because we're such different people, but the things he told me I still remember.

Like?

Well, I asked him, 'What's tonalities?' He said, 'Look, half close your eyes and some things you see darker than others. That's tonalities.' That I learned from him. I'd never learned that at the Slade. I didn't know what it was. It was so complicated. He said, 'Be true to yourself; you're your own best friend.' He said that to me. And he told me to draw. He said, 'Just draw and draw.' When I was stuck, you know; after leaving the Slade I was stuck. And he said, 'Just draw and draw.' And I did; I just drew and drew, what came in my head.

So he really accepted you as what you were and what you were going to be; there was no attempt to be a sort of Svengali and say, 'I will help this unformed creative person become something marvellous'?

A Euston Road painter? Not at all. He once put a bowl in front of me, a blue bowl with some oranges in, when I was stuck again, and he said, 'Well, if you don't know what to do, paint that.' And you know – horror, horror – I couldn't. There's no faces there, no faces. And so he said, 'You see, you can't do that. Go and do some more drawing.'

And you can't do landscape either?

Not much. I try to.

Is it the same thing, that there are no faces there?

No faces. There's so much spread around that the moment that you concentrate and try to observe a bit, you're on to the next bit but then you've missed out things. I can't do it. I have no overall feeling for landscape, really. I sometimes used to like being in the landscape; not much, because I always think I'm being followed if I'm in the countryside. I always think there's somebody behind me, and I don't like that. So I don't like being outdoors a great deal. Even when I was little and I was sent out into the garden to play, I used to stay quite near the front door. So I can't see, I can't draw, I can't do landscape now.

At a fairly early stage in your marriage, I think about six or seven years after you were married, Vic was diagnosed with multiple sclerosis, which he then had for twenty-two years. Agonising for him to experience.

Well, not at first, but it was crippling later. At first it was not; we didn't even know what it was, never heard of it, you see. So years passed by without knowing what was going to happen, which was just as well.

When did the illness become acute? How many years of really acute suffering were there for him and you?

Well, it got bad in the early seventies, and in the eighties it was pretty bad.

But even then, when he was very ill, he was making suggestions to you about paintings. And if we think of that extraordinary series of paintings called Girl with a Dog *– where girls look after a dog, they dress it, they shave it, they feed it, and so on and so forth – he suggested that idea to you?*

No, he did not.

Where did the idea come from?

A friend of mine, Colette, she said I should do something about Vic, but it wasn't from him. His idea was *The Monkey, the Bear and the One-Eared Dog*, because he had such toys as a child, and he gave me that idea. But after that he didn't give me any more ideas. After that he'd no more.

Let's talk about the Red Monkey *series. So he gave you the idea that there were these three characters. So the monkey having its tail bitten off by the wife, and either vomiting or spitting out wine, that*

ON CREATIVITY

was entirely something which you brought to that series of pictures?

Yeah, it was. The animals were his, but what happened to them was mine. What I made them do was my idea. My idea is what really happened to them.

What really happened to them?

What really happened to them in life. So the story took hold of the animals, you see, and they just acted it out for me.

Roughly how long did each one of those paintings take to do? And were you painting them all separately?

No, they were done on the floor, those pictures, because then I began to draw on the floor, like I did as a child. That was very important. And those pictures took no time at all. I would do one a day, you see.

And you painted them in sequence?

I painted them in sequence, one after the other, yeah.

And you knew when you had come to the end of the series, when, as it were, those characters had stopped telling you a story?

Yes. You can only do four. Any more is self-indulgence, and also it goes off. The first one, you're grasping for what you want. The second one, you get it. The third one, you get it very, very well. The fourth one is decadent already. You start again.

So then there was this series, Girl with a Dog, *which this friend suggested as a way of coming to terms with Vic's illness?*

Yes. I didn't know how. You see, it was so embarrassing, because it's such a personal thing, and you can't really do it directly. And so you have to find a way round it, a story. But it doesn't work like 'now I'm going to do something about this situation'! An idea comes to you, and you do the first one, and then after you've done it you realise what it is that you've done. Do you see? And the picture begins to tell you what has happened. And what has happened is, you've opened a whole corridor into the darkness; and then you follow it. And then as you go into this dark corridor it begins to light up, and you see things. But it's an adventure, and sometimes a dangerous one, and painful too. And risky, and then you're ashamed, ashamed, you see. But I think that that's how it started, and then the girls and the dogs led to more

210

religious pictures, and the pictures became really religious pictures.

Can I just hold you for a moment on the Girl with a Dog *series. What did Vic think of them – because like it or not, they are seen as being your reaction to his illness?*

Oh, he liked them.

He didn't mind being portrayed as . . .?

Well, he didn't know. I mean, he liked the pictures!

And were they a help to you in the experience of dealing with a sick and ultimately dying husband?

Not at all. They weren't any help whatsoever. The only thing was that I did some pictures that meant a lot to me, that's all. But that's quite good. If you do pictures that mean a lot to you, that's terribly good really.

You mentioned danger in the process of discovery. What sort of danger?

Well, as a thrill that you might go over the edge into some area which is fraught with danger and risk of total embarrassment; doing something that is going to reveal unspeakable things. I don't quite know what, but that's the risk of it.

Let's talk about the business of painting a little bit more. Vic, it's said, placed the brush on the canvas with precision and fastidiousness. He called you 'a monkey with a typewriter', in the sense that you splashed and splashed, and sooner or later something wonderful would come out. Was that ever a fair description of how you painted?

He said I was like a monkey with a typewriter because I did many drawings. I didn't splash around trying to see a face in the clouds like some people do, because that is just silly. You have to have an idea, you see, and then you put it down. But the idea goes wrong many times, and you do that many, many different ways until one is better than the others.

But at what stage did that stop? You'd been through surrealism, you'd been through collage. How important was the moment when you were told that collage was not helping you and that you should go for straight, figurative painting?

Well, my friend Joao said, 'What are you cutting up this stuff for?' I could not get ready-made collage that was specific enough – newspapers are too vague. So I used to do drawings of monkeys, of people, and then I used to cut them up and reassemble them to make a collage, so that it would undergo a whole process of transformation, which I thought was necessary for art, you see. What happened was that that in itself became totally academic, and the method of doing took over; so it became a method. Now, a method is no good; method stinks. So when he said, 'Why are you cutting up, why don't you just leave the drawings as they are?' I said, 'Do you think I could?' And that was fantastic, because it simplified my life a great deal.

And that in fact was when the Red Monkey *series was done, that was 1981?*

1980, even 1979 I began, because I did things before the *Red Monkey*.

Now, the journey from the way the Red Monkey *series looks (which is acrylic on paper, and quite light and almost sketched) . . . the journey from that to your later works (big figures, very often big blocks of colour), that's a journey of over twenty years. How conscious was the movement from that earlier style to the style that you have now?*

Well, you go from one thing to the next; you never know where it's going to lead you. I could have gone a different way. It just so happened that the pictures after the girls and dogs were like religious pictures, actually – there's the sort of *Deposition*, there's the *Raising of Lazarus*, all those things, they have got something – and that just took me on to the next one and the next one, really.

You've also done a lot of illustrations, illustrations of Peter Pan*, of nursery rhymes, of poems by Blake Morrison. Where does this fit into your work? Is it illustration or is it something else?*

It's something else. It's like working with stories as in the pictures, really. But I bring them into my own experience, the things I read like the nursery rhymes. They just came to my mind, actually. I used to read one at night and in the morning an image would turn up. So that's instinctive, that was not difficult, because nursery rhymes we don't know what they look like. But *Peter Pan* was more difficult because *Peter Pan* is such a classic and so

English, he's such a challenge for me. But again, I used people I knew. I cast the parts around people. Sometimes they would be miscast, which is quite a lot of fun. So it was game-playing as well.

What strikes me about the nursery rhymes is that you always manage to make even the innocent things disturbing. Children playing games, falling down slides. Are you surprised that people find them disturbing?

Some are sinister on purpose, like *Little Miss Muffet*, you know, and that fear. But the others I don't intend to be too sinister or anything like that. I think sometimes it's technical. For instance *Baa, Baa Black Sheep* and the sheep is so black; it stayed for quite a long time in the aquatint and came out all black. I thought, 'Crikey, this is the devil, and that would be bad,' but he's quite nice, quite a friendly ram. But I don't think some of them are too sinister.

But do you mind when people say they find your drawings so frightening?

I'm used to it. I mean, think of Gustave Doré, the great illustrator, marvellous illustrator. I was brought up on Dante's *Inferno*. My father used to scare me with it. Those things are sinister, full of black and full of nauseous images, very nineteenth-century nausea, which is something that's always tickled my fancy.

Do you now think that you are painting better than you were twenty years ago? Or do you just have a way of expressing what you want to express?

Well, Vic used to say, 'You never get any better, you just get better at it' and I think that's probably true. And I know that I'm better at drawing now; that's because I practise so much more in a conscious way. But whether I'm better at it . . . you know, one's as good as one is.

Do you still paint on the floor?

No, because I now use models, people I work from, and I can't see them if I'm on the floor. So I have to have an easel, and they're there, and then I copy them.

And wasn't the fact that you decided to stop smoking after Vic's death, wasn't that an important element in changing how you painted?

It was, because in order to hold a drawing board, you can't have a cigarette in your hand as well. So I held the drawing board much more and began to draw from looking at things, or people, really.

You work a lot with one particular model, Lila. She's the one who just acts things out for you and appears in many, many paintings. What's the significance?

Well, we work together and it's a collaboration. She's able to interpret what I want. By now she seems to know what it is that I want and she falls into positions that I find just right. I work through her, she's like a medium for me. Through her I can tell a story, I can do a picture. We really started with my *Dog Woman* when I realised I had to have a model because I couldn't do it without the information that I needed from another human being to copy. And she put herself in that position and it was so marvellous. Then after she was the sleeping dog; then she was the bad dog; and then slowly we began to understand a language together and now she can interpret all sorts of things for me. It's always different.

Is there something particularly important to you in the fact that she's Portuguese? She has a completely Portuguese body, heavy, stocky, solid. Does that trigger something in you that these are the physical shapes that you respond to?

Yes indeed. It's also that although she's much younger, she's also a bit like myself. So instead of doing myself I do her, which is much more fun. And we talk Portuguese together when we're working, we listen to Portuguese music, and we have an understanding. Yes, she's stocky, although she's slim but she's short limbed.

So you work with models, and you say that 'Everything I paint has to be literal; I can't make anything up'. It seems to me an extraordinary thing to say, given that your images have such imagination. They're anything but literal. If one tries to interpret your pictures in a literal way, one is completely lost. So it's a wonderfully paradoxical thing to say, but why do you say it?

Well, I dress up people who work with me. They're not models, they're my collaborators. I dress them up in the clothes I want, and we act out together things that they're supposed to be acting, like stage actors. And then: 'Now, that's just good, now stay like that,' and then I draw them. So that's why I call it literal – that it's actually real, it's from life. But it's made up in the sense that I make up the stories.

But when does the story come? Does the story come before you paint, during painting, or do you rationalise it to people like me after the painting is completed?

All of those. Before, I have to have an idea about something I really want to do, which I usually get from doing a drawing from my head on a piece of paper – where you're actually bending over this piece of paper and things pour out of your head straight into it through your hand; you draw with your hand. Then, if you like it, you try and set up a scene with chairs. Sometimes I rent chairs and everything – stuffed animals, plants – and set up a scene. And people come and act there, and then I copy them on to the canvas. So it's all that process. And the story then changes as you go along. Pictures are pictures, they're formal things. They have to be resolved as pictures, and sometimes it's very difficult to resolve them. But sometimes a formal thing will bring the story round in another way. So it's always a constant thing between the story and the formality of the picture, and in the end I'm left with something.

At the point of completion, though, would you have to say to yourself, 'I want to produce a painting which is satisfactory in formal terms'? Does the formal correctness of the picture come first?

The formal correctness. If it's formally pleasing to me, then the story has to be right.

You're very good at answering questions about what the story in a painting is. But is there only one version of the story?

Lot's of them, lots of different ones; I very often don't remember. When I finish the picture I usually have a pretty pat explanation for it. So that's OK, that's usually a help, to get people to look. But that's only a way into the picture. Because one hopes that once a person is looking into the picture, other things will come out that I'm not even aware of. That's what the picture is: it's full of telling things that I'm not aware of.

You've never belonged to any school of painting. Did you ever feel, in the years when you weren't recognised and you were looking after Vic, 'maybe I should belong to a particular school and I'd be taken more seriously'?

Well, I couldn't. I tried. Once somebody told me that I should do abstract pictures and he told me how. And he said, 'You don't want this rubbish of stories, this is all an excuse. All you need is a canvas, a long canvas, not too big but long, and you need two brushes and five colours. Dip the brush in a colour and you spread it from left to right; you dip the brush in another colour and you spread it from right to left. And when you've covered the canvas you've got a picture. That is a picture.' I cried because I thought I preferred my stories. I cried because he hadn't liked my pictures. Nevertheless I went back to Portugal for my summer holidays and I tried it. I did left to right, right to left, and left to right, and of course it was entirely meaningless. I was completely idiotic to try such a thing, and there you are: I could not do something else than I did.

For years and decades nobody bothered to do figuration. Do you get a quiet satisfaction of personal vanity at saying, 'I stuck to these things which were unfashionable and they now recognise that the work I do is good'? You must get a bit of satisfaction from that?

No. Not at all. I don't see things like that. I use figuration because it's the only way that I can put the mood across – through figures, because I like drawing people. I'm very interested in people; I like people above everything else. It's curious the cruelty and all those fascinating things that people are. And it's what interests me. But I don't think in terms of having stuck at it. I had no choice, really. I was lucky to be able to go on doing it.

Let's talk about the atmosphere of your paintings. It's been said that you paint to give terror a face. What is the terror?

Well, when one's a child, one's afraid of all sorts of things. You're afraid of the dark, you're afraid of the devil, you're afraid of all sorts of things. I guess you go on being afraid of certain things – I don't know what they are.

You've also said revenge is a theme?

Well, like in the *Amara* series; what happens to the girl who has an affair with the priest. She gets knocked up and then she has a baby and the baby is taken away from her and she dies. I wasn't aware of it, don't you see; I didn't think, 'Oh, now I'm going to revenge her.' I'm not aware of this. I then did an angel with a sword in one hand and a sponge in the other; my angel. And then I realised that I've done my angel because the angel was going to take revenge for this girl. And it's a protecting and vengeful angel. I just realised after I've done this angel that that was what it was for, it had a business in life to do that, absolutely.

And you've said that when you're painting, you are a man because 'the part of me that is male' comes into force.

Well, I stand aggressively in front of the easel, and I walk from one foot to the other with my hand in my pocket. And I swagger like people do in operas!

Why does that have to be male?

Well, females don't do that usually. They don't swagger like that, and stamp around and so on. Maybe it could be female, because that's what I am: female.

This is an important statement, about your being a man when you're painting. Is it about having the confidence to say, 'This is me and this is what I'm doing and I'm completely in control'; is there an element of that?

No, I wish there were. It's very difficult when you're drawing life. When you're drawing, it's very hard to do, and I'm not confident at all, and I just try terribly hard. And I try to get it right – which is something you're not supposed to do – but I try to get it right. I try to observe it to get it right, and I try so hard, and sometimes I actually succeed. And that gives me enormous pleasure. But that comes after, there's no confidence, it's not confidence there, no.

There's a tendency to interpret what you do as a feminist painter. But Vic Willing wrote about what he saw as the ambivalence in your paintings. He wrote 'rebellion and domination, freedom and oppression, suffocation and escape'. It seems to me that your paintings invite a superficial response that the painting is about one thing; and then the second look shows you that it's about something very different.

It's about both things sometimes. I know that it sounds odd but it's sometimes about both things – this thing and that thing which are opposites. Opposites can come together in a picture, and that is very interesting; you can have both resentment and affection – which happens in life you know. So a picture can contain many different kinds of feelings and attitudes, and even the way that you behave. A picture can contain all these contradictions. That's why it's a picture.

I certainly found that I would look at a painting and would say, 'Oh yes, that is about such and such a subject.' And then I'd read what a critic had said and it would be something completely different. And then I'd read what you had said, and it was something slightly different. But all these meanings can be read into your paintings?

Of course, yes, because one's self is full of contradictions. I mean one is a bag of contradictions from morning till night. And therefore it would not be truthful if you just selected one side – well, you couldn't; if you go into a picture, you go the whole hog, you know, and there it is – phwar!

Do you mind being called a feminist painter?

Well, I don't know what feminist painter means. Obviously, if I have a standpoint it will be from a woman's point of view on account of that's what I am. And so I can tell the story from what it was like being a little girl, for instance. That's how it's a story told by a woman.

When you did that series of paintings about abortion, did you hope that you would have a social message, particularly as the paintings were exhibited in Madrid and in Lisbon?

Yes, they were done for that, they were political. They are also political pictures because of the referendum nobody bothered to attend to vote to legalise abortion in Portugal; nobody bothered. So the rule went on being the same, and I felt indignant: why can't people go and vote, it's such an important thing, causes so much suffering. So I did a series of pictures of very young girls having illegal abortions, in their bedrooms, on their own, which is what happened in Portugal, and happens everywhere else where it's forbidden.

Where did you get the knowledge from?

Well, when I was in Portugal, when I was there first with Vic, a lot of people – local women and girls – used to come and ask me for money so that they could have an abortion because they already had lots of kids and so on. And of course one knew all about it, one saw it.

Apart from that, does painting matter first and foremost because it is important to you? Is that the ultimate explanation for why you paint?

Well, it has to matter to me. I paint because I just do one picture and then another one. And I got the habit, thank goodness. It's got to matter to me somehow!

When people ask what is the justification of having artists like yourself, would you claim any justification for it in broader terms?

It's not up to me to claim such things; it's up to me to do them. It's up to other people to claim for me. I can't claim, you see, I have no potential, I don't know. But other people may claim if they think it's right. You know, I do them . . .

Are you now capable of criticising your paintings in the way that Vic Willing used to?

I've had to. I've had to distance myself. And I was very scared that when he died I wasn't going to be able to. But I've done my best. I don't know how brave I've been, but I hope so, yeah.

Do you find yourself saying, when you've got a puzzle, 'I wonder what Vic would think of this?'

Well, I used to but I don't do that so much any more because I've gone so far different from what I used to be when he was alive that I have no point of reference any more. I'm out in the sticks now. And he's there somewhere in the background. I can't do that any more, so I just have to trust myself.

You've lived in England for many years. You've been proudly adopted by the English. How much are you English and how much are you Portuguese, or does it not matter?

There's a part of me, the part that speaks in Portuguese, brings memories back that I don't have if I speak in English. But as for poetry, for instance, I understand the language in English rather than Portuguese. In literature I get on better in English than I do in my own language. And to talk about pictures, for instance, I find it immensely hard to talk about them in Portuguese; I cannot. So English is for the grown-up more, the Portuguese is the childlike, which also comes into the grown-up and is totally precious, because without that we cannot exist.

Some people would say that a grown-up is a grown-up and you put childish things behind you. But you've insisted on keeping that connection?

Well, you can't really get rid of it. It's that the child is concertinaed into you, and it pulls out at every instance – even in the most posh places, or in the most awesome situations, this lilt comes out. And it's the bit that saves you, really. It's not a bad bit, it doesn't mean you're going to do something really rude, it means that you have more a sense of yourself. So that is in everybody, not just in me. As for being in England, I love living in London, I love it, it's brought me freedom.

And you wouldn't have had that freedom in Portugal?

Never. I had to bring my stories out in order to be able to enact them in England. England is a free place, at least I've always felt that freedom. And also London is big, anonymous, and just marvellous there. And I don't say about the countryside because I've never lived there; I couldn't. But London I love.

Apart from all the store of ideas, images, stories, myths that you have, are you still revitalising that store, are you taking in fresh images which are going to produce something in your paintings, heaven knows when? Are you still working with the reservoir of impressions you had when you were sixteen?

Very often the new images, the new experiences, find in the course of storage that they connect there somehow. And they winkle out something. And then they do join up. You see, if it connects with this reservoir, it gives it a bigger reality than a new one. A new impression can't exist without attaching itself to something that's already there. How can it? You don't know what it is, you wouldn't recognise it if it wasn't part of the past experience.

Just thinking about the look in the eyes of so many of your women: it strikes me that the women know what's going on, and that even where the overt situation is either threatening or potentially violent, you look at the way the face is held, you look at the look in the eye, and you think that the woman knows what is going on and she is ultimately in control.

Well, I think that's partly wishful thinking. My wishful thinking is that should be so. But it should be so, it should be so. The women should always be in control.

But you fear it isn't?

But not always. No!

MURIEL SPARK

'I try to complicate it even more, so that
I've got to get out of it'

Few novelists are identified by
popular catchphrases from their writing. It's a fair bet that of the
countless people who talk of 'girls of slender means', 'a far cry from
Kensington', 'the ballad of Peckham Rye', or undoubtedly most often,
'the crème de la crème', few know that they're echoing a line or a title
from a novel by Muriel Spark. Her titles, her subjects, her characters have
an insinuating quality. Her prose, which she insists is really poetry, is

spare, lean, economical. Muriel Spark's observations are sharp, often lethal. It's been said that the slivers of glass that should reside in any writer's heart are pretty large ones in her case.

She published her first novel when she was thirty-nine – a late developer, though her apprenticeship in reviewing, lit. crit., editing, jobbing journalism and running the faction-ridden Poetry Society was classic Grub Street. She was poor. She was often hungry. But the experience of falling ill and suffering hallucinations after taking slimming tablets produced her first novel, *The Comforters*. It was a huge success. 'The shape of things to come,' her editor said to her. He was right. That was a turning point.

The other was Muriel Spark's conversion to Catholicism in 1954, for she is a Catholic writer, not in the mawkish, religiose sense but in the sense that she and her characters carry with them a strong sense of the fact that everything matters but, as she puts it, nothing matters more than our humanity. Now a grand lady of English letters, Dame Muriel Spark lives in Tuscany in a former rectory. She writes intensively and, judging by her last novel *Aiding and Abetting*, about Lord Lucan, she writes without diminished sense of narrative ingenuity or moral complexity.

You've written in detail about your childhood in pretty modest circumstances in Edinburgh. What stands out from that is your awareness of life in the family household. You were never kept out of the adults' way, were you?

No, never kept out of their way, and nothing was censored. I was allowed to read anything. They didn't seem to realise that one shouldn't read something. Our paper, for instance, was the *News of the World*, which was a real scandal sheet in those days –

probably still is, I haven't seen it lately. But I used to read the *News of the World* and get all the scandal, and understand everything. I wasn't kept out of family life at all.

And you relished observing people from a very early age, didn't you?

Oh yes, I used to be a people watcher, very much.

Your parents used to give people nicknames, didn't they? They always used to talk about them once they'd left the house?

Once they'd left the house they would talk about them, yes, in front of us. Absolute hypocrisy. But there it was.

Were they bitchy, malicious?

Yes, sometimes, and sometimes not. My mother was always amiable to everybody, mostly, and so was my father. He was very amused by her and her nicknames, and everything. She was the one who was more amusing.

Were you part of this? You must have picked this up?

I picked it up but I didn't copy it really. I didn't quite like it. By the time I went to school, I didn't quite like it.

You've also said that you were an avid listener. Were you listening to people's voices, to their remarks, their turn of phrase?

I was listening to words, voices, remarks and the nuance, and various levels of meaning, not in a more sophisticated sense but in a quite elementary sense.

Looking back on it now, do you think that those were important parts of what either made you a writer or enabled you to be a writer?

Oh yes. The first things I wrote about were my brother and my mother and my father. I wrote about them, made up poems, made up stories. Then I wrote about the school, and my first writings were about the teacher who later became Miss Brodie. I wrote about her. We were given to write about how we spent our summer holidays, but I wrote about how she spent her summer holidays instead. It seemed more fascinating.

And then this continued after you left school. You got your first job. You went to that genteel Princes Street outfitters, William Small. This was a different cross-section of life.

There was a very elderly man, Mr Small, the owner, and he would confide in me and talk to me and ask my advice about what he should wear, and his shirts, and various things like that. And his son would dash in every now and again and play the piano; there was a piano in his office. I rather enjoyed that job.

And watching the people, the Edinburgh gentry?

I didn't get to see a great deal of that because I was in his office right at the top of the building – there was a wonderful view of Princes Street and the gardens. He gave me more money to stay on, sort of thing, when I thought I might get a more interesting job.

You had this awareness of people and tricks of character. You couldn't go to university because your parents were too poor. And in any case, I think you didn't want to go to university because you thought the girls were so dull and charmless!

They were very dull. At that time, the girls who went to university looked as if they'd just put on a dark-blue dress and left it at that for the whole winter. They were so dreary. And I liked to look nice and go dancing too, and things like that. And they didn't look as if they ever did any of these things. I thought them very dreary. And also when I'd talk to university people, people who really I might have got something out of, I thought them dreary too.

Do you still think them dreary?

Just occasionally I do, yes.

Instead of going to university you went to this précis-writing course at Heriot Watt. What on earth made you think that précis writing was going to be useful or interesting?

Well, I always liked to keep it short, and I thought probably I would get some ideas how to express myself as briefly as possible. It was a challenge. I just did enjoy that course, very much.

Where do you think the idea to be economical in your writing came from, because after all, usually late adolescents think they have to write in a great overblown way, don't they?

Yes. I don't know, I think that was built in, a built-in thing with me. I always wanted to keep it short and pithy. And anything I said, I wanted to make it short.

Surprisingly, you've also put in a good word for what you call managerial speech – this is when you were doing a job where managerial speech was necessary – because you thought that they also stuck to the point?

Yes, I like business speech. I often listened to it for that very purpose, to see how they stuck to the point and they were focused – they targeted a subject instead of spreading themselves all over the place with sub-clauses and that sort of thing.

Do you always strike out a sub-clause in the unlikely event that one should crop up in your writing?

No, I don't strike out much. I write on.

Even if it's an errant sub-clause?

I don't do that. I do one draft. I do the editing in my head first. Maybe it's a desire to save paper, I don't know, subconsciously.

I want to talk about the emphasis you've always put on the search for experience and the need to have experience. You left Edinburgh because you wanted different experiences, didn't you?

I left Edinburgh to get married. I went to Africa, where my fiancé was already. He was in Zimbabwe. And I went there really to get married. And also I had the happy prospect of not having to do housework. And really, I often wonder if that was the only thing, because when I got there it wasn't long before I didn't like my husband. However, I had to stay there for quite a time because war broke out.

But were you looking for experience? Somewhere else you've said that actually the reason you got married to your husband was that you wanted sex!

Yes, the only way a girl – a respectable girl – could have sex in those days was to get married.

But were you also looking for something which wasn't Edinburgh life, something which brought you in touch with the world outside?

Oh yes. I wanted to go abroad in any case. I would have gone to Paris, New York. I would have gone there if I hadn't gone to Southern Rhodesia, to Africa. I didn't intend to stay there.

But is the search for experience something that's been a constant theme in your life? The need to have things that you have lived through?

Yes, I've always looked for experience when I've got bored in any situation. I've very often had to put up with a lot of boredom, for jobs and things like that. But I've found more and more, as time goes on, that experience comes to me. If I have an idea and want to experience something connected with it, it somehow happens – it's like a magnet. One is looking for just that, and one is a magnet for experience when one has an idea fixed for writing.

That itself has been a constant experience in your life? That is how ideas and experience work together?

Yes. For instance, I'm writing a novel at the moment called *The Finishing School*. I always wanted to know what was in those enormous backpacks that young people wear; I wanted precisely to know. Well, I met someone in France just now who knew exactly that, who had to do with children, who knew exactly every item. That I wouldn't have known if I hadn't been writing this particular book!

And you feel that you couldn't have written about it unless you knew something as minutely detailed as what's in a backpacker's backpack?

Yes. This woman, she told me what girls have, what boys have, and of different ages, and what they carry in their backpacks.

You left Rhodesia as quickly as you could during the war, because you said you wanted the experience of being in Britain in wartime. What did you think you were going to find – what were you looking for?

Well, I wanted to experience wartime. I went first to Edinburgh to see my parents, naturally, after all those years. Nothing was going on there, so I came to London. There were some bombs, incendiary bombs and things like that, and I wasn't really particularly looking for that. I stayed in a club called the Helena Club, which is the background for *The Girls of Slender Means*, a book of mine. Then I had to apply for a job through a Labour Exchange, as they called it in those days, and I was sent to the Foreign Office in the country, which was very much secluded from activities of war. But it was very much into the war because it was a secret radio station which was broadcasting a lot of lies to the Germans. As much lies mixed with truth, so very much like writing a novel, something to make our stories plausible. We had to invent things.

This was the station run by Sefton Delmer, wasn't it?

Yes. With the idea of demoralising the troops who were holding out in France – the Germans. We had Germans working with us who had ratted on their army, on their country, and they were a bit unhappy. But mostly they'd found justification for what they did because they were indignant with Hitler in some way. They were either Communists or counts or something like that. I loved it. I really loved it.

What did you like about it?

I liked the mystery, and the intelligence of everybody around me. It was a really intelligent outfit. I liked it very much.

Most people wouldn't think of propaganda as having to be intelligent – that may just be a comment on the general level of propaganda. But why was this particular kind of propaganda intelligent?

Because it had to be different from the usual. The BBC were putting out plain propaganda, and this was called black propaganda because it was so demoralising and mixed with truth and really rather insidious. We said some nasty things, really nasty, but it would have been a nasty job if it hadn't been wartime.

What strikes me is that elsewhere you said how utterly important the truth is to you and especially the truth about yourself. Here you are saying how much you enjoyed working with people who were concocting ingenious lies.

Yes, because we knew we were doing it. We were lying properly because we did know the truth. Writing a novel you have to be quite aware that what you are writing is not at all true. Such a character did not cross the road at such a time; this is not true. A lot of people can't read novels from that point of view – they can't suspend disbelief and can't see that what your writing stands for is a kind of truth that you hope will emerge from it.

But would you say that there has to be a kind of psychological truth to the characters?

Oh yes. Yes, I would say so. One hopes so.

So there's no contradiction between this comparatively brief period where you relished the ingenuity of making up stories and your commitment to the truth otherwise?

Yes.

You mentioned the hostel that you stayed in during the war. There are a lot of writers who when asked, 'How much of this has come from your life?' shy away and say there's nothing autobiographical. You've always been absolutely open about it. Why is this?

Because I use the background but I invent a great deal. It's not the very fact, but it's the sort of thing. Two weeks ago I was at Norwich University giving a reading, and in Norwich among the people there – the audience – two women were at that hostel with me in the forties. It was an amazing thing. And of course they recognised the place in my book but they knew it wasn't them.

Did they think that they recognised some of the characters?

I think they did, yes, but they recognised the characters as the sort of thing, rather than that person. It would be rather like taking an eye here and a nose there, as the police make an Identikit.

Is this process of transforming your experience into fiction semi-conscious; it's just going on the whole time?

It goes on the whole time while I'm writing a novel. But I exclude automatically – unconsciously, I think – I exclude what is of no use to me, and take in what is of use, and write notes and write it down. I sometimes refer to notes, not always.

And you yourself crop up in your novels, in some form?

I think I must crop up through every character in a way.

Barbara Vaughan in The Mandelbaum Gate?

Yes. I don't see where, otherwise, one's knowledge comes from. One has to feel things. And so I suppose one is in every character, a bit. Barbara Vaughan?

Yes, a Catholic convert, half-Jewish.

Well, in fact I had somebody else in mind but it was a situation that I was interested in – half-Jewish is interesting, I think.

You say you are half-Jewish, because you are. In strictly Orthodox circles you aren't half-Jewish because your father was a Jew and your mother wasn't. So why does the half-Jewishness matter to you?

I really don't know, except I was very fond of my father. But I don't know how it comes out.

But you're not prepared to have people deny that you should call yourself half-Jewish?

Either a full Jew or you're nothing – well, that's according to Jewish usage or law. But I'm talking in the English language and we talk about half-Jews, or part-Jews. I think that's perfectly plain and I don't see that I shouldn't. It's a very important part of my self-identity, because I had a Jewish family, and still have, and a Christian family. And I still have cousins and rather more children because I'm old now, but rather more children of cousins, second cousins and once removed – there are plenty of them.

Are there Jewish observances and rituals and things like that which you still have a fondness for?

Well, I wasn't brought up with a great many of those. It was more just a family thing. I had one aunt who was more observant and used to take me to their feasts and their house, and I'd be there with my brother, and we'd take it all in, and I felt quite happy that way. There was no conflict between the two families – that was another nice thing. When I was very young, they were young people, and they all seemed to call each other by their first name. I never was aware of the conflict between the Jews and the Christians in our family.

Now, your writing. Precision – we've discussed that, one characteristic of it. The sense of poetry is the other that you've always insisted on. How do you define the poetry that you believe is implicit in your use of language?

It's not so much the use of language, it's the fact that I am aware when writing of rhythms, music, and a poetic vision of things. I do see things in a different way from ordinary fictional vision. I know that I have a poetic turn of mind. I claim that. Whether it's right or not I don't know, but that's what I feel. And I think language certainly has to do with it because it's a musical thing; and the composition of my books is really musical, to my mind. I know when I'm coming to the end and what I should do, and various things like that, through a musical sense, although I've never studied music seriously.

I think you've also described it as being about construction and lyricism and a reversal of circumstances at the end.

Yes, I like that. Reversal of circumstances is what Aristotle called Peripetea. I like that very much, towards the end, a reversal of circumstances.

Is there an element of the perverse, almost; of catching the reader by surprise?

Yes. Yes, I think it's perverse. It's got to appear to be true. I like a plausible book. I don't like a book where it couldn't possibly happen. If not, if I'm fictional, I like it to be absolutely fictional. I can give you an example. The last book I wrote was called *Aiding and Abetting* and it was about Lord Lucan, and I didn't know what to do with him at the end. And so I did a fictional end, and I arranged for him to be eaten by cannibals in Africa. And it's extremely fictional, that bit, but I wanted it there, to say to people, 'You know, you don't need to believe it but this is what I'm saying.'

But you say partly it was because you weren't quite sure what to do with the book at that stage?

I had no idea what to do with him. I wanted him to have some form of just reward, and I thought this was an amusing one.

Your novelist character in Memento Mori, *Charmian Colston, says that in many of her books she gets into a tangle about halfway through. Then one of her friends says, 'I know that Charmian is now going to say "but at a certain stage the characters take over"' and that is what she then says. Very naughty, of course. But an element of truth in this with yourself?*

I don't find so much that the characters take over, no. But I do find that in the middle of a book I do get into a tangle, and then I make it worse as a way of getting out of it somehow. I just complicate it again, even more, and then get out of it.

You wouldn't stop and go back?

No. I very seldom change paragraphs and things around. Having thought about it, I don't move things about constructionally or anything like that. I've heard that it's very useful for people who do move things about to have a computer, but it wouldn't suit me because I just write on.

So once you've got into a tangle, you write your way through it?

Well, I rather try to complicate it even more so that I've got to get out of it.

It is remarkable (if you weren't the writer that you are) that you don't say, 'I'll now chuck all that up and try a different direction.' That never enters your mind?

I think it might have happened with a short story or two. It could happen. It has happened in my life but hardly ever.

Have you ever had writer's block?

Well, yes, I have had writer's block, but not really when I sit down with a pen. You know, I really have to sit down to it and then something happens.

And how do you start a novel, or when do you know that there's a novel ready to come out?

I really don't know. Just when I've got a clear day with nothing else to do, I see to it that I clear the decks and then I can start, having thought about the theme, so I just start. I don't think there's any difficulty in starting, for me at least, because I've been doing it so often.

But is there always a novel or two in the queue almost writing itself in your mind?

There used to be but now I've only got one at a time. I used to have two at a time, three at a time. I left it so late in life that everything was bursting out and I'd do two novels a year. But now I don't have the energy to write as I used to.

Which was how?

I used to write twelve hours a day; now I do three, if I'm lucky, three hours.

And you'd sometimes get up, in the old days, in the middle of the night and write?

Yes. In the old days I used to do that but I don't do it now. Besides, I write in the morning now, if I write at all. I used to write at night best, when everyone was asleep.

You've described yourself as a writer in action, and you've said you pause and you think, and then you strike like a cat.

Yes, that's it. I strike. I'm absolutely aware of striking.

You're striking at the image, or the phrase?

The whole concept. I would say the whole concept of the book. I like to begin that way, to get it down and then flow on.

You've said that your ideas take form as if you're shuffling the cards of your ideas. And the cards are a sort of sacrament. Is that part of the Catholic nature that people write about in your writing?

Yes. Well, I'm wondering if Catholicism does come out in my writing, unless I make a Catholic character or a situation. I don't know that. It's just that Catholicism gives me an inner stability which enables me to write better, I feel. But the idea that in order to express anything spiritual – which is partly in a novel, there's a spiritual element – you have to have something material; that's the sacramental side. So in fact the material aspect is really just pens, notebooks, time, me, energy and a desk – that sort of thing. And that's the sacramental element, I think.

But you say Catholicism gave you 'a certainty and a stability which enabled you to write better'?

Stability, yes. I was very tentative before. I wrote biographies and I was very tentative about creative work.

Were you frightened of the word creation or the thought that you were creative?

I'm really not sure about that. I was just a little worried, tentative. Would it be right, would it not be right? Can I write a novel about that? Would it be foolish, wouldn't it be? And somehow with my religion – whether one has anything to do with the other, I don't know, but it does seem so – I just gained confidence, and I don't care if it's foolish or anything, I just write.

But you're not a preaching, moralistic sort of Catholic?

No. I've never had any desire – probably I should have – but I've never had any desire to change people's characters or to convert them to any idea of mine. I like to express my ideas but I have no idea to proselytise. I haven't got it in me. People are what they are, you know. I don't like to go round changing people.

There's an awkward squad side to your belief, isn't there? Your admiration for Job, the first man in the Old Testament to challenge God. Explore that a bit.

Well, Job is every author's character, he's wonderful. It's the most beautiful poem anyway. It's almost comic the way he says to God, 'Come out like a man and reason with me! You're not saying anything, you're not doing anything, I'm here.' I love the satire of it, trying to talk to God, which is absolutely impossible.

Is there an element of that in yourself as well, of your Catholicism?

Yes, very much.

Do the priests approve?

I don't see priests a great deal but I think they approve. If they don't, they keep quiet about it.

And you have a very strong sense of the devil, don't you?

Yes, I do. I really do think that the devil exists. I think evil exists. I think we see it everywhere.

And people who are possessed by the devil, in whom the devil works?

Yes, there are people possessed by the devil in whom the devil works, and there are people who are fiendish themselves. I'm quite sure of that. You can't do anything with them because that is their nature.

But some of the characters in your books who have a devilish element to them, you give them some of the best lines. Some of them are very funny. Like Dougal in The Ballad of Peckham Rye.

Yes. I've never really said that he was the devil. He's got horns on his head, but they might be cysts, you know, that sort of thing.

Were you conscious of conceding that there is something in the devilish character that is almost attractive because of the black humour?

Yes, there's an ambiguity about that, the fiendish character can be very, very entertaining.

In your books, some people say that the men are usually pretty weak.

I don't know. I think it's natural that a woman should write better about women than about men because I can't really probably conceive what it's like to be a man, and try as I might I can't really get a strong character. I can't think of one. There is a male character in one of my books who I thought was a strong but a sensitive male, a book I wrote called *Reality and Dreams*, about a producer. He's the nearest I could get.

But let's just go back to the fact that you yourself said, after your second or third not very successful relationship with men, that you are a rotten chooser of men!

Awful. Really terrible. Better when I stop!

But the interesting thing is that you look at people through sex or sexuality. Not sex in the sense of having sex but that everybody has a sexual personality.

Everybody has a sexual personality, yes. Yes, I do. I think it would be insulting not to attribute some form of sexuality to everyone one meets. One has to take the whole person.

You've moved a lot in your life, sometimes moving towards experience as we've discussed, sometimes moving away from experience, when you moved from London, away from New York. Has this been both a moving towards and a moving away process?

I went to New York because I really wanted freedom from family preoccupations, but I found it was too distracting after four years. I wrote two books there. I wrote a book called *The Mandelbaum Gate*, after having been in the Middle East; and then I wrote *The Girls of Slender Means* in New York. Here I've written all the other books. I've been in Italy over thirty years. It really is a good place for a writer because I'm away from the literary ambience. I like literary life and I've got a lot of friends who are authors and good ones. But I'd rather be an unknown person here.

You said you have given up a lot in the way of not going to parties and all that in order to write.

I suppose one does as one gets older anyway, but I'm not very keen.

In the book that you wrote about Lord Lucan, Aiding and Abetting, *all that happened more than twenty years ago. That was experience that you gathered at second hand, from newspapers, from television and broadcasting. Is this also another source of taking in experience?*

Yes, it was quite an acute experience when I read it first. I read it over and over again. I wanted to see what happened, and how it could have happened, this strange battering of the nanny in the dark. I always meant to write about it but I thought Lucan will turn up, and there'll be complications of various kinds. And then I thought of a way of doing it where it didn't matter if he did turn up. With *Aiding and Abetting* I very much wanted to get off my chest also the story of the fake stigmatic. I always wanted to write about that.

What appealed to you about that?

Well, I remember I knew some nurses at the time because they were staying at a boarding house I was staying at, Irish nurses. And they were sending off their poor little bits of money to this girl in Bavaria, this woman who was supposed to have stigmata. And they used to hand me out prayer sheets and all sorts of things and say how she'd work miracles. I used to try to dissuade them, I said, 'Oh, don't waste your money on that.' And years later I heard that she had been exposed as a fake, and she covered herself with menstrual blood every month and just held up her hands. But she did apparently do miracles. I suppose, psychologically, it would happen that people would be impressed to feel it, you know. And apparently she did do some good. I don't know what happened to her.

Does that raise problems for you as a Catholic? Because on the one hand, what could be more abusive of the Catholic faith than the fake stigmata, but then, some people were cured. It's very tricky, isn't it?

Yes, it's amazing. I don't know. I think there's a lot of that going on, fakery in the Catholic Church. It's a big Church. It's full of all sorts of things. But I think there's a lot of fake. And I don't base my faith on fakes and miracles and things. It is a problem: if indeed there were miracles, she did do some cures, curing someone miles and miles away, just by praying for them.

Do you believe in miracles?

Well, I believe that there can be miracles, yes, but I've never seen one, never experienced one. I've never had a psychic experience in all my life although I've written about ghosts and things.

And yet you've had a sense of things outside you and bigger than you, and things almost directing you?

Yes. I have great faith in the supernatural, the existence of something bigger than myself. And the Catholic Church seems to me to sum it up. Besides, I like Christianity as a religion. I think it's awfully good. It's the best that there is, as far as I'm concerned.

In your own experience it is a benign influence and a benign experience, this supernatural?

Yes. Yes.

And you also felt it very strongly in the physical world. The Victoria Falls, you said, gives you an incredible sense.

Yes, that was really an intensely, almost religious experience. But I'm not alone there. A lot of people felt that, especially the Africans. They have an intensely religious awareness of the Falls. It's an enormous mile-long thing – you look up and down, and you can't see the beginning of it or the end. But it was very amazing. I found that the Africans were equally moved.

Do you think that we lack in general a sense of the numinous, the spiritual, in our lives today?

Well, I think we notice it when it does come, when it's there. It's just that we've lost touch with natural things. I also felt very much that sense of being in touch with nature once in India. I was on an island outside Bombay, and my friends had gone away to take photographs and things, and I was sitting alone, and some monkeys came on a rock opposite me and looked at me. And I looked at them. And it was an amazing experience. They were saying, 'Look at her.' And I was looking at them.

Did you have any spiritual experiences when you were looking at the Christian sites in Israel and Jordan?

Yes, I thought that you have to be there to realise that miracles could happen. There is a sense that the miracles of the Bible could happen on those spots. It was quite different from learning about it far away, you know. Especially at Mount Sinai, and where the Sermon on the Mount took place. The miracles of the Bible became more plausible to me.

Are there other aspects of the world around us that you're taking in intensively through your newspapers and television?

At the moment it's just, I think, *The Finishing School*. I'm in that sort of ambience at the moment, thinking of it.

Is it your credo that you feel you've done enough to realise yourself and you've said, 'The really important thing is to start, it doesn't always matter if you finish'?

No, but it can't matter if you finish, because we die in the middle of something, usually. And it can't be an obligation to finish anything. But one hopes to finish things, complete things. Yes, I feel I've realised myself but I'm never happy, you know. I want to finish something else, a number of things.

Is it a question of doing what Eliot said, the need to justify your existence?

Probably. Yes, one likes to justify an existence, but I don't know, I think sitting in the sun is justifying your existence. Quite honestly, he was very puritanical, Eliot!

Which you're not?

No, I'm not. But I'd like to do more. I want to finish this and a few other things. I've started a play. I'd like to finish that too.

DAVID SYLVESTER

'Somewhere between prayer and sex'

In general, I have been talking to people who create – a painter, a sculptor, a composer. Most people don't regard the job of criticism as either creative or constructive; indeed, they probably see it as the reverse of creative. But in the field of the visual arts, there was one critic who was widely regarded as standing head and shoulders above his colleagues. He was David Sylvester, not just a critic but a writer, an interpreter, by no means uncritical, of the works of artists and sculptors of the last century. A curator, too, of major exhibitions, and a consultant to collectors of modern art. Francis Bacon was his friend. Giacometti used him as a model. Howard Hodgkin has called him the only sacred monster who has ever existed in the English art world. He had that kind of grandeur, and sadly he died not long after I spoke to him.

You've interviewed many artists in your life: De Kooning, Motherwell, David Smith, and Bacon, of course, extensively. You've written that you like interviewing them because 'one has the illusion that one is helping the artist to speak for himself'. How do you feel about being interviewed, because you certainly don't need to be helped to speak for yourself?

Well, to be honest, I feel pretty alarmed.

Alarmed about what?

The prospect of being interviewed.

But you're not bad at putting your thoughts into words in an extempore way in front of the microphone?

And on the whole, not talking about myself.

Haven't you written about yourself?

In a book of my essays, I wrote a short introduction in which I tried to put the book into the framework of a context and I have lately started to write an autobiographical book. Maybe, as people get older, as they begin to run short of ideas, they turn to autobiography.

Well, you don't seem to be short of ideas, but we'll come back to that later. It's been said that the interesting times in people's lives aren't those where things go right, but the times when they seem to go wrong. Now, you left school at fifteen without a School Certificate. You could have gone up to Trinity, Cambridge to read Moral Sciences; you didn't. You spent some years painting, very intensively, until you found out that you were no good. Do you regret any of those dead ends?

The dead end that I mostly regret in my life was that I spent about five years or more in the 1950s, when I was in my early thirties, backing horses and dogs. I spent those years on the race-course and the greyhound track. I had an obsession with beating the bookmakers and, apart from losing a lot of money, I spent a lot of time in ridiculous remorse. I don't mean remorse at the fact that I was doing it, but remorse that I backed the wrong horse. And I think that that was a pretty fruitless time. I don't think I learned much from it, certainly in proportion to the amount of time I expended on it. But I got an obsession with it.

It's remarkable that you cured the obsession, because usually if somebody has been betting obsessively for five years, they'd be very lucky to get out of it scot-free.

Well, I got out of it in the following way. At the beginning of one year I decided to keep precise accounts of my turnover, winnings and losses and expenses. I put down even every copy of the *Sporting Life* and the telephone calls and everything. And in the middle of July, after the first July meeting at Newmarket, I realised that I was losing too much and that my smaller bets tended to be on winners and my larger bets tended to be on losers. And I decided, as I'd decided with painting, that I was no good at it. And I gave it up overnight.

Whose money were you losing?

My own. Partly it came from money I'd earned and partly it came from having bought works of art well and then they'd gone up in price, gone up in value, and I was able to sell them to fuel my betting.

Do you look back at any particular work that you sold then to fuel this obsession and bitterly regret that you sold it?

I regret that less than I regret the waste of time. Because after all, that period of one's life is a very fruitful period and I was writing very little.

You left school at fifteen without a School Certificate and by the age of eighteen you were starting to write about art. Where did your knowledge come from? Was there a teacher, some influence that said, 'Look, if you're really interested in art, this is where you should start looking, this is what you should start reading'?

I think that I was destined to practise criticism. I'll tell you why I think so. There were various things I wanted to do when I was a boy. Above all, I wanted to be a professional cricketer, but I wasn't good enough at that. I wanted to be a jazz musician, primarily composer and arranger rather than an executant; I wasn't good enough at that. When I was fifteen, just before I left school, I wanted to do something very modest and quiet and scientific; I wanted to be an analytical chemist, which would have been a quiet and obscure life. But I think that I was doomed to be a critic for this reason. The first time I went to a professional football match – and of course, the interesting thing about this is that a boy of eleven going to a football match today would have seen hundreds of games on television – all I'd seen of professional football was the odd thirty seconds, when a bit of an international appeared on a news reel.

Which was the most exciting moment that one could possibly think of, wasn't it?

Yes. But I went to this match and I could only completely experience it by going home and writing about it, writing a report of the match. I must say that I showed myself to be a journalist, rather than a writer, a real writer, because I think if I'd been a real writer, I would have written a report on one's first experience of a professional football match. But I didn't do that. I did an imitation of a newspaper report of a match, in which I wrote that Arsenal were playing West Bromwich Albion and I wrote about Arsenal as if I'd already seen them play a hundred times. I did a total imitation, a total fake, of a genuine football report by an experienced watcher. And then it seemed to me that there was somehow a need to complete the aesthetic experience by reporting on it, analysing it, putting it into words. And then, too, I was very obsessed with making lists in order of merit. I did this with jazz musicians; I did it with cricketers and footballers. By the time I was thirteen or fourteen, I'd produced my World All-time Eleven, both First Eleven, Second Eleven, Third Eleven, Fourth Eleven, Fifth Eleven – all based on reading and the study of statistics.

You were doing fantasy cricket long before it was invented in the papers. I think every schoolboy was, weren't they?

But it was a particularly obsessive quality, in my own case. I think I did it more than most. And I think that, after all, two of the characteristics of the critic are the need to analyse and describe what one has seen and the other, the need to make evaluations. And these were both strong in me at that time.

Can you remember what your top ten list of the world's greatest painters was?

No, that didn't come until much later – by the time I was about twenty-five years old and had seen a good deal of art around Europe, a good deal of the old masters because of course, you know, growing up, I didn't see any old masters. In the first place I became interested in art, in looking at painting, through a modern painting. A black-and-white reproduction of Matisse's *La Dance*.

What book were you looking at?

I was looking at Robert Goldwater's *Primitivism in Modern Painting*.

Why did you have that? Was it in the house? Was it in the library?

No. I knew a young man, slightly older than myself – he was a student. He converted me to Communism, though I didn't join the Party, and we talked about a lot of things, besides politics. He had this book by Robert Goldwater – who became a friend of mine in later years. I looked at this book, I saw this Matisse, it gave me a visceral experience – the linear tension of the forms of this circle of dancers – and suddenly I was turned on to painting and a week later I started to paint. Now, I was only interested in modern art at first. You see, you were cut off from the old masters during the war. I had this experience in 1941.

The old masters from the National Gallery were all in store in those Welsh slate quarries, weren't they, because of the bombing?

Exactly. By the time I had seen some painting, say by 1950, I would say that my top ten . . . I know that Titian came top of the list. Others among the first three or four were Michelangelo and Rembrandt and Velazquez. I think Rubens, too, Piero della Francesca, and Masaccio.

Where did the poor old moderns come in?
Should I tell you how I didn't become art critic of *The Times*?
Yes.

The critic of *The Times* was a wonderful man, but he sometimes enjoyed himself too much at lunch. And one afternoon after lunch, he insulted the president of the Royal Academy and became *persona non grata* at the Royal Academy. Well, in those days, in the mid-fifties, it was impossible for the art critic of *The Times* not to be *persona grata* at the Royal Academy – there was an establishment in those days. And for a time *The Times* had a marvellous entertainments editor (so John Lawrence was proud to call himself – he was very insistent he was the entertainments editor, not the arts editor) and he employed three or four of us writing, trying out to see who would be a likely successor. I think I was his favourite choice and I was asked one day to a lunch, which confirmed more than anything the existence of the establishment. They were all senior civil servants, or ex-senior civil servants, like Lord Bridges, or generals or bishops. And there they were, these regular *Times* Thursday lunchers, all round the table. At the centre was old Mr Walter, the owner. On his right was the guest of honour, Sir Mortimer Wheeler. On his right was William Haley. On his right was me and on my right was a man called Lawrence Irving, whose only real claim to fame was that he was a nephew of Henry Irving. And he was supposed to be *The Times*'s art expert. And Haley talked to me – we were both shy, but within those limits we got on all right. Then, Lawrence started on me. Now the thing is, this is the important thing, I had been writing the most avant-garde criticism ever to appear in *The Times*. And I'd been writing articles in that spirit for some time. That morning, an article of mine had appeared in the *Listener* about a Cézanne exhibition at the Tate, which I'd raved about. Cézanne is my favourite painter to this day. And he said, 'Do you really think Cézanne is as great as you say?' 'Oh yes,' I said, 'and he's the last really great painter.' I didn't get the job of art critic at *The Times* – which I desperately wanted, because I wanted respectability – I didn't get the job and I was confidentially told the reason was that

I was thought to be too 'retardataire' in my views. But I would still say that I don't think that any twentieth-century artists, even Picasso, Matisse and Mondrian, are the equal of the great old masters. I think Cézanne was the last of the pantheon.

I want to get you to talk about looking, because that's what we all do more or less imperfectly when we go to galleries. Can you tell me how you look at a painting – or is it so instinctive that you can't?

I look.

Yes, but how? In a systematic way?

Oh no. Not at all. I just look.

At the whole, or at parts? And how do you start to put it together?

Well, by what my eye's attracted to. I mean, in certain art it might be to the brush strokes. In certain art it might be the total thing. In the case of Poussin, one of my favourite painters, it would be the architectural structure. In another case it might be in response to a mood.

If you're puzzled by a work, if you're coming to something completely new, do you fall back on your professional skill at looking and the ingredients in your professional skills are such and such?

I don't have any sense that I have professional skills that I can resort to. The experience is instinctive. It's somewhere between prayer and sex.

Between prayer and sex, or both prayer and sex?

Both prayer and sex. When I say 'sex', what I mean is responses that one feels in one's body.

And if you don't feel that sort of response in your body, does that say to you that there's something in the work which is less good than it might be?

Not necessarily. The response is no different from one's response to poetry or drama or music. It can occur in various parts of the body, it can occur in one's spine, it can occur in the back of one's neck, it can reveal in one's hands, it can occur in one's solar plexus.

At best, there's real physical reaction?

Yes. Oh yes. And sometimes, when I was young, when I was really at my best, when I got the acutest responses, I would sometimes go into a gallery and look at paintings and I was so sensitive to them that I sometimes felt that I had two or three skins less than normal. The thing was going through my body so forcefully. But I don't necessarily reject what doesn't happen to turn me on and sometimes being turned on is a long thing. For example, with Matisse, I've been very moved by Matisse. I used to go regularly to the Barnes Foundation, near Philadelphia, where there are some great Matisses. And there was a series of mural paintings there and I could go and look at them for an hour and nothing would happen. I'd go out to the delicatessen across the road and I'd come back and look again and after a time – this sounds terribly pretentious, but it is true – I would have a feeling like that of elevation.

That's where the prayer bit comes into it?

No. I think the prayer is more the concentration.

Elevation is the fulfilment of the prayer, if you're lucky?

Yes, exactly. Exactly. But it took time and I learned to be patient with Matisse. Now, Picasso is the exact opposite. Picasso hits you immediately in the solar plexus and then often fades. But Matisse comes gradually. And so often one has to be patient and wait. But I don't necessarily assume that the things that don't turn me on most are less good. The artist who turns me on most regularly, it's almost as good as a drug, it can be counted on, is Barnett Newman. When I was installing the exhibition of Picasso at the Tate, and earlier at the Pompidou, there were some Newmans in other rooms. And I would go and look at the Newmans and I'd have a physical response much stronger than I had to the Picassos. And the same happened when I was installing De Kooning in Washington at the MGA and there were the Newman *Stations of the Cross* in another room. They turned me on more. But that does not necessarily mean that I think that Newman is a greater artist than Picasso. It's just that there's some ingredient in it that turns me on.

Most of us, when we're going through a gallery, spend a minute looking at each picture. Now clearly we should spend longer, but what do you feel about that statistic? Either 'that's life, that's people' or 'that's sad'?

I would say that the average is probably less than a minute. Michael Compton, when he was working at the Tate, computed that the average time that people spend in front of a picture was about three seconds. But I want to say this: very often, the thing grabs you at once, instantaneously. There are cases where one has to wait, but there are other cases where the thing grabs you immediately and shatters you immediately. It varies. The final intensity of the experience can come quickly, can come slowly.

So it's not necessarily wrong? Somebody might go to it and see in three seconds that that's a shattering picture.

I think that often happens with artists. Artists respond very fast and don't necessarily stay long.

How do you stay fresh in looking at works of art? Do you find that the sheer weight of what you know and what you've seen is so intense, that the moment you start looking you're already saying 'there's a bit of X and a bit of Y and a bit of Z there', rather than reacting as you did when you were younger?

No. I think I still react to the thing itself, though not so intensely. But I have to own up, with some shame, to something. And that is I find it very difficult to suppress the critic in me. Often, when I'm deeply moved by a piece of Beethoven or Bach, I'll say to myself, 'Now, this is not like Eliot's "music hurt so deeply that you are the music while the music lasts",' because one suddenly detaches oneself and thinks, 'well, of course Bach is the greatest composer,' or 'of course, Beethoven is the greatest composer' and that means you're not actually listening. And I'm afraid that I do have a habit of losing contact with the work itself and getting involved in evaluation.

Yes, but you'd be superhuman if you didn't. And in any case, you have a job to do as well as reacting to the work, don't you?

I don't in the case of music, but I still tend to get involved in evaluation. I'm rather ashamed of it. I do certainly get struck by resemblances to other works of art. I don't necessarily go looking for them, but I certainly get struck by them. Would you agree with Eliot that the idea of looking at art is 'music hurt so deeply that you are the music while the music lasts'? How often does one

249

actually manage that? How often does one get that total immersion in a work of art, whether it's a play or a work of music or a work of art?

Less and less. And I guess for very much the same reasons as you say. And I also regard it as part of my own professional de-formation!

There is one thing I'd say, though, about standing back and analysing. I think that one of the things that enables me to perform as a critic is this: I'm not talking about this silly business of evaluation, but I do have a capacity while being deeply, physically moved by the experience, at the same time of being able to analyse the experience and analyse the work. I can be incredibly involved; I can be feeling, tingling all over, but at the same time be able to detach myself and observe what's happening. And I think that that is a useful characteristic if one is a critic.

Where do you stand between your role as somebody who serves the public, and your role vis-à-vis the artists, many of whom you know very well?

It doesn't help things, to be writing about living artists. It doesn't help. I prefer writing about dead artists. It's easier. You don't get that feeling that the chap who made it is going to read what you've written. It's very, very difficult to eliminate from one's thought the fact that the artist is going to read it!

But do you believe, do you hope, that what you write, perhaps especially when it is critical, is going to help that artist?

No, I don't believe that. At best, I believe that I'm writing a love letter to an artist. If you've been moved by the work, sometimes one does feel that one is writing him a love letter.

Is it significant that when you thought for a period that Bacon had gone off the boil, that you really didn't like what he was painting, that you wrote nothing about him for four years?

Yes. I must be specific about the date. It was from 1955 or 1956 on, until the early sixties.

And your response to what you saw as the shortcomings of his work was to say 'I won't write about him at all'?

I also avoided him personally. But there was another thing in that alienation from Bacon and that was I was angry with him about his ridiculing Jackson Pollock. I thought that his dismissal of Jackson Pollock – who is a greater artist than Bacon, of course – I just found it impossible to take. And I felt alienated from him. Of course, Bacon never stopped pouring scorn on Pollock.

What was the compulsion? It must have been a defensive reaction, wasn't it?

Well, I don't know if it was defensive. Bacon was pretty scornful about most artists and he rejected most of his own work, too. But he did reject most things. Two of the artists, both of whom I admire most and with whom I've been friendliest, Bacon and Giacometti, I disliked the way in which they found so little other art that pleased them and that they accepted. I also liked De Kooning, he was an artist of similar stature. De Kooning's ability to appreciate other artists – I enjoyed that in him.

But you then came back to Bacon and you admitted that the years when you hadn't liked what he was doing were an essential period of transition and you wrote that. And you've also been very candid about the artists that you didn't recognise at the time, of whom Jackson Pollock was one and Rauschenberg was another. Have you found that difficult, or do you regard that as a piece of professionalism, that when you get something wrong it is your responsibility to explain to the public that that's what you've done?

I think one has got a responsibility to do that, yes.

But have you found it difficult?

No. It's not a secret shame.

But you've been very directly active in the art world in other senses. You have been a major curator of exhibitions. How much does that matter to you?

When I started writing about art, I didn't think that this was something that was going to happen. It happened because I was asked to do a big show in 1951 and it is certainly the part of my work that I most enjoy by far.

What do you enjoy about it?

One of the last conversations that I had with Henry Moore, before he became senile, I said, 'The older I get, the less I like writing about art and the more I like choosing and installing exhibitions.' When I'm writing about art I always feel that what I have to say is beside, it's to one side. I never get it. I can never grasp the artist. When I do the exhibition, I have the feeling that I can really present an artist in a way that shows his work at its best. I feel I have an ability to choose the best works, and to place them well and tellingly. And that whole business of taking a group of works and taking a space, putting the works in the space, the different configurations one can make in different spaces, is absolutely marvellous. It's the nearest one comes to making art, because an exhibition is a kind of collage.

Aren't you overwhelmed by the process, by the task of selection?

Much less than I'm overwhelmed by having to write about a great artist. But the thing was, I said this to Henry and Henry said, 'Oh, I disagree. Words are the most powerful instrument of communication. Not images, words. Tolstoy's novels, those are the most powerful instruments of communication.'

There was an occasion – one of your first really seminal meetings with various artists in Paris when you were a comparatively young man – and you were introduced by Kahnweiler, weren't you, to the whole group of them. You just came into this room and there they all were, the legendary names of the contemporary art world.

Two of the greatest French writers of the time were in the room. It was an amazing experience.

Did you meet Giacometti on that occasion?

Yes. He painted my portrait in 1960 and I think there were about twenty-four sittings, something like that. And I was always touched by this. He had two models at the time, whom he was painting. One was myself and the other was Yanaihara, the Japanese professor of philosophy. And I would sit for Giacometti in daylight. He would get up, you know, about lunchtime because he went to bed about six in the morning and he'd paint me until the light failed, about seven o'clock at night. Then I'd go off and then Yanaihara would arrive and Giacometti would paint him for a few hours. And after that, Yanaihara would disappear to make love to Giacometti's wife. I'm not being indiscreet; this fact is in the public domain. Giacometti encouraged this. But Giacometti would suggest at the end of the session we worked together, towards the end of my posing, 'Let's meet for dinner at midnight'. And I'd say, 'You've seen enough of me today. You don't want to see me again later!' And he said, 'Those who work together, eat together.'

You've written about the extraordinary direct gaze that his sculptures have, those incredible tiny heads are full frontal. He demands that gaze. They look at the viewer and he demands them back. Was that how he painted you? Was that the sort of engagement between you?

No, he couldn't paint me that way, because you're sitting opposite me in exactly the same way as Giacometti was when he painted me, only two or three feet nearer. And you'll notice that I'm not looking at you full in the face. I'm looking at you with my head turned very slightly to one side.

That's because we're not sitting exactly opposite one another.

No, it's not that at all. It's because I have a defect of eyesight and if I look straight in front of me with both eyes, I get double vision. And it's a defect of eyesight that I've had since birth. So, when Giacometti painted me, I wasn't frontal. I was just slightly, halfway towards a three-quarter view.

Did that irritate him?

He dealt with it and Theriad who was a great man in the art world, said that he thought that Giacometti's portrait of me was his greatest portrait. And one or two writers have suggested that Giacometti deliberately varied his usual practice, but he didn't. The only way I could sit for him was looking slightly askew. And actually, I think that possibly it was a help to him not to follow the usual. I think if Giacometti had a fault – he was a very great artist – but I think if he had a fault, it was because he was too formulaic in approach to the subject. And I think in a way that maybe his drawings are the greatest part of his work, because there he didn't insist – with drawings you can't, when you're drawing a portrait, but anything else – on that intense frontality.

You say somewhere that towards the end of his life there was a feeling among some, certainly Picasso, that perhaps what Giacometti was doing was less interesting. And somebody said to Picasso, 'That is because Giacometti is looking for a new solution to figuration.' And Picasso said, 'There isn't a solution. There never is a solution. And that is as it should be.' Is that, in a sense, the key statement about art? The person who looks for the answer certainly is not going to find it, and shouldn't be looking for it.

I think it's a marvellous statement. And you agree, don't you?

I certainly recognise it. But is that one of the reasons why you are ready to go back and review what you yourself have said? Because anything that you have written is never ex cathedra and finished? It's the best response you can make at the time?

Oh yes. That would certainly be the case.

I've often thought that you can judge a person, or have an interesting view of them, according to their enemies. You had this very public row, which I think you've still kept up, with John Berger. What really divides you and do you regret anything about the public nature of your disagreement?

I think that Berger was a wonderful writer. A marvellous writer. And I thought that his judgement of contemporary art was very bad. And because he was such a good writer he had a lot of influence, and I thought his influence was distracting the public's attention from the best art towards less good art. And I thought that that was not a good thing. So I thought he was a dangerous figure.

Am I fair to say that you regarded him as an enemy?

As a personal enemy, certainly not. We started by being friends. Ideological differences came between us. But then, I think it was his first novel *A Painter of Our Time*, he wrote a caricature of me (I was a character in the book) and I thought it was an unkind caricature, and not only unkind but unfair, because he suggested that I was corrupt. And I don't think I am especially corrupt. The one thing that has corrupted me is friendship with artists. I haven't been corrupted by the temptations of money, but I have been corrupted by feelings of kindness towards artists whom I like, and haven't been as tough with them as I ought to have been.

As you've raised the question of money, does the fact that you write within the context of an increasingly commercialised art world ever

result in you saying to yourself, 'I know that certain people want this
new artist to be valued and I'm not going to let them make some easy
money'?

First of all, I must say that the amounts one is paid for writing
about art are derisory. If, for example, my advice is sought by a
collector on a purchase he wants to make and I give that advice, I
can be paid a fee for that. I'm not in the least ashamed of doing
that. I have sometimes advised a collector not to buy a work by an
artist I both like and whose work I admired, but I've said, 'You
should not buy that work.' And one gets a fee for that kind of
advice. The difference between the speed with which one makes
money as soon as one gets involved in the commercial side of the
art world, and the sort of money one makes by sweating over a
book for two years, or an article for two weeks and ends up by
getting £200, is appalling and it constantly appals me. Or by
working on an exhibition in the public sector. The amount one is
paid is derisory.

It appals you, but does it upset you personally?

Yes.

But still, you would never say, 'Damn it! I'll go into dealing, just be a
commercial consultant and charge a thousand pounds a day!'

In the 1950s my admiration for Kahnweiler led me to think that
I wanted to become a dealer, because one can be very creative as
a dealer. And I admire dealers, the best dealers, on the whole more
than I admire the best museum people. They have to have enormous courage, they have to put their money where their mouth
is. And I respect good dealers and I respect dealing as a profession.
Although it's a dirty profession, at the same time it's a valuable
profession.

Why is it dirty?

Because you have to get the better of other dealers and dealers
tend to be unscrupulous in the way they do that. They're often
dirty to artists and they're often dirty to people selling works to
them, not giving them as much value as they should do.

I wonder though, David, how good a dealer you would have been?
And that's on the basis of something that you said a little while ago –

*that you have hated being cruel to and critical of artists whom you know
as a critic. As a dealer, presumably you have to be honest and perhaps
rather brutal with artists.*

The answer is that after entertaining this thought for a little in
the mid-fifties – I wasn't only gambling, but it was about that time
that I did entertain the thought of becoming a dealer – I decided
that I couldn't be. For this reason: once or twice I'd been given
works by artists to try and sell on their behalf. And in one or two
cases I was successful and I would make a profit out of the
collector, to whom I sold the thing. Now the collector would, in
most cases, be a rich person. But I was ashamed of taking a profit.
The successful dealer is somebody who, when he's made a million
dollars out of selling a collector work, feels he's done the collector
an enormous favour. And he probably has. But in my case when I
felt that, I felt an irrational sense of guilt that I was making a profit
out of selling something.

It's your Communist training, isn't it?

I suppose it is. But it was an irrational sense of guilt and I knew
that it was therefore impossible for me to be a dealer.

*Have your critical sympathies stopped developing? Do you find that
the work of the Damien Hirsts, the Rachel Whitereads, the Gillian
Wearings, people like that, that you come to that as fresh, relatively
speaking, as to the work that you first saw in your twenties and thirties?*

I think that I'm able to respond, viscerally, to the work of artists
born until about 1945–50. After that I tend to feel a bit lost and
don't trust my responses. I used to have, when I was young,
tremendous confidence in my ability to pick winners among the
younger generation. And I find that it's now got out of reach.

*So there is a sense in which what the new generation are doing is
more difficult for you?*

The National Portrait Gallery decided that they wanted to put
me in the gallery and they asked me whom I'd like my portrait to
be done by, which was a wonderful privilege. And I chose Jenny
Saville, who's thirty years old.

*There's been extraordinary change in our lives from the wartime
experience when there was virtually no art for people to see. Today,*

when you can hardly get into Tate Modern and many other galleries, does this present any sort of a problem? Is there a sense in which modern art might now be too popular?

I think all art is much too popular. If I go to a great concert and I see empty seats, I am annoyed. I regret that there are empty seats, and my own response to the music is heightened by the sense of being one of a number of people who are all sitting in that space responding to the same work. But you see, the presence of other people in the concert hall doesn't get in the way. It may increase the coughing a bit, but you get silence. But art needs silence as music needs silence. Not quite as much, but it does need silence.

It certainly needs space.

And it certainly needs space. And one cannot – I cannot – enjoy a work of art with people jostling around me to see it.

So how do we reconcile these two contradictions, as far as the experience of modern art today is concerned?

I don't know the answer to how you give access to works of art and to exhibitions or museum displays which I can see in solitude. But the problem is a terrible problem and I don't know the answer to it.

Are art galleries the new cathedrals? That is where people go to find their spiritual or quasi-spiritual experience?

But in a cathedral at High Mass, people attend to the service and they go there to pray. And they go to become involved.

Is there an element of that in going to a modern gallery?

Not much. Or people wouldn't behave the way they do. They talk too much, they jostle too much, they look too short a time, despite what was said before. They treat it as a theme park. I think a museum should be a temple. But there is a simple, practical problem of the crowds. A cathedral is built – and again, like a concert – it's wonderful when a cathedral is full for a service, but the problem with art is people getting in one another's way, getting in the sight lines of other people. And it's a problem that has to be taken very seriously.

ON INTERVIEWING

We all know what an interview is; or at least we think we do. Almost everyone has been interviewed at some stage in their life: for a market research questionnaire, a job application, a street 'vox pop' – we can all oblige a television reporter with a soundbite. Yet very few people, by contrast, have been involved in the broadcast interview, where ideas or actions are challenged – and must be defended – on the most exposed and public stage. Since the greater part of the contemporary debate on political, social and moral issues takes place on radio or television through exactly this form of exchange, however, it is an activity that deserves closer examination. The interview, and the art of interviewing, now play such an important part in public life that they deserve a second and a third thought.

The interviews that form the basis of this book reflect the experience of a lifetime of interviewing – and a lifetime of change, evolution and development in the way interviews are conducted, and in how I conduct them.

It is more than forty years since I first did an interview on radio. On a basic BBC Course for General Trainees, the course leader, the formidable Miss Macleod, told me not to bother with any thoughts of broadcasting in voice since I had a 'glottal stop'. She was dead wrong but I didn't find that out for some years. Oddly, I was less mortified by her total rejection of my faltering efforts than

I should have been. After all, those dreams of being one day 'the voice that a nation recognised' had no sooner been glimpsed than they were cut off. In the event, her withering dismissal of my first interview attempts had the beneficial effect of putting me off a front-of-microphone career for a decade. However my radio ambitions might shape themselves, being a personality interviewer would not be one of them.

As a current affairs producer in the BBC General Overseas Service in the early 1960s, though, jobbing interviews were simply part of one's role – paying for professional interviewers was too expensive. This kind of interviewing was functional, utilitarian, austere, self-effacing, and entirely dedicated to the cause of giving the listener around the world as much information and clarification as possible. The listener wanted to know, needed to know, 'what, how, why, when, where' and possibly 'what if', though such questions were often frowned on either for being too speculative or, more probably, for skirting too close to an expression of opinion on the part of the interviewer. The BBC in those days, and by extension BBC producers as the Corporation incarnate, had no opinions; or if they did, the proper place to leave them was at the door of the studio. If you wanted to voice your own views, then the press was the place for you, or more likely Parliament.

It is easy to smile at the attitudes of a different era and culture; and, of course, producers could not have, or could not display, 'attitude' in the contemporary sense – a wholly unknown posture at the time. The rules and conventions were limiting and restrictive. They set the interviewer's legs in concrete boots, clogged his mind in glue. They were not designed to bring the best out of the studio exchange. And yet there is something rather admirable about the austerity and self-effacement of the philosophy behind such an approach. It put the interviewer, the broadcaster, the journalist squarely at the service of the audience. Displays of temperament, flashes of exhibitionism, any flirting with the cult of personality interviewing were discouraged and kept in check. The only easing of restraints at the BBC World

Service occurred in the African Service, where the broadcasters understood that live, rolling news and entertainment programming demanded a more characterful, personality-driven approach. The African audience had no truck with Anglo-Saxon stiff-upper-lip broadcasting, the sound of the strangled tonsils, the choked throat. They wanted to hear the whole person communicating his or her whole personality to the whole listener. That is what the BBC African Service gave them and very successful it proved to be.

I have never regretted being trained in such a tight framework. It demanded a severe, intellectual discipline in the preparation and organisation of interviews. Time on air was limited and precious. Much needed to be explained and communicated. Sacrificing the pubescent ego of the interviewer to these higher ideals seemed a small price to pay in order to deliver to listeners what they needed.

When I started interviewing for radio's *Ten o'Clock* programme in 1966 – the predecessor to *The World Tonight* – a more overt studio and microphone style was both demanded and allowed. It was certainly instructive to work with such experienced journalists and fellow presenters as George Scott, Anthony King, the Oxford psephologist David Butler and the constitutional expert Norman Crowther Hunt. All possessed and displayed that bedrock of professional knowledge that allowed interviews to take place on the basis of intellectual equality with the interviewee. The studio challenge was less the personalised confrontation, more that the interviewer's knowledge allowed him or her to interrogate the studio guest with an authority the audience could hear for themselves.

To be sure, there was one well-known broadcaster, already famous on television, whose approach to the radio interview was to arrive in the *Ten o'Clock* office and say breezily to his producer, 'Just five questions on a card, please, dear boy!' He duly read the prepared studio script, read the prepared questions to his studio guest, rarely deviating from what the producer had put in front of him, picked up his fee, drank a glass or two of wine and went on his way. It was deeply disillusioning to me that the subsequent broadcast often sounded perfectly adequate. What was the point of my own painfully researched, laboriously devised questions if a thoughtless production-line approach could achieve almost as much? A lightly adjusted 'Speak Your Weight' machine would have done the job as well.

By the early 1970s that seminal transformation of the radio networks, 'Broadcasting in the Seventies' – which created the present pattern of radio networks from Radios One to Four – replaced the historic rigidities of *Ten o'Clock* – four interviews of four and a half minutes in a twenty-minute slot – with the new-style, flexible formats of *The World Tonight*. Further disillusion lay in store. A key *World Tonight* stalwart not only typed out all his questions in advance, but filed them for future use should he interview the same person twice. He was anxious not to repeat himself, a somewhat irrelevant anxiety given the nature of politics and journalism. Worse still, he stuck to his typed, prepared questions rigidly on air. You could always tell when – as occurred frequently – the studio guest had already answered the question that came next on the pre-planned sheet because the interviewer had to preface his (already answered) question by saying 'Nevertheless . . .' Frustratingly, this style also managed to produce results and was taken seriously by many.

By the late seventies the major inhibition on effective engagement in radio interviewing derived from the fact that the majority of interviews were pre-recorded; in the editing process, the producers worked to deliver the 'tidy' interview. This meant a neat three to four minutes without repetition, deviation or messy inconclusive exchanges. In the process of sanitisation, inevitably, challenge, argument, exchange were left on the editing suite floor because 'they didn't get us anywhere'! They did, of course. They revealed inconsistency, they demonstrated challenge and they revealed the personality under challenge. But the sheer tidiness of the prevailing, and increasingly obsolete, disciplines gave messy interactions a lesser priority than the maximum transmission of information. The BBC has always had a strongly anal-retentive side to it.

I was particularly stung on one occasion when the Foreign Office BBC Governor criticised me for 'letting a Soviet journalist off the hook' in an interview. What had happened was that we had a fairly rowdy exchange during the recording but the producer felt that the argument 'got nowhere' and removed it in its entirety from the final edited tape. What he lost in doing so was just the sense of challenge and engagement that I had wanted, that was required in interviewing a Soviet official and that the BBC Governor rightly noted was missing. In editing as he did, the producer deprived the listener of a crucial ingredient of meaning – emotional meaning rather than pure informational meaning, but the stuff of live broadcasting nevertheless.

I was more than ready for a change of style and direction, for a release from these archaic inhibitions, when I joined the newly devised *Newsnight* at its creation on BBC Two in 1979. The exchanges were live; they were visible; there was no hiding for either the questioner or the questioned. Research, knowledge and personal briefing were even more important. So was a carefully thought-out strategic line of questioning, anticipating responses and the necessary follow-up to those responses. Together with my colleagues Peter Snow and Donald McCormick, we had rambunctious exchanges on air with fractious politicians, though in the early 1980s the most lurid moments came as rival members of the Labour Party, including Eric Heffer and Tony Benn, queued up to proclaim their internecine hatred for one another in the studio. On such occasions our role was less to interview than to hold the coats as the two fraternal opponents squared off. The Social Democratic Party breakaway, it was said, was born in the *Newsnight* studios, with the Labour left acting as enthusiastic accoucheurs.

Though the three main presenters were the 'personalities' who gave the programme its character, I do not think any of us thought of ourselves as 'celebrity interviewers' in the current meaning. We were active journalists, rather, with professional specialisms, who conducted authoritative interviews on the basis of our long acquired knowledge and hard daily research. While I enjoy watching today's prize fight interviews as much as anyone, I do wonder if relentless aggression is the best way of approaching every interviewee, be they never so innocent. Lesser television personalities who ape the aggressive style merely because it is the dominant alpha male one, end up looking strident and petulant rather than frightening and effective.

Equally, on the essential *Today* programme where guilt is assumed the moment the interviewee enters the studio, when the questions become almost as long as the permitted answers, you wonder if the balance has not become a little skewed? This is not to suggest for a moment that the deferential interview is either desirable or possible: it is not. The obstreperous interviewer is the essential counterweight to the pre-briefed, spin-directed Minister. But the dangers of creating a kind of Frankenstein of broadcasting egoism lurks in the corners of many studios.

My own view of the correct role of the interviewer was clarified when Valerie Solti told me of a conversation that the young George Solti had with the great composer-conductor Richard Strauss, who gave the young Hungarian the benefits of his lifelong experience in the orchestra pit. 'Always remember,' said the great composer-conductor, 'when you are conducting, you are not there to enjoy yourself.' That reminder should be plastered on the walls of every studio in broadcasting.

But I'm worried about other aspects of broadcasting as political communication. Very few politicians have not been at the receiving end of the robust studio interview. Why, therefore, have politicians not learned more from their experiences, as their generally ineffective cross-examination of Government Ministers suggests they have failed to do? Of course, Ministers can evade questions on the floor of the Commons even more easily than they can in the studio; they are not exposed to the sustained interrogation from one person as they are when on air. But politicians have not adapted their experiences to their parliamentary behaviour. As a result, the expert robustness of political broadcasters, whatever its occasional shortcomings, has shifted the arena of active political debate away from the House of

Commons and on to the airwaves. Ministers and politicians have contributed to – even connived at – this shift both through their readiness to broadcast at the drop of a telephone, as well as their inability to challenge effectively in their own environment, the Commons debating chamber.

If that raises issues for broadcasters, the questions it raises for politicians are far larger and more profound. Why have MPs allowed their grip on the political debate to be loosened in this way? The only answer can be because of a huge failure of institutional will. There is a democratic price to be paid for this combination of inadvertence, laxity and professional laziness.

What makes the interview such a compelling form of exchange is the continuous nature of the challenge. It does not always occur in real time, but more often than not it does. There is no hiding moment, no respite. Evasions are transparent; failures to deal with a question immediately noticed. Incoherence, insincerity, bluster, bombast reach the listener's ears in a microsecond of their utterance. Character is exposed as much as knowledge and intelligence. There is no time for second thoughts, for backtracking, for the equivalent of rewriting, for the second version, or the chance to reach for the better phrase. Any answer, once made, is in the airwaves and on the record. It cannot be withdrawn. It is a high-risk, high-adrenalin, high-reward activity.

But so it is for interviewers, even if they stick to the safe ground of the obvious and predictable – this too is instantly recognisable. Taking on a politician who should know more about his or her subject than you do involves the risk of looking callow and superficial in your assumptions, lazy and inadequate in preparation, slow in response, leaden in mental footwork. The unselfcritical interviewer can appear self-important, puffed up with synthetic indignation, bullying, overbearing and irritatingly too big for his – or her – boots. The wise interrogator should always remember that it is far easier to ask questions than to answer them. In this sense only, asking questions, even in the public interest, is an irresponsible activity because the questioner is only responsible for his words. The responsibility of the interviewee remains deeper, more serious, more profound and far more difficult.

When I moved from the journalism of asking questions on *Newsnight* to the totally different task of managing the BBC World Service, I rapidly discovered that this particular boot was now on a very different foot. It was my turn to provide the answers to journalists' and politicians' questions. It was harder, far more demanding, more personally testing, but ultimately more satisfying. I felt – and still feel in the heart and heat of the debate about the role and funding of the arts – that to answer questions, to offer solutions to problems is a more mature activity than to ask the questions without ever addressing the possible solutions. The interviewer never has to confront the reality that there are usually no conclusive answers to the questions put. That is the perspective of life from within the studio box; that is the nature of life outside the small studio box.

Where does this place the type of interview contained in this book? The very idea of challenge in its obvious sense is almost impertinent – no artist is obliged to answer for his or her actions or activity. They speak with their art, in whatever form it appears, and can leave it at that if they so wish. There is no obligation to speak out, to be accountable except in their artistic expression. But being human, many of them – though not all – enjoy talking about what they do and even, so they say, learn something from the result. That is not why they talk, but the process of rationalisation can assist, marginally, in the creation process. One of my interviewees spoke for many when he would not talk about future projects in case he 'lost' them by premature and inappropriate verbalisation.

My own assumption was that many creative artists would enjoy, even if they did not need to value, the chance to talk about their life and how they work. Most of them have considerable portfolios of their utterances, catalogue introductions, learned essays about them. There was nothing exclusive in the journalistic sense to be found in the exchanges I sought. So what could I deliver that was different from the already known, or at least could be heard and read as being additional?

In part, it was the very lack of journalistic topicality – the forthcoming book, piece or show – that helped, though some of my guests only realised what we were doing a few minutes into the talking. There were subtle shifts of approach as they changed gear from the familiar promotional dialogue to the more self-reflective conversation I was inviting. But this could only occur when they recognised that my questions and approach were based on a good deal of direct experience of their work, gained as a matter of pleasure over the years, as well as on further research to fill the inevitable gaps in my acquired knowledge.

If the presumption of overt challenge, in the political sense, was not a prime feature of my interviews, the assumption of informed enquiry and hoped-for revelation were central. I am sure you cannot explain creativity or genius, but I am sure that certain traits of behaviour, outlook and character run like a vein through the make-up of many artists. Setting out my questions in great detail was the path to coaxing such moments of understanding. For each interview I prepared some five pages of questions in sequence, grouped in headings that themselves were part of the hoped-for sequence of the conversation. By formulating my questions in precise word form, a thought sequence was locked into my mind, a sequence that I hoped my guest would find logical but from which I would deviate if he or she did not.

Hearing your interviewees respond to a line of questioning is reassuring. You are on the same wavelength. Hearing them deviate from it is joy – the element of surprise, the opening of real dialogue, the opportunity for discovery. Something new has surfaced, something that I did not know might be said, something that my interviewee may only have thought of in response to my questions. These are the moments when the interview becomes such a rich experience. For talking face to face, person to person, is a very intimate activity. Both partners in the dialogue offer something of themselves. It is part courtship, part self-examination, part jousting, part self-justification, part self-revelation.

The best times are when I set aside my carefully prepared

questions. They are there as a guide, as a reassurance, as a safety net. But the interviews work best when the ideas offered by my guest are so interesting that a previously unexpected avenue of questioning opens up before us. Galloping down those avenues are the moments to be cherished and relished. For similar reasons, I always read my studio introduction to my guest as part of the recording – part courtesy, part reinsurance, part challenge. Best of all is when they pick up something I have said in the introduction and challenge it. It shows that they were listening, that it matters enough to want to put a nuance or alteration on one of my judgements.

So what I have valued in these interviews – apart from the chance to talk to people of such creative stature – has been the ability to be organised but not circumscribed, prepared but not hidebound, disciplined but not inhibited; in short, free in the best sense of the word, carrying with it the responsibility of being true also to the person facing me, to the art he or she practises, and to the listeners who are the essential eavesdroppers on the conversation. This is what the interview as dialogue is about. I like listening. I like starting with what I think I know about people; and ending with things they may not have known themselves before we started talking.